# THE TIMELINE ATLAS

## WORLD HISTORY
### +MAPS & FLAGS OF TODAY'S WORLD

# The
# TIMELINE
# ATLAS

## WORLD HISTORY
## +MAPS & FLAGS OF TODAY'S WORLD

This edition published 2016 by Geddes & Grosset, an imprint of

The Gresham Publishing Company Ltd., Academy Park, Building 4000,

Gower Street, Glasgow, G51 1PR, Scotland, UK

ISBN: 978-1-910965-21-4

Printed and bound in India by Gopsons Papers Ltd

**Atlas of World History:**
Co-authors: Liz Wyse and Caroline Lucas
Design and illustration: Ralph Orme
Maps by Malcolm Porter (assisted by Andrea Fairbrass) and András Bereznay

Image credits:
Courtesy of Shutterstock: — page vi (Atlas) © PerseoMedusa, (Zion Narrows) © Doug Meek, (cutaway Earth) © Johan Swanepoel; page vii (flags) ArtisticPhoto; page viii (Tungurahua volcano) © Fotos593; page 9 (Earth) © Tatiana Shepeleva; page 12 (winter and summer soltices) © Peter Hermes Furian; page 13 (pollution) © Tatiana Grozetskaya; page 14 (paths of the planets) © John David Bigl III; pages 16-17 (solar system) © LSkywalker; page 19 (Earth's magnetic field) © Snowbelle, (Earth) © Lightspring; page 20 (tectonic plates, continental drift), page 21 (atmosphere) © Designua; page 23 (hydrological cycle) © Merkushev Vasiliy; page 25 (geyser) © Denis Kichatof; page 27 (sun) © Triff, (eclipse) © Ethan Daniels, (sunspots) © MarcelClemens; page 28 (full moon) © Quaoar, (phases of the moon) © David Carillet; page 30 (Milky Way) © Alessandro Colle; pages 34-5 (star maps) © shooarts; page 36 (Earth) © 360b; page 37 (Angel Falls) © Alice Nerr; page 38-9 (Mt Dhaulagiri and Mt Annapurna) © Daniel Prudek; page 40 (Colorado River) © Christopher Boswell.

# CONTENTS

# INTRODUCTION

In Greek mythology, Atlas, said to have been the leader of the Titans in the war against the gods, was condemned, as a punishment, to the task of bearing the heavens on his shoulders. The same name, atlas, is given to a collection of maps and charts and was first used by Gerard Mercator in the sixteenth century, the figure of Atlas bearing the globe being placed on the title pages of such works.

*The Timeline Atlas* is appropriately named and brings together historical and up-to-date facts and figures reflecting an ever-changing world.

Below: Nature and structure in *Our World.*

It does so in five complementary ways:
- providing basic geographical information about our world
- giving an overview of history which shows graphically the major movements and events that have transformed the world
- detailing a timeline that relates the various events taking place simultaneously worldwide
- supplying up-to-date physical and political world maps including a comprehensive index
- providing flags of the world pages that have helpful labels and thumbnail 'quick facts'

## Our World

This introductory section concisely summarizes geographical facts about our physical world, including our place in the universe, our neighbours in space, the origin, structure and dynamics of our planet, its enveloping atmosphere and its vast oceans of water.

Atlas, leader of the Titans.

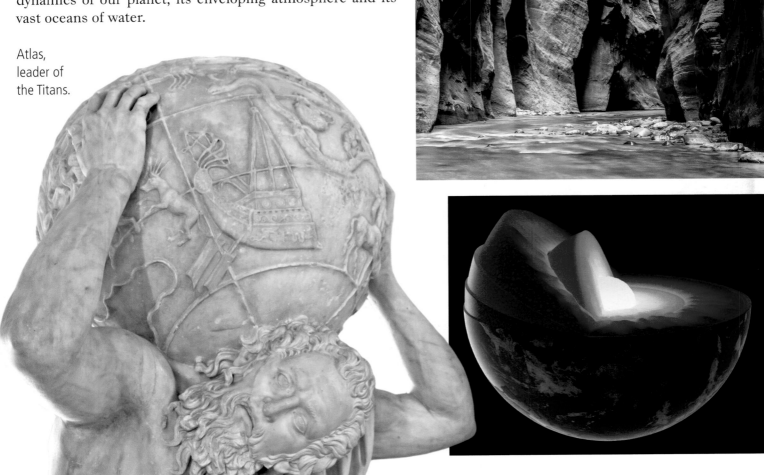

vi

## Atlas of World History

From the early environments and lifestyle of the first humans to the world of today with its ever-advancing technology and its ever-shortening lines of communication, this section uses meticulous illustrations showing people and places at all stages of history. Clear and stimulating maps plot the great changes made by human beings in all parts of the world.

Right: Roman soldier, *Atlas of World History.*

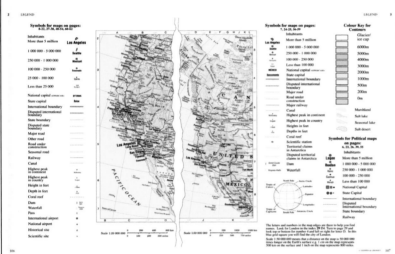

## Maps of the World

The world maps bring alive in full colour the 3-D art of the cartographer with a map coverage that extends to every part of the world. Each continent is treated systematically.

Below: Legend from *Maps of the World.*

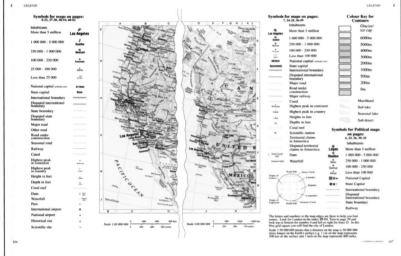

Each double-spread or single-page map has been planned carefully to include an entire physical region or political unit.

Generous overlaps allow for continuity between maps. Maps consist of different kinds of symbols which are explained in the key. These include guides to population numbers, national capitals, state capitals, boundaries – whether state, national, international or disputed – and features such as major international and national airports, historic and scientific sites, roads and railways, highest peaks, passes, dams, coral reefs and waterfalls.

There is an 11-colour key for contours from 0 metres to glacier/ice cap level, and further colour coding reveals marshland, salt lakes, seasonal lakes and desert.

Grid letters and numbers at the edges of a map make it easy to find places. These are needed when using the index.

Map scales are a way of showing an area at a reduced scale, since it is impossible to show a country at its true size on a map. All maps in this atlas are therefore drawn at a reduced scale. To fit the area to be shown on one page, many different scales are used. The amount of information given and the area covered by each map are affected by the scale of the map. For example, at a large scale, regions are shown, at a medium scale, countries, and at a small scale we are able to map the continent of Europe.

Finally there is an index to most of the place names to be found on the maps. Each entry in the alphabetized index starts with the name of the place, followed by the page where it is located (the number of the most appropriate page on which the name appears, usually the largest scale map) and the alphanumeric reference of the map grid on that page.

## Flags of the World

In addition to giving an accurate up-to-date illustration of each of the flags of the world, the 'quick facts' provide information on each country with statistics on area, population, capital, government, religion and currency.

Lava erupts from Tungurahua (Ecuador), one of South America's most active volcanoes (see *The Earth's Structure*, p 18).

# OUR WORLD

This section of illustrated and informative text concisely summarizes recent scientific discoveries and conclusions about our physical world: our place in the universe; our neighbours in space; the origin, structure and dynamics of our planet; its enveloping atmosphere; and its vast oceans of water, so crucial to life on Earth.

## THE PLANET EARTH

Earth is the planet which we inhabit, a nearly spherical body which every 24 hours rotates from west to east round an imaginary line called its axis. This axis has at its extremities the north and south poles, and in the course of a year it completes one revolution round the Sun.

The Earth is around 4.54 billion years old and most probably took over 100 million years to form into a ball of rock, at which time the surface cooled to form the crust, with the first tiny signs of growth appearing some 3.5 billion years ago. Life as we know it has evolved over the last 40 to 50 million years.

Volcanic eruptions produced gases which formed the Earth's atmosphere – the layer of gases surrounding the Earth that is retained by Earth's gravity. The atmosphere is approximately 1000km (620 miles) high and its various layers shield the Earth from the harmful ultraviolet rays emanating from the Sun and protect it from extremes of temperature.

These eruptions also produced huge volumes of water vapour which condensed to fill the hollows in the Earth's crust to form the seas and oceans.

The Earth's surface layer of rock is known as the crust, around 30 to 50km (20 to 30 miles) deep in areas of land mass and 5 to 10km (3 to 6 miles) deep under the oceans. Beneath the crust is the mantle, a rock layer some 2900km (1800 miles) deep. The core of the Earth has two further layers, the outer core and the inner core. The outer core is made up of molten iron, around 2000km (1240 miles) deep. The inner core is of solid iron and nickel, a great ball at the centre of the Earth.

To an observer on Earth, the visible part of the Earth appears as a circular and horizontal expanse. Accordingly, in remote antiquity, the Earth was regarded by man as a flat, circular body, floating on the waters. But gradually the spherical form of the Earth began to be suspected. The mere fact that the Earth could be circumnavigated did not prove it to be round. Its surface, land and ocean

Below: This diagram shows the inner structure of the Earth. The thickness of the Earth's crust may be likened proportionally to the skin of an apple. The top 15km (9.5 miles) of the crust is mostly made up of igneous rocks and metamorphic rocks. Beneath the crust lie the rocks of the mantle and the two-layered core, which is mostly liquid iron.

were explored and accurately mapped, and the relative distances and directions found to be consistent only with its possessing a spherical shape.

The Earth is not, however, an exact sphere, but is very slightly flattened at the poles, so as to have a form known as an oblate spheroid. In this way the polar diameter, or diameter from pole to pole, is shorter than the diameter at right angles to this – the equatorial diameter. The most accurate measurements make the polar diameter almost 42km (27 miles) less than the equatorial, the equatorial diameter being 12,756km (7926 miles), and the polar 12,714km (7900 miles).

The Earth is regarded as divided into two halves – the northern and the southern hemispheres – by the equator, an imaginary line going right round it midway between the poles. In order to indicate with precision the position of places on the Earth, additional circles are traced upon the surface in such a way that those of the one set all pass through both poles, while those of the other are drawn parallel to the equator. The former are called meridians or lines of longitude, the latter parallels or lines of latitude, and by reference to them we can state the latitude and longitude, and thus the exact position, of any place.

The surface of the Earth covers 510,000,000 sq km (196,900,000 sq miles) of which about 29% is dry land, the remaining 71% being water. The land is arranged into masses of irregular shape and size, the greatest connected mass being in the eastern hemisphere. The chief masses receive the name of continents, detached masses of smaller size being islands. The surface of the land is variously diversified with mountains, valleys, plains, plateaux and deserts. The water area of the Earth is divided into oceans, seas, bays, gulfs, etc., while rivers and lakes are regarded as features of the land surface. The great phenomena of the oceans are the currents and tides. The Earth's seas and oceans have an average depth of 3.5km (2.2 miles).

The Earth is one of eight planets which circle around the Sun, completing its revolution in about 365 days and 6 hours. The orbit of the Earth is an ellipse. Earth is the third planet from the Sun and the only one which we know that supports life. Scientists and astronomers estimate that there could be as many as 100 to 200 billion galaxies in the universe. The Sun is but one of around 100 billion stars in our galaxy.

The Earth's daily motion about its own axis takes place in 23 hours, 56 minutes and 4 seconds of mean time. This revolution brings about the alternation of day and night. For all places removed from the equator, day and night are equal only twice in the year (at the equinoxes). At the summer solstice in the northern hemisphere, the north pole of the Earth is turned towards the Sun, and the south pole away from it, and for places within 23.5° of the north pole there is a period of longer or shorter duration during which the Sun is continually above the horizon throughout the 24 hours of each day. Round the south pole there is an equal extent of surface within which the Sun for similar periods is below the horizon. The reverse occurs at the winter solstice. The circles bounding these regions are called respectively the arctic and the antarctic circles, and the regions themselves the polar or frigid zones. Throughout a region extending to 23.5° on each side of the equator the Sun is directly overhead at any place twice in the year. The circles which bound this region are called the tropics, that in the northern hemisphere being the tropic of Cancer, that in the southern the tropic of Capricorn, while the region between is the torrid zone. The regions between the tropics and the polar circles are the north and south temperate zones respectively.

**SUMMER SOLSTICE (BETWEEN JUNE 20 AND JUNE 22)**

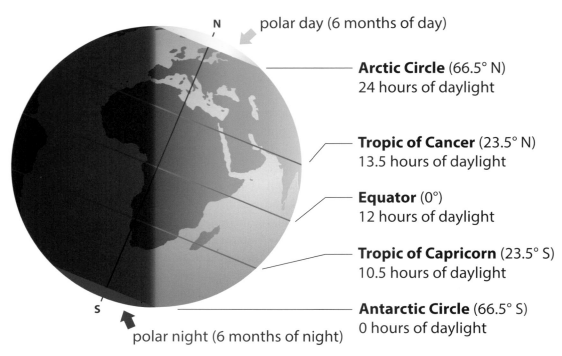

polar day (6 months of day)

**Arctic Circle** (66.5° N)
24 hours of daylight

**Tropic of Cancer** (23.5° N)
13.5 hours of daylight

**Equator** (0°)
12 hours of daylight

**Tropic of Capricorn** (23.5° S)
10.5 hours of daylight

**Antarctic Circle** (66.5° S)
0 hours of daylight

polar night (6 months of night)

**WINTER SOLSTICE (BETWEEN DECEMBER 20 AND DECEMBER 23)**

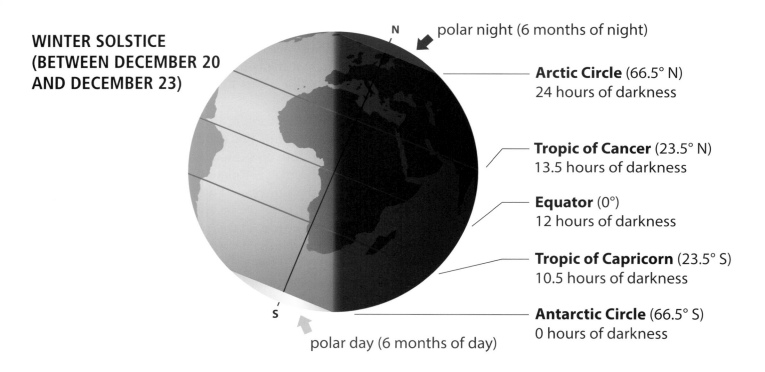

polar night (6 months of night)

**Arctic Circle** (66.5° N)
24 hours of darkness

**Tropic of Cancer** (23.5° N)
13.5 hours of darkness

**Equator** (0°)
12 hours of darkness

**Tropic of Capricorn** (23.5° S)
10.5 hours of darkness

**Antarctic Circle** (66.5° S)
0 hours of darkness

polar day (6 months of day)

Above: The axial tilt of the Earth. As the axis on which the Earth rotates is inclined towards the plane of its path about the Sun at an angle of 66.5°, and the angle between the plane of the ecliptic and the plane of the Earth's equator is therefore 23.5°, the Sun ascends, as seen from our northern latitudes from 21st March to 21st June (the summer solstice), to about 23.5° above the celestial equator and descends again towards the equator from 21st June to 23rd September. It then sinks till 21st December (the winter solstice), when it is about 23.5° below the equator, and returns again to the equator by 21st March. This arrangement is the cause of the seasons and the unequal measure of day and night during them. The solstice dates vary — see above.

The Earth is a complex, evolving system with many interacting parts. To understand fully how our planet works and to ensure that its resources can be sustained we need to explore and come to understand (under the umbrella of Earth science) a wide range of topics, including the evolution of the solar system, the Earth and life, the nature of planetary interiors, the causes of earthquakes and volcanic eruptions, earth-surface processes and the origin and behaviour of oceans and the atmosphere.

The relatively short existence of man, compared to the age of the Earth, has caused alarming levels of pollution, and our planet is under increasing threat from the results of human activity. Two main areas of concern are global warming and the depletion of the ozone layer. The burning of fossil fuels and clearing of forests have intensified the natural greenhouse effect, causing global warming (a term used to describe a gradual increase in the average temperature of the Earth's atmosphere and its oceans – a change that is believed to be permanently changing the Earth's climate). While the release of chlorofluorocarbons (chemicals found mainly in spray aerosols heavily used by industrialized nations for much of the past 50 years) has led to a breakdown in the ozone layer in the atmosphere which normally serves as a shield from the harmful ultraviolet B radiation emitted by the Sun.

The World sustains just under 7.3 billion people – a population which has more than doubled since the early 1950s and it is believed by many experts that the population could grow to over 9 billion by 2050. We must learn to sustain this growth, and face the growing ecological crisis.

Below: Industrial pollution is damaging our environment.

# THE SOLAR SYSTEM

The first astronomers, long ago, noticed five special 'stars' that gradually moved through the constellations. The Greeks called them planetoi, the wanderers, from which came our word 'planet'. Planets shine with a steady light, but real stars often twinkle. This is because a planet is, in fact, a disc of light, whereas a star is so distant that it is always just a point of light. The light from a point source shimmers as it passes through the Earth's atmosphere.

Planets are not like stars at all. The Sun is a typical star. It radiates heat and light of its own, but the planets shine only by the light they reflect from the Sun. Most stars are much larger than planets. The Sun is a thousand times more massive than the biggest planet, Jupiter. The twinkling stars are other suns, much farther away from Earth than any planet.

All the planets visible in the night sky are members of the Sun's family or solar system. Our solar system is part of a spiral galaxy called the Milky Way. The five planets that can be seen without the aid of a telescope are Mercury, Venus, Mars, Jupiter and Saturn. Mercury is closest to the Sun. It is not easy to pick out because it is never far from the Sun in the sky. Venus is also closer to the Sun than is the Earth. This brilliant planet is seen at its best at dawn or dusk and is often called 'the morning star' or 'the evening star'. Mars is the 'Red Planet', so named because of its colour. Jupiter and Saturn, both of them giant planets, can often be seen shining with a steady yellow light.

After the invention of the telescope, astronomers found three, more distant planets. Uranus was discovered in 1781, Neptune in 1846 and Pluto in 1930. In 2006, Pluto was recategorized as a dwarf planet along with Eris and Ceres, the biggest asteroid in our solar system. All planets travel in orbits around the Sun. They all journey in the same direction. The planets closest to the Sun take

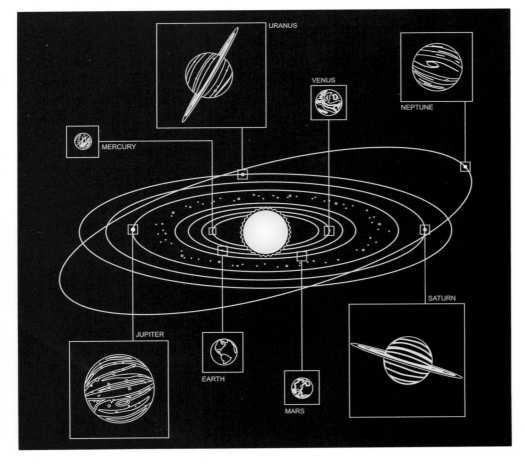

Left: The path of planets around the Sun.

the least time in orbit. Mercury, nearest to the Sun, makes a circuit in only 88 days, Earth takes a year, and Jupiter almost 12 years.

Studying the motion of the planets, the German astronomer, Johannes Kepler, discovered in 1609 that the orbits of the planets are slightly stretched circles, called ellipses. An ellipse has two focal points. For each planetary orbit the Sun is at one of the focuses. This means that the distances of the planets from the Sun change slightly as they travel in their orbits.

Kepler found out how the planets move, but it was Isaac Newton, the seventeenth-century English mathematician, who realized that gravitational force holds the planets in their orbits. The Earth's gravity makes objects that are dropped fall to the ground. If the Sun's gravity did not constantly keep tugging at the planets, they would fly off into the depths of space.

The Sun's family has other members apart from planets. Swarming between Mars and Jupiter are thousands of asteroids or minor planets. Comets with their streaming tails approach the Sun from the farthest parts of the solar system. In addition, dust is scattered in the space between the planets, as well as stones called meteoroids. These space rocks burn up if they crash through the Earth's atmosphere, creating a meteor trail or shooting star. Many of the planets have moons orbiting them, rather like miniature solar systems. Jupiter has at least sixteen moons, four of which can be seen with a small telescope. Gravitation holds the moons in their orbits around their planets, just as it keeps the whole of the solar system together.

The exploration of most of the planets in the solar system is a major scientific achievement of the twentieth and the twenty-first centuries. While the study of space is carried out mainly by astronomers with telescopes, the physical exploration of space is conducted both by unmanned robotic probes and spacecraft/space stations manned by humans. Space explorers have landed on the Moon and brought back samples from its surface. There are two space stations currently in orbit round the Earth: the International Space Station (manned) and Tiangong 1 (unmanned most of the time). Interplanetary flybys have been made past Venus, Mars, Jupiter, Mercury, Saturn, Uranus, Neptune and Pluto and interplanetary surface missions to return at least limited surface data have been made to Venus and Mars.

Right: This table lists the eight planets in the order of their distances from the Sun.

Distance from the Sun is measured in millions of kilometres (miles).

The comparisons of the characteristics of the other planets to those of the Earth are given in decimal ratio, that is, Mars is 1.52 times farther from the Sun than is the Earth.

| Name | Distance from the Sun | Distance from the Sun compared to the Earth | Time to orbit the Sun in years | Mass compared to the Earth | Radius compared to the Earth |
|---|---|---|---|---|---|
| Mercury | 58 (36) | 0.39 | 0.24 | 0.06 | 0.38 |
| Venus | 108 (67) | 0.72 | 0.62 | 0.82 | 0.95 |
| Earth | 149.5 (93) | 1.00 | 1.00 | 1.00 | 1.00 |
| Mars | 228 (142) | 1.52 | 1.88 | 0.11 | 0.53 |
| Jupiter | 778.5 (484) | 5.20 | 11.86 | 318.00 | 11.00 |
| Saturn | 1427 (887) | 9.54 | 29.46 | 95.00 | 9.00 |
| Uranus | 2870 (1783) | 19.18 | 84.00 | 15.00 | 4.00 |
| Neptune | 4497 (2794) | 30.06 | 165.00 | 17.00 | 4.00 |

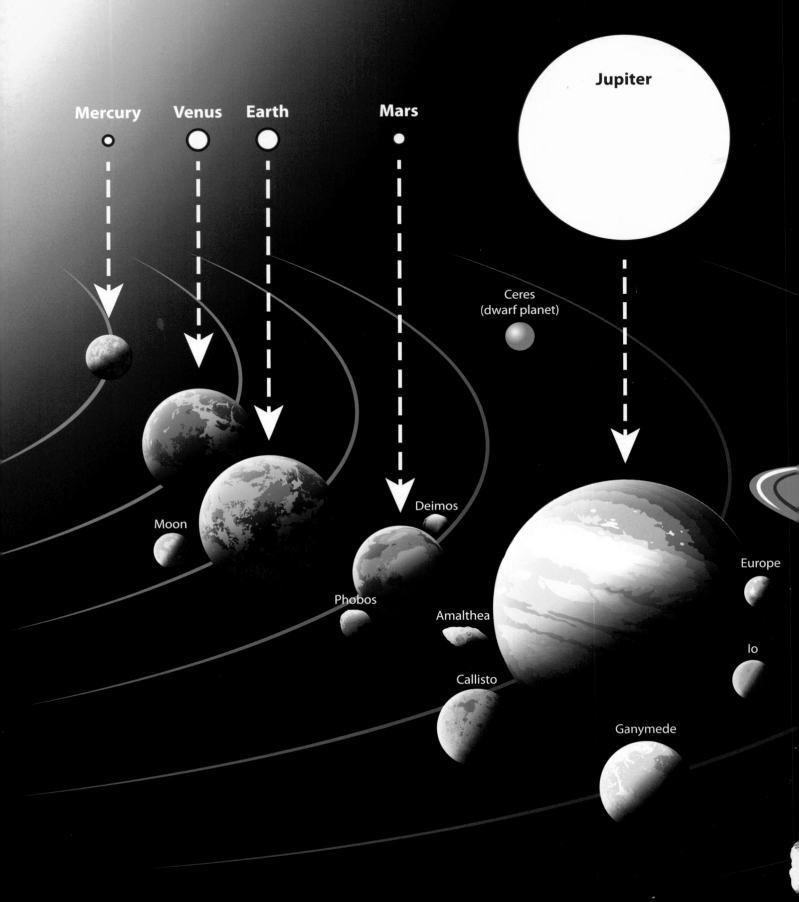

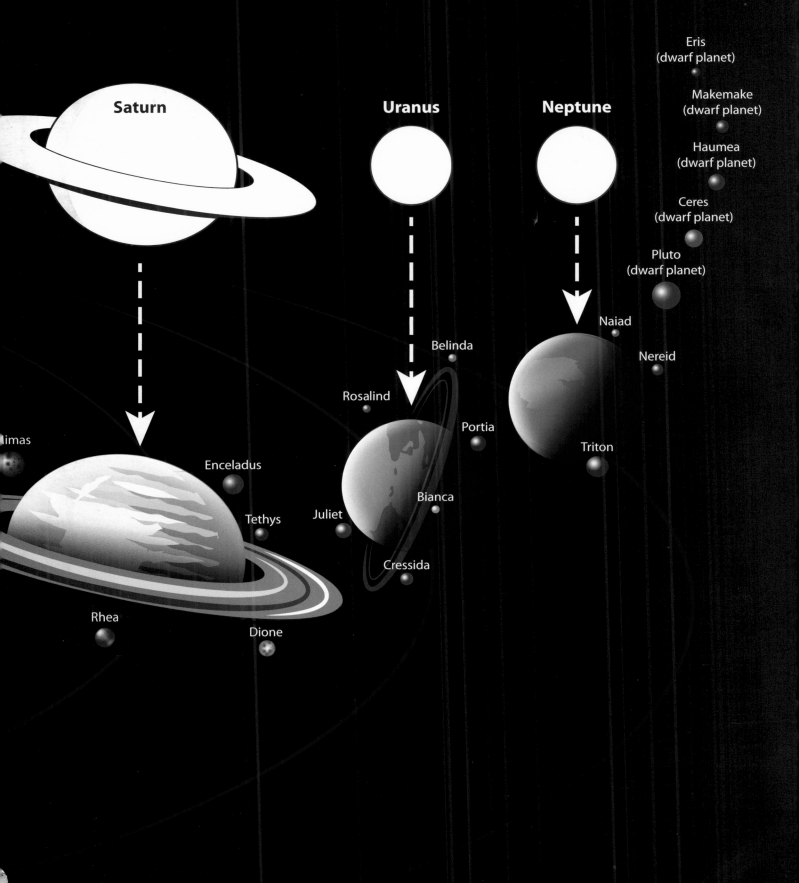

The solar system: The Sun (top left) and its orbiting planets, with their major moons.

# THE EARTH'S STRUCTURE

Man has been able to study the surface of his own planet for as long as the Earth has been inhabited. Yet it is strange to think that before orbiting space-craft had actually returned colour photographs of Earth, nobody had predicted accurately what it would look like from space. Now the Earth can be seen and photographed as a beautiful blue and white planet. From beneath the spiralling patterns of brilliant white clouds, the shapes of the continents come into view.

Many factors make the Earth unique in the solar system. It is the only planet with substantial amounts of liquid water. Oceans cover almost three-quarters of the surface. This vast quantity of water is a powerful force of erosion – the wearing away of the Earth's surface. Weather behaviour and long-term changes in climate gradually wear down the continental rocks. Mountains are eroded by land rains, carrying sediment away from one place and depositing it in another.

Erosion has given the Earth a quite different appearance from that of the other planets in the inner solar system. For example, there is little evidence now that Earth was once as pitted with meteorite craters as the Moon. But it is hard to imagine that Earth escaped this tremendous bombardment. Erosion by wind and water has helped heal such wounds.

Unlike the older rocky planets, the Earth has inner layers containing tremen-dous forces that are very active. Volcanoes and earthquakes, for example, permit Earth to let off pressure from friction and heat that build up inside as the great plates of rock comprising the Earth's surface slowly slide about. Earthquakes, sudden, unpredictable and lethal though they may be, teach geologists about the inner structure of the Earth. Vibrations spreading out from an earthquake are measured and analysed by scientific instruments all over the globe. These vibrations reveal that Earth is made of several layers. On top is a thin crust of rock that is nowhere more than 50km (30 miles) thick. The crust lies atop a thick layer of rock 2900km (1800 miles) deep: the mantle. Inside that, there is an inner core 3000km (2000 miles) deep. This inner core is thought to consist of a nickel–iron alloy and it is divided into two different zones. The outer core is a liquid because the temperatures there are adequate to melt the iron–nickel alloy. However, the inner core is a solid even though its temperature is higher than the outer core.

Earth's magnetic field is generated by the motion of molten iron alloys in its outer core. This flow of liquid iron generates electric currents, which in turn produce magnetic fields. A compass needle lines up with the Earth's magnet-ism and points to the north.

Compared with most of the other rocky worlds in the solar system, Earth is a hive of geological activity. Mountains are constantly being thrust up, earth-quakes make the globe tremble and volcanoes cough out liquid rock. Even the continents are slowly gliding about. Only Io, a moon of Jupiter, shows similar activity. Why does the Earth differ from Venus and Mars?

The answer is that within the Earth's crust there are several large rigid segments called tectonic plates that are continually moving (at a rate of a few centimetres per year). According to theory, heat flowing from underneath the plates causes this motion, which is like that of a conveyor belt. In certain places the plates push into each other, and cause tremendous buckling. This crumpling of two continental plates has caused the formation of the Alps and Himalayas. Along the west coast of North and South America the continental plates are being forced against the oceanic plates and this has formed a great range of coastal mountains from Alaska to southern Chile.

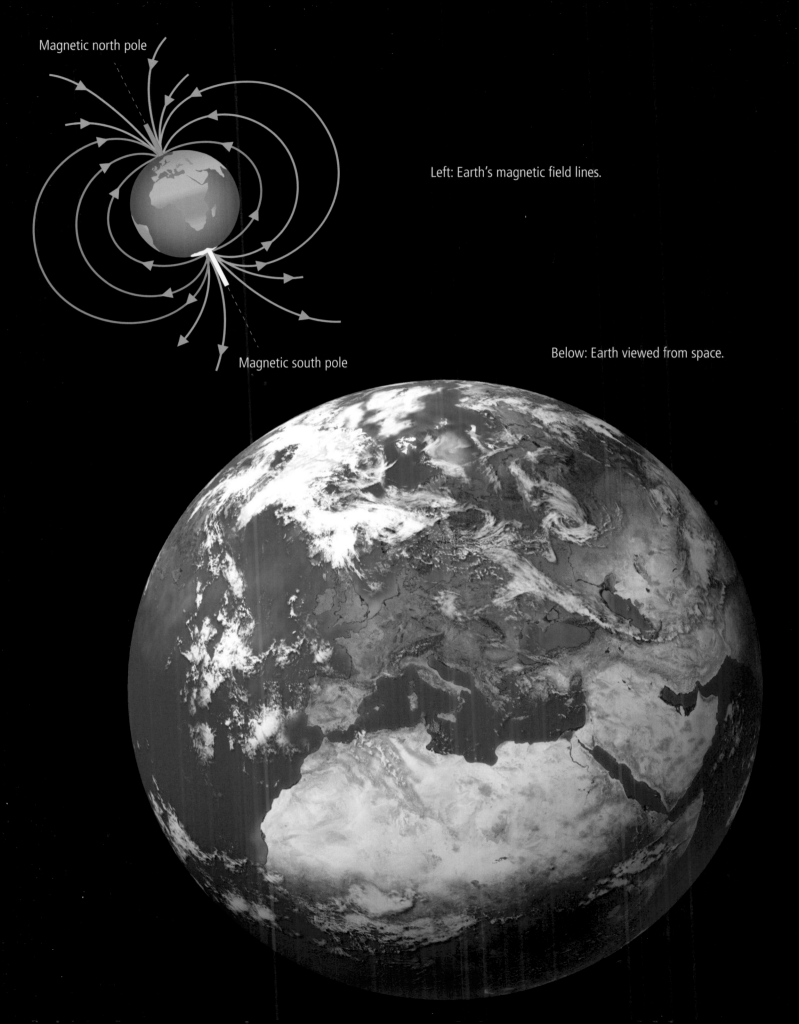

Magnetic north pole

Magnetic south pole

Left: Earth's magnetic field lines.

Below: Earth viewed from space.

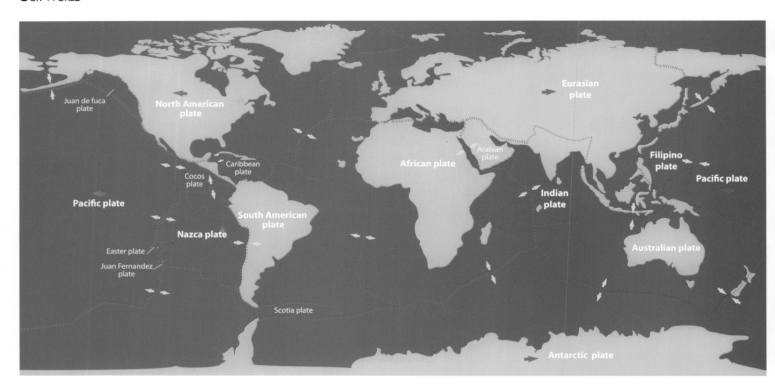

Above: Earth's tectonic plates.

Another effect of these movements in the Earth's crust is to generate friction. This may melt the rock below the surface; molten material works its way upward through cracks and erupts as a volcano.

The motion of continental and oceanic plates is not noticeable in a human lifetime. But it is fast enough to change the face of the Earth. For example, all the present continents resulted when two enormous land masses shattered about 200 million years ago. South America and Africa are still moving about but a look at the map below shows how they once fitted together.

Below: How the planet's land masses once fitted together, drifted apart and how they look in the present day.

*Pangaea supercontinent (300 million years ago)*

*Laurasia and Gondwana supercontinents (200 to 180 million years ago)*

*Modern world*

# THE ATMOSPHERE

Earth's atmosphere, which surrounds and sustains life, is the stage setting within which the drama of weather is played. Extending from the Earth's surface to 10,000km into space, the atmosphere divides into several layers, each comprised of gases in varying quantities and densities that are held in place by Earth's gravity. The predominant gases in the lowest layer, the troposphere, are nitrogen and oxygen, with small concentrations of trace gases, including carbon dioxide, and – most important for the weather – water vapour.

Virtually all of our weather as we know it – with constant changes from wet to dry, clear to cloudy, hot to cold, windy to still and vice versa – takes place in the troposphere. This is mainly because all but the tiniest traces of water vapour – the stuff of which fog, clouds, rain and all other forms of precipitation are made – occur in the troposphere. Without this water vapour there would be no life on Earth.

The troposphere varies in height from about 8km (5 miles) over the poles to about 17km (10.5 miles) over the equator. The Earth and the water vapour in the troposphere act as radiators, both absorbing and giving off the Sun's heat. The trace gases in turn absorb heat from the infrared energy given off by the Earth and so warm the Earth to the temperatures we experience today. However in more recent years because we are now producing too many of these

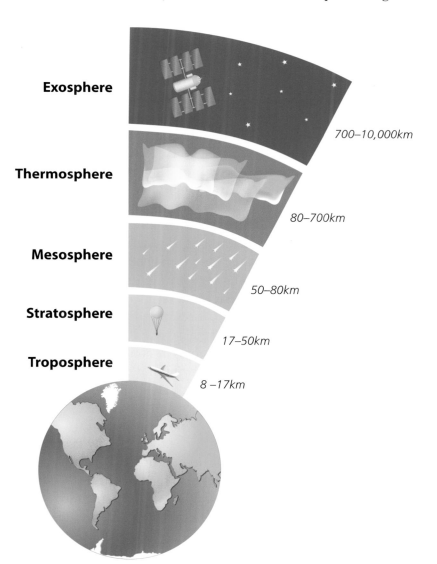

**Exosphere**

*700–10,000km*

**Thermosphere**

*80–700km*

**Mesosphere**

*50–80km*

**Stratosphere**

*17–50km*

**Troposphere**

*8 –17km*

Right: The layers of atmosphere

heat-trapping gases, in particular carbon dioxide, the Earth is being warmed too much, causing changes to our climate. To stabilize this global warming, emissions of carbon dioxide need to be reduced by as much as 70% throughout the world.

Above the troposphere is the stratosphere and here there is very little water vapour. This layer of the atmosphere is where jet-powered aircraft fly. In the stratosphere the temperature becomes warmer with increased altitude because of the dominance of solar radiation. Then, in the next layer, the mesosphere, the temperature turns cold again, in part because of the reaction of a gas called ozone. It is the ozone layer that blocks out the Sun's ultraviolet rays. The temperature continues to drop until it reaches 85°C or more below zero. Then, at perhaps 80km (50 miles) over the Earth, where the thermosphere begins, the gases – under the direct influence of the Sun – become so thinly concentrated that they all but disappear.

Although these upper layers contain no weather in the popular sense of the term, they affect events in the troposphere by shielding the Earth from the searing rays of the Sun. More recently, high levels of chlorofluorocarbons (CFCs) in the atmosphere caused a hole in the ozone layer and these chemicals are now banned. It was expected that the ozone layer would begin to repair itself after the banning of CFCs but some chemicals used to replace them still damage the ozone layer and climate change may be making the situation worse. It seems possible that the increased amount of heat-trapping green-house gases in the lower atmosphere could start to cool the stratosphere, accelerating further ozone loss.

In addition, these upper layers together contribute about 25% of the atmospheric weight that presses down upon the Earth's surface while the troposphere contributes the other 75% through the presence of the relatively dense gases – including water vapour. Vapour enters the atmosphere by evaporation from oceans, seas and lakes, and to a lesser extent from wet ground and vegetation (transpiration). Heat is needed for evaporation to occur, and this heat is taken from the surrounding atmosphere and the surface of the Earth, which therefore becomes cooler.

This heat is not lost, but is stored in the vapour as hidden, or latent, heat. The vapour is carried by winds to higher levels of the atmosphere and to different parts of the world. As a result, water vapour may be found throughout the troposphere and over all regions, oceans and continents. Eventually, water vapour condenses into liquid water or solid ice and falls to the ground as precipitation – rain, snow or hail. In condensing, it releases its latent heat to the atmosphere. Thus if water evaporates into the air from a tropical ocean and winds then carry it to a temperate continent, where it condenses and falls as rain, this provides a very effective means of carrying not only water but also heat from places that have plenty to places that are short of both.

In the air around us, the temperature, pressure and moisture content are affected by another critical ingredient that makes up our weather: the wind. As we know, wind is the name for a moving mass of air. Nearly everyone is familiar with winds that blow from north, south, east or west – that is across the Earth's surface, or horizontally. But winds also blow vertically – as bird-watchers know from seeing gulls or crows sail upwards on rising currents of warm air, or from watching a hawk sink down rapidly on a descending cold current.

Most vertical air currents are much gentler than horizontal winds. But they are vitally important, because they can generate many different types of weather. When air rises it expands, because the pressure on it becomes less. As it rises, the air cools. Because it cools, its moisture content increases. Eventually the rising air may reach a level at which it becomes saturated with moisture. If it rises still further, water vapour starts condensing to form clouds. Nearly all clouds and rain originate in up-currents of air.

One reason why air starts to rise is because of temperature differences from place to place. Such differences are very marked on sunny days over land, when the air above some surfaces, such as asphalt or bare soil, becomes warmer than that over adjacent surfaces, such as trees or lakes. The warmer masses of air, which can be called bubbles, then start to rise. The air between the rising bubbles sinks to compensate. This type of air movement is called convection.

Once a bubble of air has started to rise, it will continue to do so as long as it remains warmer than its surroundings. As it rises, it cools, initially at a rate of 15°C per 90 metres. But its surroundings also cool with height. Eventually the bubble will reach its condensation level and clouds will start to form. The condensation in such clouds releases latent heat, making the rising air even warmer. This increases the difference in temperature between the rising air and the surrounding air. The atmosphere is then said to be unstable. As long as the atmosphere remains unstable, the bubble will grow bigger and rise further, producing a tall cloud. This cloud may become so saturated with moisture that rain or snow begins to fall from it.

Right: The hydrological cycle.

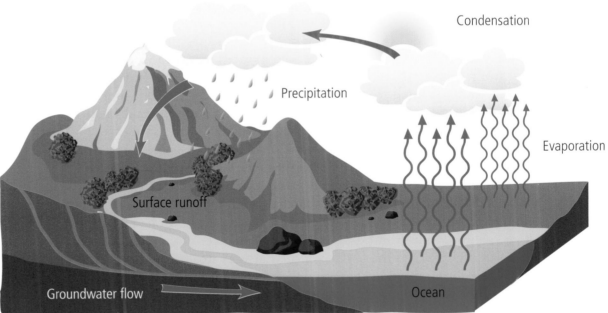

On the other hand, if the rate of decrease of temperature in the air surrounding the bubble is quite small, or if the temperature actually rises with height – as it sometimes does – then the rising air bubble will soon become colder than its surroundings. The bubble will then stop rising. In this situation the atmosphere is said to be stable. Bubbles may never reach their condensation level, in which case no clouds will form – or the bubble will produce only small, shallow clouds. When clouds do form, condensation may stop before the air becomes so saturated that precipitation begins. This is typically the case in stable air.

## SEAS AND OCEANS

The water on the Earth's surface that now fills the oceans got there as part of a process that started with the origin of the Earth itself. This is the opinion of most Earth-scientists today. To understand that process, we need to know something about the origin of the solar system. The material from which the Earth and the other planets were later to be formed probably began as a cloud of gases spinning around the Sun. These gases gradually condensed, making solid particles. Many of them collided, and built up larger and larger concentrations of matter.

The part that was eventually to become the Earth seems to have cooled and begun solidifying about 4.54 billion years ago, and as the spinning movement shaped the matter into a ball, it contracted even further. Under these pressures, matter at the centre of the newly formed Earth began to heat up again and became molten. When this happened, water that had been contained inside the Earth was released to the surface as vapour and was added to the primitive atmosphere. When it cooled and condensed, it fell to the surface as rain and eventually formed the first oceans. We do not know how much of the water in the oceans came from this source. Estimates range from a third to almost all of it – there is no way we can determine the exact amount. Neither can we tell when this happened, but some indication comes from rocks. The oldest rock discovered so far on the Earth's surface is from Greenland and is 3.8 billion years old. It is a kind of rock formed from pebbles laid down under water and later compressed. This shows that water must already have condensed and fallen to Earth during the millions of years that had passed since the Earth was formed.

The rest of the water in the oceans also came from the interior of the Earth, but was forced to the surface by volcanic eruptions and hot springs. There are many volcanoes and hot springs on land and even more in parts of the ocean, and they are still spewing out water. Only a small proportion of this water is new, or juvenile, water coming from deep inside the Earth for the first time. Most of it is groundwater or seawater that seeped down into the Earth, was heated up through contact with hot rocks and then returned to the surface in a volcanic eruption or a hot spring. Although only a small proportion of this water is juvenile, the total amount of new water brought to the surface in the billions of years this process has been going on has been enough to help fill the oceans.

Was the water that came from the Earth's interior to fill the oceans the same salty seawater we know today? As far as we can tell, the oceans never had fresh water. Salt, or salinity, comes from gases and other substances dissolved in the water. When water first rose to the surface of the Earth as steam, it contained gases, some of which dissolved in the original oceans. Since then, volcanoes have supplied other gases along with water and added them to the oceans. Other substances in seawater reached and still reach the ocean by a different process. They come from rocks on land which slowly break down to produce tiny fragments that flow in rivers into the oceans.

Although the ocean, like the atmosphere, had very little oxygen up to about 1.9 billion years ago and had differing amounts of gases and metals in the past, the total amount of all dissolved substances in the ocean – and salinity – was probably similar to the present. And about 1 billion years ago the oceans reached a composition very similar to what it is today.

Just as substances are being added to seawater, so also are they being removed. If they were not, the concentration would go on building up. Water is still being added to the oceans by volcanoes, rain and rivers, and is being lost again by

Below: This fountain geyser, Strokkur, in southwest Iceland erupts every 4–8 minutes sending a tall column of water and steam into the air to a height of 15–20m.

evaporation. The salinity of seawater remains at the same level because some of the solids sink to the bottom or are thrown into the air in sea spray. Salt particles attract water in the atmosphere and droplets grow on them, some of which are blown away over the land as rain. By these means, water and solids are recycled through the atmosphere, rivers, sediments, seawater, rock and the Earth's interior to maintain the overall composition of the oceans.

# THE SUN

To the planets, animals and people of the Earth, the Sun is a unique and vital star. Every living thing on the Earth owes its existence to the fact that the Sun is nearby and keeps shining, and has done so for about five billion years. The energy from the burning of coal, oil and natural gas was once sun energy. These fuels are the remains of plants and animals that grew in the warmth of the Sun's energy millions of years ago. Earth's nearest star, apart from the Sun, is 300,000 times more distant than the Earth is from the Sun, and the weak star energy we receive from it cannot possibly replace the Sun's energy.

The Sun is far larger than the Earth and also a great deal more massive. One hundred and nine Earth-planets placed side by side would stretch from one side of the Sun to the other. Its volume is 1.3 million times greater than the Earth and the mass 330,000 times as great.

The distance from Earth to the Sun is about 150 million km (93 million miles). Light and heat take 8 minutes and 20 seconds to race across inter-planetary space and reach the Earth from this distance. Although this seems a great separation, only a handful of stars exist within a million times this distance from the solar system.

The Sun's gravity pulls much harder than the Earth's gravity. A person who was able to venture to the surface of the Sun would weigh about one-and-a half tons. However, this is an impossible adventure since the Sun has no solid surface and the temperature there is about 10,000°F. This exceeds the melting temperature of every known substance. The temperature of the surface seems high, but inside the Sun it is much hotter. Its entire globe is a glowing mass of gas. At the centre the temperature is about 27 million degrees Fahrenheit.

The gas inside the Sun is three-quarters hydrogen, the lightest gas. Deep inside the hot Sun, hydrogen atoms crowd together. In the jostling a group of them collides so violently with another group that they fuse together and make a completely different substance, helium. Each second, 650 million tons of hydrogen become helium. A small part of this mass of material is transformed in the process and reappears as pure energy, as Einstein has predicted would be the case. In one second, the Sun's mass falls by four million tons. In fifty million years the lost mass is equal to the mass of the Earth. Flashes of energy burst forth as the hydrogen turns to helium. The great density of matter traps the energy flashes inside the Sun. It wanders through the interior for a million years or so before reaching the surface. The energy then streams off into space.

Along with heat and light, the Sun emits radiation that can be harmful to living creatures. Ultraviolet rays and X-rays damage the cells in plants and animals. The Earth's blanket of atmosphere soaks up almost all of this radiation, although the small amount that reaches the ground on a fine day will make fair skin tan or cause painful sunburn if exposure is too long. Astronauts journeying into space have to be protected from the Sun's harmful rays.

Sunspots look like holes in the fiery surface of the Sun. In fact they are areas that are about 3000°F cooler than the surrounding surface. This makes their temperature roughly 7000°F. Something that hot is actually extremely brilliant: sunspots only look dark because they are cooler and dimmer than the rest of the Sun. If a sunspot could be plucked from the Sun and examined separately it would seem a hundred times brighter than the full Moon. An average spot is 32,000km (20,000 miles) across; most spots are more or less as big as the Earth, and huge spots span 145,000km (90,000 miles).

Opposite: The main picture is an ultraviolet photograph showing the Sun's surface as a mass of swirling eruptions and flares of superheated gases escaping into space.

The bottom left image shows a solar eclipse, when the Moon blocks out the Earth's view of the Sun, revealing the star's corona.

The bottom right image shows sunspots, which, although they appear dark, are still extremely bright.

The chromosphere, the cool layer of the Sun's atmosphere that sits just above the photosphere, can be seen readily only during total eclipses. The temperature in this thin layer is about 8000°F. Above the chromosphere is the intensely hot and invisible corona, where the temperature soars to an amazing 2 million degrees Fahrenheit. The gas in the corona is boiling away into space. This gas rush is called solar wind.

## THE MOON

Moon soil is not like Earth soil, it is made entirely from finely pulverized rock – the dust from meteoroid crashes. Moon soil has no water, decaying plant material or life. But it does contain something beautiful and unusual. Moon soil has many glass beads, emerald green and orange-red in colour, shaped like jewels and teardrops. These are made when a meteoroid impact sprays liquid rock in every direction. When the droplets of rock solidify, they turn glassy.

On the surface of the Moon a man weighs only one-sixth of his Earth weight. This is because the Moon's mass is a mere one-eightieth of the Earth's, so the gravitational pull is considerably smaller.

It was once feared that if a spacecraft landed on the Moon it would rapidly sink without trace into the deep dust layers. However, the lunar soil is well packed down to provide a reasonably firm surface. The main hazard of Moon travel is finding a smooth place to land. At close quarters the surface looks much like a bomb site, with small craters everywhere.

Moon rocks are distinctly different from Earth rocks. A geologist could easily tell them apart. The difference between them suggests that the Moon was once hotter than the Earth has ever been, and emphasizes the fact that the Moon has no air and no water. The oldest rocks found on the Moon are 4.6 billion years old. In comparison, the most aged rock yet discovered on Earth dates from only 3.8 billion years ago.

Astronauts left scientific apparatus on the Moon, including sensors that have detected numerous 'moonquakes' as well as the impacts of meteoroids, some spacecraft and man-made debris slamming into the surface. Several small reflectors, like those on a car or bicycle, were placed on the Moon. Scientists can now measure the Moon's distance to within an inch or so by aiming a powerful laser beam at these reflectors and timing the beam's round trip from Earth to Moon and back again. This distance on the average is 385,000km (240,000 miles.)

Geological maps of most of the surface are now available, a possibility undreamed of before about 1960. Samples, mainly from the Apollo program, have been sent to laboratories throughout the world for very detailed examination. Nevertheless, this analysis of lunar material has shown that the surface has never supported life in the past. However, astronauts brought back to the Earth a piece of the Moon lander, Surveyor 3, which had landed on the Moon three years previously. Bacteria on this craft were still alive after several years of exposure to the harsh lunar environment. These bacteria did not flourish, but neither did they die. Thus there is a faint, extremely remote possibility that spacecraft are contaminating the Moon, planets and deep space with microscopic life from Earth, even though the equipment is given a complete cleaning before its launch.

Two or three times a year, the full Moon moves into the Earth's shadow, and the Moon is eclipsed. During this so-called lunar eclipse, the shadowed part of the Moon looks dimly red because Earth's atmosphere scatters reddish sunlight into the Earth's shadow. Eclipses do not take place every month because the Moon's orbit is tilted at an angle to the Earth's path around the Sun.

Opposite: The surface of Earth's Moon and the phases of the Moon as it orbits the Earth.

Opposite: The Milky Way as seen from the Earth's surface.

The Moon's gravitational pull has the important effect of creating ocean tides. The water surrounding the solid Earth is distorted into the shape of a squashed ball under the influence of the Moon's attraction. As the Earth spins on its axis, the bulges in the water seem to sweep around the Earth, causing two tides each day in most places. The Sun, too, influences the tides. When the Moon and the Sun are both pulling from the same direction, the highest tides are formed.

## THE STARS

### *Autumn and Winter*

A good starting point for recognizing stars in autumn is the constellation Cassiopeia (see below). The five main stars of this group make the very obvious shape of the letter W, even though none of them reaches the first magnitude of brightness. This starry W is situated high in the sky during autumn evenings. Observers who are located at latitudes around 50° to 60° North see it right overhead.

Two stars in the W of Cassiopeia point to Cassiopeia's husband, Cepheus; and on the other side of Cassiopeia is their daughter, Andromeda. The W is also a signpost to the large constellation of Pegasus, the winged horse. The principal stars in this constellation are part of the Square of Pegasus. Looking for this square, bear in mind that it is large and that none of the stars reach the first magnitude of brightness.

Andromeda includes an object of unique interest. The great spiral galaxy M31 is just visible to the eye as a hazy patch of light. Two faint stars in the constellation of Andromeda lead to the galaxy M31, far beyond the edge of the Milky Way. Its light has taken two million years to reach the Earth. The M31 Galaxy is the most distant object visible to unaided human eyes. In a small telescope M31 is a soft glow of light.

Right: This typical star locator map shows how astronomers use the position of one constellation, and the stars within it, to locate other heavenly bodies. In the autumn sky of the northern hemisphere two arms of the W-shaped constellation Cassiopeia point to Cepheus and Pegasus (red lines). M31 can be found by following the map from Pegasus to Andromeda.

The bright constellations of winter, when the nights are long, are the best known, as well as being simple to learn. One splendid view is that of the south on a January evening. Ahead is Orion, marching across the sky, with three stars forming a neat swordbelt for this mythical hunter. In Orion, seven stars of second magnitude and brighter make a memorable pattern. Betelgeuse, upper left, is distinctly red. It contrasts well with Rigel, lower right, which sparkles blue-white. Orion's belt points to twinkling Sirius, also called the Dog Star, the brightest star visible from northern latitudes. Procyon is a zero magnitude star, forming a triangle with Betelgeuse and Sirius. Near Orion's belt is a glowing cloud of gas or nebula – a fine sight through binoculars.

Above Orion are Taurus, the Bull, and Gemini, the Twins. Aldebaran in Taurus is red. Near the Bull's head lies the star cluster called the Pleiades, or Seven Sisters. Six or seven stars can be seen by the unaided eye, but a small telescope or binoculars will reveal dozens more. Higher still lies Auriga, the Charioteer, with the yellowish first magnitude star, Capella.

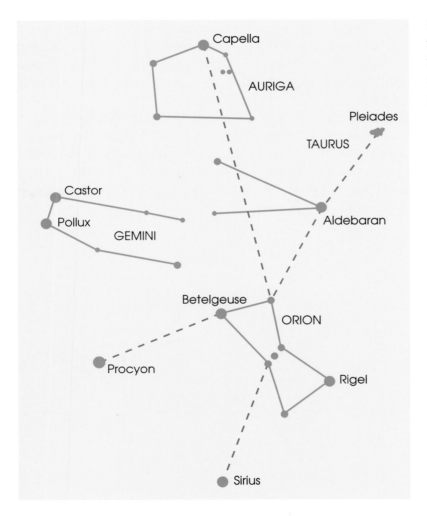

Left: This locator map shows major stars and constellations that can readily be found after Orion has been identified in the winter sky. The dotted lines lead to Procyon and Sirius, to Capella in the constellation Auriga, and to the star Aldebaran and the Pleiades, a star cluster, in Taurus.

## Spring and Summer

In April the constellation Ursa Major reaches its highest point in the sky in the early evening. Observers between latitudes 50° and 60° North, in Canada or Alaska, for example, see it directly overhead. A section of Ursa Major, the Big Dipper, can be used to find three of the first magnitude stars in spring skies in the following manner. Following the curve of the Big Dipper's tail leads to Arcturus, one of the brightest stars in the northern part of the sky. A reddish star, Arcturus belongs to the constellation of Boötes, the Herdsman. The eye, continuing to sweep in an arc from the Big Dipper through Arcturus, turns the observer's face to the south and leads to Spica. This white star, the brightest in constellation Virgo, is a first magnitude star.

Yet another star of the first magnitude, Regulus, can also be seen by facing south. Regulus is the major star in the constellation of Leo, the Lion. It appears in the south in winter time and remains there through the spring. One way to find this star is to follow a line through the bowl of the Dipper, pointing away from the North Star. Regulus will be the brightest foot – just below the lion's head.

In the skies on summer evenings three stars of first magnitude or brighter stand out: Deneb in Cygnus, Vega in Lyra, and Altair in Aquila. For an observer facing south, these map the Summer Triangle. Deneb is the brightest star in the constellation of Cygnus, the Swan. This group of stars is sometimes called the Northern Cross. It lies right within the Milky Way. Binoculars or a small telescope can be swept slowly around this part of the sky. Rich star fields, many of them thousands of light years away, will come into view. They make up the soft glow of light from the Milky Way. Close to Cygnus there are dark patches where dust clouds in deep space cut out the faint background of light from distant stars. Vega is a member of the small constellation of Lyra, the Lyre, and Altair belongs to Aquila, the Eagle. The other stars in these two constellations are much fainter than Vega and Altair. The attractive grouping of stars making up Delphinus, the Dolphin, lies close to Aquila.

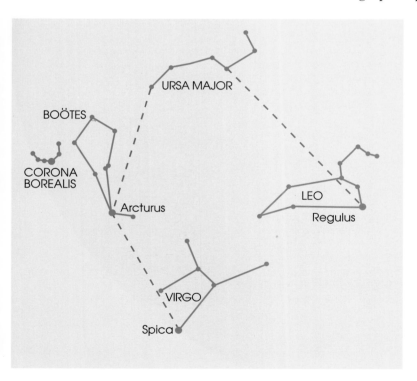

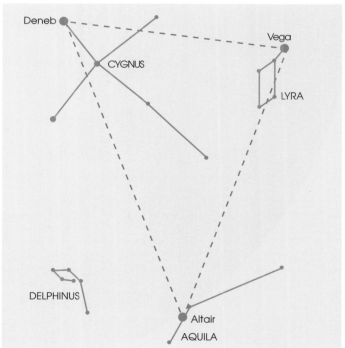

Above: Stars in the Big Dipper (within Ursa Major or the Great Bear) can be used in the spring to find Regulus, the brightest star in the constellation of Leo, Arcturus, the brightest star in Boötes, and its neighbouring constellation of Corona Borealis, the Northern Crown. Arcturus, in turn, points to Spica, the brightest star in the constellation of Virgo.

Above: The locator map right traces a triangle of very bright stars that are visible in the northern hemisphere in summer: Deneb, in the constellation of Cygnus; Vega, in Lyra; and Altair, in Aquila. Stars in the small constellation of Delphinus are not nearly as bright as those of the triangle, but the compact constellation is easy to find near Altair.

# Northern Hemisphere

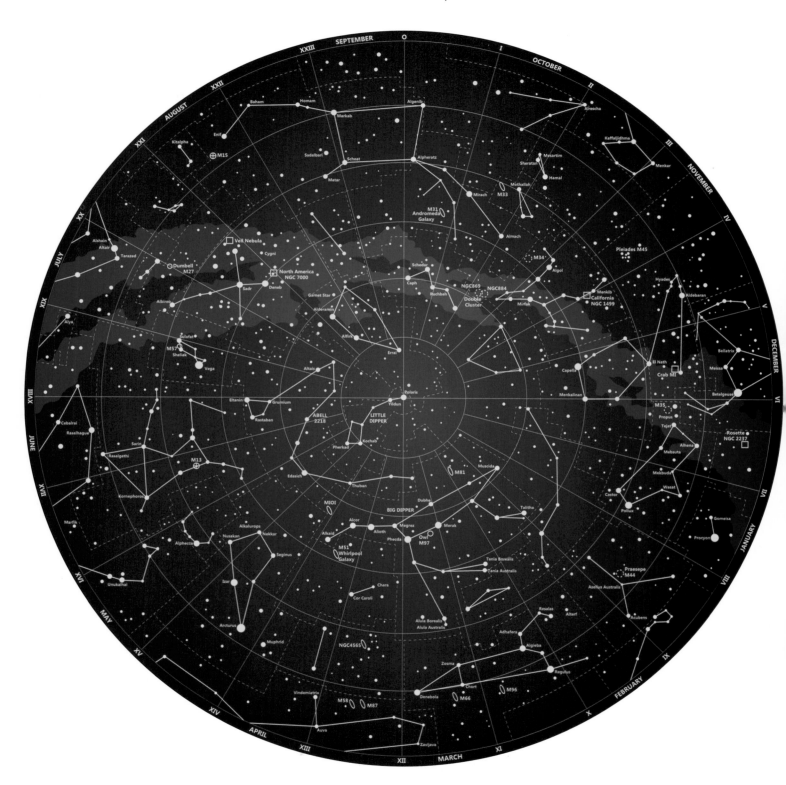

Above: Stars of the northern hemisphere.

## Southern Hemisphere

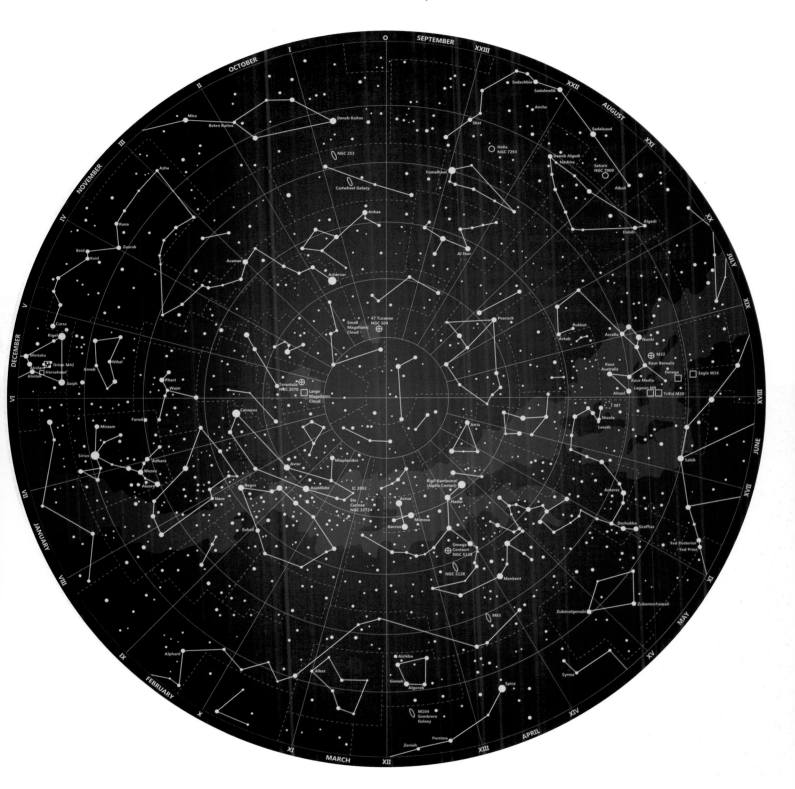

Above: Stars of the southern hemisphere.

# EARTH'S VITAL STATISTICS

Age: Approx 4540 million years (4.54 billion years)

Weight: Approx $5.9722 \times 10^{24}$ kg (5.9 sextillion tonnes)

Diameter: Pole to pole through the centre of the Earth 12,714km (7900 miles)
Across the equator through the centre of the Earth 12,756km (7926 miles)

Circumference: Around the poles 40,008km (24,860 miles)
Around the equator 40,030.2km (24,874 miles)

Area: Land 148,182,000 sq km (57,213,390 sq miles) 29% of surface
Water 361,900,000 sq km (139,730,371 sq miles) 71% of surface

Volume: 1,084,000 million cubic km (260,160 million cubic miles)

Volume of the oceans: 1335 million cubic km (320 million cubic miles)

Average height of land: 840m (2756ft) above sea level

Average depth of ocean: 3682m (12,080ft) below sea level

Density: 5.513 times water

Mean temperature: Around 14.5°C (58°F)

Length of year: 365 days 6 hours (365.26 days)

Length of one rotation: 23 hours 56 minutes and 4 seconds (23.934 hours)

Mean distance from Sun: 149,597,870km (92,955,807 miles)

Mean velocity in orbit: 29.8km (18.5 miles) per second

Escape velocity: 11.2km (6.96 miles) per second

Atmosphere: Main constituents: nitrogen (78.5%), oxygen (21%)

Crust: Main constituents: oxygen (47%), silicon (28%), aluminium (8%), iron (5%)

Known satellites: 1 (the Moon)

Angel Falls in Venezuela

# PRINCIPAL WATERFALLS OF THE WORLD

| Name (location) | Height (m) | Height (ft) | Name (location) | Height (m) | Height (ft) |
|---|---|---|---|---|---|
| Angel Falls (Venezuela) | 979 | 3212 | Salto Kukenan (Venezuela) | 674 | 2211 |
| Tugela Falls (South Africa) | 948 | 3110 | Yutaj Salto (Venezuela) | 671 | 2201 |
| Three Sisters Falls (Peru) | 914 | 2999 | Kahiwa Falls (Hawaii) | 660 | 2165 |
| Olo'upena Falls (United States) | 900 | 2953 | Browne Falls (New Zealand) | 619/836 | 2030/2742 |
| Yumbilla Falls (Peru) | 896 | 2940 | Sutherland Falls (New Zealand) | 580 | 1904 |
| Vinnufossen (Norway) | 860 | 2822 | Kjellfossen (Norway) | 561 | 1841 |
| Balåifossen (Norway) | 850 | 2789 | Ribbon Falls (United States) | 491 | 1612 |
| Pu'uka'oku Falls (United States) | 840 | 2756 | Mardalsfossen (Norway) | 468 | 1536 |
| James Bruce Falls (Canada) | 840 | 2756 | Kaliuwaa/Sacred Falls (Hawaii) | 463 | 1520 |
| Browne Falls (New Zealand) | 836 | 2743 | Della Falls (Canada) | 440 | 1443 |
| Kaieteur Falls (Guyana) | 822 | 2697 | Gavarnie (France) | 422 | 1384 |
| Strupenfossen (Norway) | 820 | 2690 | Hunlen Falls (Canada) | 401 | 1316 |
| Ramnefjellsfossen (Norway) | 818 | 2684 | Giessbach Falls (Switzerland) | 400 | 1312 |
| Uitgordsfossen (Norway) | 800 | 2625 | Takakkaw Falls (Canada) | 380 | 1246 |
| Waihilau Falls (United States) | 792 | 2598 | Krimmler Falls (Austria) | 380 | 1246 |
| Colonial Creek Falls (United States) | 788 | 2585 | Papalaua Falls (Hawaii) | 366/500 | 1200/1640 |
| Mongefossen (Norway) | 773 | 2536 | Widow's Tears Falls (United States) | 357 | 1170 |
| Gocta Cataracts (Peru) | 771 | 2530 | Cachoeira do El Dorado (Brazil) | 353 | 1158 |
| Mutarazi Falls (Zimbabwe) | 762 | 2500 | Cachoeira do Fumaça (Brazil) | 340 | 1115 |
| Kjelfossen (Norway) | 755 | 2477 | Honokohau Falls (Hawaii) | 341 | 1120 |
| Johannesburg Falls (United States) | 751 | 2464 | Dudhsagaar Falls (India) | 310 | 1017 |
| Yosemite Falls (United States) | 739 | 2425 | Staubbach Falls (Switzerland) | 300 | 1000 |
| Cascades de Trou de Fer (Réunion) | 725 | 2379 | Vettisfossen (Norway) | 275 | 902 |
| Ølmåafossen (Norway) | 720 | 2362 | Wallaman Falls (Australia) | 268 | 879 |
| Mana'wai'nui Falls (United States) | 719 | 2359 | King Edward VIII Falls (Guyana) | 260 | 840 |
| Kjeragfossen (Norway) | 715 | 2346 | Jog/Gerosoppa Falls (India) | 253 | 829 |
| Avalanche Basin Falls (United States) | 707 | 2320 | Cascada de Basaseachi (Mexico) | 246 | 807 |
| Haloku Falls (United States) | 700 | 2297 | Kalambo Falls (Zambia/Tanzania) | 235 | 772 |
| Chamberlain Falls (New Zealand) | 700 | 2297 | Feigumfossen (Norway) | 218 | 715 |
| Alfred Creek Falls (Canada) | 700 | 2297 | Tin Mine Falls (Australia) | 213 | 699 |
| Døntefossen (Norway) | 700 | 2297 | Silver Strand Falls (United States) | 175 | 574 |
| Brufossen (Norway) | 698 | 2290 | King George VI/Oshi Falls (Guyana) | 152/213 | 500/700 |
| Spirefossen (Norway) | 690 | 2264 | Wollomombi Falls (Australia) | 150/230 | 490/750 |
| Lake Unknown Falls (New Zealand) | 680 | 2231 | | | |

# PRINCIPAL MOUNTAINS OF THE WORLD

| Name (location) | Height (m) | (ft) | Name (location) | Height (m) | (ft) |
|---|---|---|---|---|---|
| Mount Everest (Asia) | 8848 | 29,028 | Denali/Mount McKinley (N Amer) | 6168 | 20,237 |
| K2/Godwin-Austen (Asia) | 8611 | 28,250 | Mount Logan (N Amer) | 5951 | 19,524 |
| Kangchenjunga (Asia) | 8586 | 28,170 | Cotopaxi (S Amer) | 5896 | 19,344 |
| Makalu (Asia) | 8485 | 27,766 | Mount Kilimanjaro (Africa) | 5895 | 19,341 |
| Dhaulagiri (Asia) | 8167 | 26,795 | Mount Huila (S Amer) | 5750 | 18,865 |
| Nanga Parbat (Asia) | 8125 | 26,657 | Mount Elbrus (Europe) | 5642 | 18,510 |
| Annapurna (Asia) | 8091 | 26,545 | Pico de Orizaba/Citlaltépetl (C Amer) | 5636 | 18,491 |
| Shishapangma (Asia) | 8027 | 26,335 | Mount Damarand (Asia) | 5610 | 18,410 |
| Nanda Devi (Asia) | 7816 | 25,643 | Mount St Elias (N Amer) | 5489 | 18,008 |
| Namcha Barwa (Asia) | 7782 | 25,531 | Popocatépetl (C Amer) | 5426 | 17,802 |
| Kamet (Asia) | 7756 | 25,446 | Mount Foraker (N Amer) | 5304 | 17,400 |
| Tirich Mir (Asia) | 7708 | 25,289 | Ixtaccihuati (C Amer) | 5230 | 17,160 |
| Gurla Mandhata (Asia) | 7694 | 25,243 | Dykh Tau (Europe) | 5203 | 17,070 |
| Kongur Tagh (Asia) | 7649 | 25,095 | Mount Kenya (Africa) | 5200 | 17,058 |
| Mount Gongga/Minya Konka | 7556 | 24,790 | Mount Ararat (Asia) | 5137 | 16,854 |
| Kula Kangri (Asia) | 7538 | 24,731 | Mount Kazbek (Europe) | 5047 | 16,558 |
| Muztagh Ata (Asia) | 7509 | 24,656 | Mount Bona (N Amer) | 5005 | 16,421 |
| Jengish Chokusu/ Pobedy Peal (Asia) | 7439 | 24,406 | Vinson Massif (Antarctica) | 4892 | 16,050 |
| Jomolhari/Chom Lhari (Asia) | 7326 | 24,035 | Puncak Java (Asia) | 4884 | 16,024 |
| Lenin Peak (Asia) | 7134 | 23,405 | Mount Vancouver (N Amer) | 4812 | 15,787 |
| Khan Tengri (Asia) | 7010 | 23,000 | Mont Blanc (Europe) | 4808 | 15,774 |
| Aconcagua (S Amer) | 6961 | 22,837 | Klyuchevyskaya Sopka (Asia) | 4750 | 15,580 |
| Ojos del Salado (S Amer) | 6893 | 22,615 | Puncak Trikora (Asia) | 4750 | 15,580 |
| Huascarán (Asia) | 6769 | 22,205 | Monte Rosa (Europe) | 4634 | 15,203 |
| Llullailaco (S Amer) | 6739 | 22,110 | Mount Meru (Africa) | 4562 | 14,967 |
| Mount Kailash (Asia) | 6638 | 21,778 | Ras Dashen (Africa) | 4550 | 14,930 |
| Mount Garmo (Asia) | 6595 | 21,637 | Mount Karisimbi (Africa) | 4507 | 14,787 |
| Tupungato (S Amer) | 6570 | 21,560 | Belukha (Asia) | 4506 | 14,783 |
| Sajama (S Amer) | 6542 | 21,463 | Weisshorn (Europe) | 4506 | 14,783 |
| Chimborazo (S Amer) | 6268 | 20,564 | Matterhorn (Europe) | 4478 | 14,692 |

| Name (location) | Height (m) | (ft) | Name (location) | Height (m) | (ft) |
|---|---|---|---|---|---|
| Mount Whitney (N Amer) | 4421 | 14505 | Mount Adams (N Amer) | 3743 | 12,281 |
| Mount Elbert (N Amer) | 4401 | 14,440 | Mount Cook/Aoraki (Oceania) | 3724 | 12,218 |
| Mount Massive (N Amer) | 4398 | 14,428 | Mount Teide (Europe/Africa) | 3718 | 12,198 |
| Mount Rainier/Tacoma (N Amer) | 4392 | 14,411 | Semeru/Mahameru (Asia) | 3676 | 12,060 |
| Markham (Antarctica) | 4350 | 14,271 | Mount Assiniboine (N Amer) | 3618 | 11,870 |
| Longs Peak (N Amer) | 4346 | 14,259 | Mount Hood (N Amer) | 3429 | 11,249 |
| Mount Elgon (Africa) | 4321 | 14,177 | Aneto (Europe) | 3404 | 11,168 |
| Mount Wrangell (N Amer) | 4317 | 14,163 | Mount Etna (Europe) | 3329 | 10,922 |
| Pikes Peak (N Amer) | 4300 | 14,110 | Cirque Peak (N Amer) | 2993 | 9820 |
| Finsteraarhorn (Europe) | 4274 | 14,022 | Mount Pulag (Asia) | 2922 | 9587 |
| Gannett Peak (N Amer) | 4209 | 13,809 | Mount Tahat (Africa) | 2908 | 9541 |
| Mauna Kea (N Amer) | 4205 | 13,796 | Mount Shishaldin (N Amer) | 2857 | 9373 |
| Mauna Loa (N Amer) | 4169 | 13,679 | Mount Roraima (S Amer) | 2810 | 9220 |
| Jungfrau (Europe) | 4158 | 13,642 | Mount Ruapehu (Oceania) | 2797 | 9177 |
| Mount Kinabalu (Asia) | 4096 | 13,438 | Mount Catherine (N Amer) | 2629 | 8625 |
| Mount Fridtjof Nansen (Antarctica) | 4070 | 13,350 | Doi Inthanon (Asia) | 2565 | 8415 |
| Mount Cameroon (Africa) | 4040 | 13,250 | Mount St Helens (N Amer) | 2549 | 8363 |
| Volcán Tacaná (S Amer) | 4060 | 13,320 | Galdhøpiggen (Europe) | 2469 | 8100 |
| Mount Waddington (N Amer) | 4019 | 13,186 | Mount Parnassus (Europe) | 2457 | 8061 |
| Truchas Peak (N Amer) | 3995 | 13,108 | Kosciuszko (Oceania) | 2228 | 7310 |
| Wheeler Peak (N Amer) | 3982 | 13,065 | Harney Peak (N Amer) | 2208 | 7244 |
| Mount Robson (N Amer) | 3954 | 12,972 | Mount Olympus (N Amer) | 2100 | 6900 |
| Granite Peak (N Amer) | 3904 | 12,807 | Clingman's Dome (N Amer) | 2025 | 6643 |
| Borah Peak (N Amer) | 3861 | 12,668 | Mount Washington (N Amer) | 1917 | 6288 |
| Monte Viso (Europe) | 3841 | 12,602 | Mount Rogers (N Amer) | 1746 | 5729 |
| Mount Kerinci (Asia) | 3805 | 12,482 | Mount Marcy (N Amer) | 1629 | 5343 |
| Mitchell Peak (N Amer) | 3805 | 12,482 | Mount Pelée (C Amer) | 1397 | 4583 |
| Grossglockner (Europe) | 3798 | 12,461 | Ben Nevis (Europe) | 1344 | 4409 |
| Mount Erebus (Antarctica) | 3794 | 12,448 | Mount Vesuvius (Europe) | 1281 | 4203 |
| Mount Fuji (Asia) | 3776 | 12,388 | | | |

Mount Dhaulagiri and Mount Annapurna, Nepal

# PRINCIPAL RIVERS OF THE WORLD

| Name (location) | Length (km) | (miles) | Name (location) | Length (km) | (miles) | Name (location) | Length (km) | (miles) |
|---|---|---|---|---|---|---|---|---|
| Nile (Africa) | 6853 | 4258 | Snake (N Amer) | 1735 | 1078 | White (N Amer) | 1162 | 722 |
| Amazon (S Amer) | 6437 | 4000 | Tobol (Asia) | 1660 | 1031 | North Platte (N Amer) | 1152 | 716 |
| Yangtze (Asia) | 6300 | 3915 | Xingu (S Amer) | 1640 | 1019 | Salado (S Amer) | 1150 | 710 |
| Missouri-Mississippi (N Amer) | 6275 | 3902 | Churchill (N Amer) | 1609 | 1000 | Gambia (Africa) | 1130 | 700 |
| Yenisei (Asia) | 5539 | 3442 | Ohio (N Amer) | 1579 | 981 | Cimarron (N Amer) | 1123 | 698 |
| Yellow River/Huang He (Asia) | 5464 | 3395 | Magdalena (S Amer) | 1528 | 949 | Yellowstone (N Amer) | 1114 | 692 |
| Ob-Irtysh (Asia) | 5410 | 3360 | Oka (Europe) | 1500 | 930 | Cumberland (N Amer) | 1107 | 688 |
| Paraná (S Amer) | 4880 | 3032 | Pecos (N Amer) | 1490 | 926 | Pilcomaya (S Amer) | 1100 | 680 |
| Congo/Zaire (Africa) | 4700 | 2922 | Darling (Oceania) | 1472 | 915 | Elbe (Europe) | 1094 | 680 |
| Lena (Asia) | 4472 | 2779 | Godavari (Asia) | 1465 | 910 | Donets (Europe) | 1053 | 654 |
| Mekong (Asia) | 4350 | 2703 | Ucayali (S Amer) | 1460 | 907 | Tennessee (N Amer) | 1049 | 652 |
| Niger (Africa) | 4200 | 2622 | Canadian (N Amer) | 1458 | 906 | Vistula (Europe) | 1047 | 651 |
| Missouri (N Amer) | 3767 | 2341 | Blue Nile (Africa) | 1450 | 900 | Gila (N Amer) | 1044 | 649 |
| Mississippi (N Amer) | 3734 | 2320 | Parnaíba (S Amer) | 1400 | 870 | Tagus (Europe) | 1038 | 645 |
| Volga (Europe) | 3692 | 2294 | Fraser (N Amer) | 1375 | 854 | Loire (Europe) | 1012 | 629 |
| Murray-Darling (Oceania) | 3672 | 2282 | Dniester (Europe) | 1362 | 846 | Sava (Europe) | 990 | 615 |
| Madeira (S Amer) | 3250 | 2020 | Narmada (Asia) | 1312 | 815 | Ouachita (N Amer) | 974 | 605 |
| Yukon (N Amer) | 3190 | 1982 | Ottawa (N Amer) | 1271 | 790 | Tisza (Europe) | 965 | 600 |
| Indus (Asia) | 3180 | 1980 | Athabasca (N Amer) | 1231 | 765 | Neman (Europe) | 900 | 560 |
| Salween (Asia) | 3060 | 1901 | Rhine (Europe) | 1230 | 760 | Oder (Europe) | 854 | 531 |
| St Lawrence (N Amer) | 3058 | 1900 | Green (N Amer) | 1170 | 730 | | | |
| Rio Grande (N Amer) | 3051 | 1896 | | | | | | |
| São Francisco (S Amer) | 2914 | 1811 | | | | | | |
| Brahmaputra (Asia) | 2900 | 1800 | | | | | | |
| Danube (Europe) | 2860 | 1777 | | | | | | |
| Amur (Asia) | 2824 | 1755 | | | | | | |
| Euphrates (Asia) | 2800 | 1740 | | | | | | |
| Zambezi (Africa) | 2693 | 1673 | | | | | | |
| Tocantins (S Amer) | 2640 | 1640 | | | | | | |
| Araguaia (S Amer) | 2627 | 1632 | | | | | | |
| Ganges (Asia) | 2525 | 1569 | | | | | | |
| Juruá (S Amer) | 2414 | 1500 | | | | | | |
| Arkansas (N Amer) | 2364 | 1469 | | | | | | |
| Colorado (N Amer) | 2334 | 1450 | | | | | | |
| Dnieper (Europe) | 2287 | 1421 | | | | | | |
| Aldan (Asia) | 2273 | 1412 | | | | | | |
| Rio Negro (S Amer) | 2250 | 1400 | | | | | | |
| Syr Darya (Asia) | 2212 | 1374 | | | | | | |
| Red (N Amer) | 2189 | 1360 | | | | | | |
| Irrawaddy (Asia) | 2170 | 1348 | | | | | | |
| Orinoco (S Amer) | 2140 | 1330 | | | | | | |
| Kolyma (Asia) | 2129 | 1323 | | | | | | |
| Orange/Senqu/Gariep (Africa) | 2092 | 1300 | | | | | | |
| Brazos (N Amer) | 2060 | 1280 | | | | | | |
| Columbia (N Amer) | 2000 | 1243 | | | | | | |
| Xi (Asia) | 1957 | 1216 | | | | | | |
| Don (Europe) | 1950 | 1212 | | | | | | |
| Peace (N Amer) | 1923 | 1195 | | | | | | |
| Tigris (Asia) | 1850 | 1150 | | | | | | |
| Uruguay (S Amer) | 1838 | 1140 | | | | | | |
| Pechora (Europe) | 1809 | 1124 | | | | | | |
| Kama (Europe) | 1805 | 1122 | | | | | | |
| Angara (Asia) | 1779 | 1105 | | | | | | |
| Mackenzie (N Amer) | 1738 | 1080 | | | | | | |
| Marañón (S Amer) | 1737 | 1079 | | | | | | |

The Colorado River.

# ATLAS OF WORLD HISTORY

# Timelines

| EUROPE | AMERICAS | ASIA | AFRICA |
|---|---|---|---|
| BC | BC | BC | BC |
| *c.* 20,000 Paintings showing hunting scenes in caves in southern France and Spain | | | |
| *c.* 6500 Agriculture in Greece | | *c.* 8000 First farming in the Middle East | *c.* 5000 Agricultural settlements in Egypt |
| | | *c.* 4000 Beginning of Bronze Age in the Near East | |
| | *c.* 3000 First ceramics in Mexico | *c.* 3100 First writing on clay tablets | *c.* 3200 King Menes unites Egypt |
| | | *c.* 3000 First cities in Sumer | *c.* 2658 Beginning of 'Old Kingdom' in Egypt |
| *c.* 2200 Beginnings of Bronze Age Minoan civilization in Crete | *c.* 2000 First metal-working in Peru | *c.* 2750 Growth of civilizations in Indus valley | *c.* 2650 First pyramid built for King Zoser of Egypt |
| *c.* 1600 Mycenaean civilization in Greece | | *c.* 1750 Collapse of Indus Valley civilization | |
| | | *c.* 1600 Rise of Shang Dynasty in China | *c.* 1552 Beginning of 'New Kingdom' in Egypt |
| *c.* 1000 Destruction of Minoan Crete | | | 1361–52 Rule of Tutankhamun in Egypt |
| *c.* 1200 Collapse of Mycenaean Empire | 1200 Rise of the Oltec civilization | *c.* 1100 Chou Dynasty supplants Shang in China | |
| *c.* 1100 Phoenicians develop first phonic alphabet | | | |
| *c.* 800 Rise of city states in Greece | | *c.* 720 Height of Assyrian power | *c.* 800 Carthage founded by Phoenicians |
| 753 Foundation of Rome | | *c.* 650 First iron used in China | |
| 510 Foundation of Roman Republic | | 586 Babylonian captivity of Jews | |
| | | *c.* 486 Death of Siddhartha Gautama, founder of Buddhism | |
| 431–404 Peloponnesian War between Athens and Sparta | | 476–221 'Warring States' period in China | |
| 334–327 Alexander the Great of Macedonia conquers Persia | | *c.* 320 Mauryan Empire in India | |
| 290 Roman conquest of central Italy | | | |
| 264–146 Three Punic Wars between Rome and Carthage | | 221 Ch'in Dynasty | |
| 146 Greece becomes part of Roman Empire | | 202 China under control of Han Dynasty | |
| 31 Roman victory at the Battle of Actium | | | |

| EUROPE | AMERICAS | ASIA | AFRICA |
|---|---|---|---|
| AD | AD | AD | AD |
| 43 Roman invasion of Britain | | c. 0 Buddhism spreads from India to South East Asia and China | |
| 116 Roman Empire at greatest extent | | 25 Han Dynasty restored in China | 30 Egypt becomes Roman province |
| 238 First raids on Roman Empire by Goths | | 131–36 Jewish revolt against Rome | |
| 285 Roman Empire divided into Eastern Empire and Western Empire | | 220 End of Han Dynasty: China splits into three states | |
| | c. 300 Mayan civilization rises to prominence in Central America | 214 Great Wall of China built | |
| 370 Huns from Asia begin to invade Europe | | 330 Constantinople becomes capital of Roman Empire | |
| 410 Visigoths sack Rome | c. 400 Pre-Inca civilizations in western South America | 350 Huns invade western Central Asia | 429–535 Vandal kingdom in northern Africa |
| 449 Angles, Saxons and Jutes invade Britain | | 407–553 Early Mongol Empire | 533–552 Justinian restores Roman power in North Africa |
| 486 Frankish Empire founded by Clovis | | 552 Buddhism introduced to Japan | |
| 497 Franks converted to Christianity | | c. 570 –632 Muhammad: founder of Islamic religion | |
| 597 St Augustine's Christian mission to England | c. 600 Height of Mayan civilization | | 641 Conquest of Egypt by Arabs |
| 711 Second Muslim conquest of Spain | | 618 China reunited under T'ang Dynasty | c. 700 Rise of Empire of Ghana |
| 793 Viking raids begin | | 622 First year of Islamic calendar | |
| 800 Charlemagne crowned Holy Roman Emperor | | 635–74 Muslim conquests of Syria and Persia | |
| 843 Treaty of Verdun divides Carolingian or Frankish Empire into three parts | | 730 First printing in China | |
| 874 First Viking settlers in Iceland | | 821 Conquest of Tibet by Chinese | |
| 886 Danelaw established in England | | | 920 –1050 Height of Ghana Empire |
| 911 Vikings granted Duchy of Normandy by Frankish king | | 907 Last T'ang Emperor deposed in China | 969 Fatamids conquer Egypt and found Cairo |
| c. 1000 Vikings discover North America | | 939 Civil wars in Japan | |
| 1016 King Cnut rules England, Denmark and Norway | | 960 –1127 Northern Sung Dynasty | c. 1000 First Iron Age settlement at Zimbabwe |
| 1054 Great Schism finally divides Church into Western Church and Eastern Church | | 1127 –1279 Southern Sung Dynasty | |

| EUROPE | AMERICAS | ASIA | AFRICA |
|---|---|---|---|
| **1066** Defeat of Anglo-Saxons by William the Conqueror | | | |
| **1071** Normans conquer Byzantine Italy | | **1071** Asia Minor conquered by Seljuk Turks | |
| | | *c.* **1100** Polynesian Islands colonized | *c.* **1150** Beginnings of Yoruba city states (Nigeria) |
| **1095–99** First Crusade | **1100** Toltecs build capital city at Tula in Mexico | **1156–59** Civil wars in Japan | |
| **1147–49** Second Crusade | | **1174–87** Ottoman Turks under Saladin conquer Syria and Levant | **1174** Ottoman Turks under Saladin conquer Egypt |
| **1189–92** Third Crusade | | | |
| **1202–04** Fourth Crusade and capture of Constantinople | Cuzco founded by the Incas | | *c.* **1200** Rise of Empire of Mali in West Africa |
| **1217–21** Fifth Crusade | | **1206** Mongol Empire founded under Genghis Khan | |
| **1228–29** Sixth Crusade | *c.* **1250** End of Toltec Empire in Mexico | **1234** Mongols invade and destroy Northern China | Emergence of Hausa city states (Nigeria) |
| **1237** Mongols invade Russia | | | |
| **1241** Mongols invade Poland, Hungary, Bohemia then withdraw | | | **1240** Collapse of Empire of Ghana |
| **1248–54** Seventh Crusade | | | |
| **1250** Collapse of Imperial power in Germany and Italy on death of Holy Roman Emperor, Frederick II | | **1261** Beginning of Greek Palaeologian dynasties: ruled the Byzantine Empire until 1453 | |
| **1270–71** Eighth Crusade | | | *c.* **1300** Emergence of Ife kingdom, city state of the Yoruba (West Africa) |
| **1271–72** Ninth Crusade | | | |
| **1305** Papacy moves from Rome to Avignon | **1325** Rise of Aztecs in Mexico | *c.* **1334** Black Death in China | |
| **1337 –1453** Hundred Years' War between France and England | Founding of city of Tenochtitlán | **1336** Revolution in Japan | |
| **1378 –1417** Second Great Schism: break between Rome and Avignon, rival Popes elected | **1370** Expansion of Chimu kingdom in South America | *c.* **1370** Tamerlane begins conquest of Asia | |
| | *c.* **1375** Beginning of Aztec expansion | **1368** Ming Dynasty founded in China | |
| **1381** Peasants' Revolt in England | | **1380** Tartars (the Golden Horde) defeated by the Grand Duke of Moscow | |
| **1385** Portugal's independence from Spain assured | **1438** Inca Empire established in Peru | **1398– 1402** Tamerlane conquers kingdom of Delhi and Ottoman Empire | **1415** Portuguese begin to establish colonies in Africa |
| **1415** Henry V of England defeats French at battle of Agincourt | **1440–69** Montezuma I rules Aztecs | | **1450** Height of Songhai Empire in northwest Africa |
| **1453** England loses all her French possessions except for Calais | **1450** Incas conquer Chimu kingdom | **1453** Ottoman Turks capture Constantinople | |
| **1455–85** Wars of the Roses in England | **1493** First New World settlement by Spanish | | **1482** Portuguese settle Gold Coast (now Ghana) |
| **1492** Last Muslims in Spain conquered by Christians | | **1498** Explorer Vasco da Gama reaches India around Cape of Good Hope | **1492** Spain begins conquest of North African coast |

| EUROPE | AMERICAS | ASIA | AFRICA |
|---|---|---|---|
| **1517** Martin Luther nails '95 theses' to church door at Wittenberg | **1502–20** Aztec conquests under Montezuma II | | **1505** Portuguese begin establishing trading posts in East Africa |
| **1520** Zwingli leads Protestant Reformation in Switzerland | **c. 1510** First African slaves taken to America | **1517** Ottoman Turks conquer Syria, Egypt and Arabia | |
| **1522** First circumnavigation of world by Portuguese navigator, Magellan | **1521** Cortes conquers Aztec capital, Tenochtitlán | | |
| **1529–36** Reformation Parliament begins in England | | **1526** Foundation of Mughal Empire (till 1857) | |
| **1532–36** Calvin starts Protestant movement in France | **1533** Pizarro conquers Peru: end of Inca Empire | **1533** Ivan the Terrible succeeds to Russian throne | |
| **1540** Potato introduced to Europe from New World | **1535** Spaniards explore Chile | | |
| **1545** Council of Trent marks start of the Counter-Reformation (till 1563) | | | **1546** Destruction of Mali Empire in northwest Africa by the Songhai |
| **1558** England loses Calais to French | | | |
| **1562–98** Wars of Religion in France | | | **1570** Kanem-Bornu Empire in the Sudan flourishes |
| **1568 –1648** Eighty Years' War or Dutch Revolt | | | **1571** Portuguese establish colony in Angola (Southern Africa) |
| **1571** Battle of Lepanto: end of Turkish sea power | | | |
| **1588** Spanish Armada defeated by English | **1607** First successful English settlement in America at Jamestown, in Virginia | | **1591** Moroccans destroy Songhai Empire |
| **1600** Foundation of English East India Company | **1608** French colonists found Quebec | | |
| **1618–48** Thirty Years' War in Europe | **1620** Puritans (Pilgrim Fathers) land in New England | | |
| **1649** Execution of Charles I in London | **1624** Dutch settle New Amsterdam | **1630s** Japan isolates itself from the rest of the world | |
| | **1654** Portuguese take Brazil from Dutch | **1644** Ch'ing Dynasty founded in China by Manchus | **1652** Foundation of Cape Colony by Dutch |
| **1688** England's 'Glorious Revolution' | **1664** New Amsterdam seized by British: later renamed New York | **1690** Foundation of Calcutta by British | **1686** French annex Madagascar |
| | **1693** Gold discovered in Brazil | | |

| EUROPE | AMERICAS | ASIA | AFRICA |
|---|---|---|---|
| 1700–14 War of Spanish Succession | | 1707 Break-up of Mughal Empire | 1700 Rise of Ashanti power in the Gold Coast) |
| 1704 Battle of Blenheim | | 1724 Hyderabad in India gains freedom from Mughals | |
| 1707 Union of England and Scotland | | 1757 British rule in India established by battle of Plassey | |
| 1740–48 War of Austrian Succession | 1759 British capture Quebec from French | | |
| 1756–63 Seven Years' War | 1775–83 American War of Independence | 1768 Captain James Cook begins exploration of the Pacific | |
| 1765 Invention of James Watts' steam engine | 1776 Declaration of American Independence | 1773–75 Peasant revolts in Russia | |
| Beginning of Industrial Revolution in Britain | 1789 Washington becomes first US president | 1784 India Act gives Britain control of India | 1787 British acquire Sierra Leone |
| 1789 French Revolution | 1791 Slave revolt in Haiti | 1788 British penal colony at Botany Bay, Australia | 1798 Napoleon attacks Egypt |
| 1804 Napoleon proclaimed Emperor | 1803 Louisiana Purchase doubles size of USA | 1799 Napoleon invades Syria | 1811 Muhammad Ali massacres Mameluke leaders and takes control in Egypt |
| 1812 Napoleon's Russian campaign | 1808–26 Independence movements in South America | 1804–15 Serbs revolt against Ottoman Turks | |
| 1815 Napoleon defeated at Waterloo | | 1819 British establish a trading post at Singapore | 1814 British acquire the Cape Colony in South Africa from the Dutch |
| 1821–29 Greek War of Independence | 1821 Spain grants Mexico independence | | 1818 Zulu Empire founded in southern Africa |
| 1825 First commercial steam railway | 1840 Union of Upper and Lower Canada | | 1822 Liberia founded on the west coast of Africa for freed American slaves |
| 1830 Revolutions in France, Germany, Poland and Italy | 1845 Texas annexed by US | 1840 Britain establishes sovereignty over New Zealand | 1830 French begin conquest of Algeria |
| | 1846–48 War between US and Mexico | 1840–42 First Opium War between Britain and China | 1835–37 Great Trek of Boers in South Africa |
| 1845–46 Irish potato famine | 1848 Gold is found in California | 1842 Hong Kong ceded to Britain by China | 1860 French expansion in West Africa begins |
| 1848 Year of Revolutions | | 1854 and 1858 Trade treaties between Japan and the US | |
| 1854–56 Crimean War | 1861–65 American Civil War | 1856–60 Second Opium War | 1869 Opening of Suez Canal |
| 1861 Kingdom of Italy proclaimed | 1865 Assassination of US president, Abraham Lincoln | 1857 Indian troops mutiny against British Army | 1879 Anglo-Zulu War |
| | 1867 Dominion of Canada formed | 1877 Queen Victoria proclaimed Empress of India | 1880–81 First Anglo-Boer War |
| 1870–71 Franco-Prussian War | Alaska is purchased by the US from Russia | 1885 Indian National Congress formed | 1882 British occupy Egypt |
| 1871 German Empire created | | 1886 Upper and Lower Burma united under British India | 1884 Germany acquires African colonies |
| | | | 1885 Belgium acquires Congo |
| 1882– 1914 Triple Alliance between Germany, Austria and Italy | 1898 Spanish-American War | 1894–95 First Sino-Japanese War | 1886 Germany and Britain divide East Africa |
| | | | 1899 –1902 Second Anglo-Boer War |

| EUROPE | AMERICAS | ASIA | AFRICA |
|---|---|---|---|
| 1904 Anglo-French Entente | | 1901 Unification of Australia | |
| 1905 First Revolution in Russia | 1911 Revolution in Mexico | 1904–05 Russo-Japanese War | |
| 1912–13 Balkan Wars | 1914 Panama Canal opens | 1906 Revolt in Persia | 1910 Union of South Africa formed |
| 1914–18 First World War | 1917 US enters First World War | 1910 Japan annexes Korea | 1911 Italy takes Libya from the Ottoman Empire |
| 1917 Russian Revolution | | 1911–49 Chinese revolution | 1914 Egypt a British Protectorate |
| 1919 Treaty of Versailles | | 1922 Republic proclaimed in Turkey | 1919 Nationalist revolt in Egypt against British occupation |
| 1920 League of Nations established | 1929 Wall Street crash heralds the Depression | 1928 Chiang Kai-shek unites China | 1922 Egypt achieves independence |
| 1922 Irish Free State created by Anglo-Irish Treaty of 1921 | 1933 Roosevelt introduces New Deal in the US | 1931 Japanese occupy Manchuria | 1935 Mussolini invades Abyssinia (Ethiopia) |
| Mussolini takes power in Italy | | 1934–35 Mao Tse-tung's Long March | |
| | | 1937–45 Second Sino-Japanese War | |
| 1926 General Strike in Britain | 1941 US enters Second World War | 1940 Japan allies with Germany | |
| 1933 Hitler becomes German Chancellor | 1945 US drops two atomic bombs on Japan and ends the war in the Pacific | 1941 Japanese attack US fleet at Pearl Harbor | |
| 1936–39 Civil war in Spain | | 1942 Japanese fleet defeated by US at battle of Midway | |
| 1939–45 Second World War | | 1945 Nuclear bombs dropped on Japan | 1949 Apartheid is established in South Africa |
| 1945 United Nations established | | 1946–49 Civil war in China | |
| 1948 Communists seize power in Czechoslovakia | | 1947 India, Pakistan and Burma gain independence | |
| | 1959 Cuban revolution | 1948 Jewish state of Israel founded | |
| | | 1948–49 First Arab-Israeli War | |
| 1956 Hungarian revolt crushed by Russians | 1962 Cuban missile crisis | 1950–53 Korean War | |
| | | 1954–75 Vietnam War | |
| 1958 European Economic Community (EEC) comes into being | 1963 President Kennedy assassinated | 1956 Second Arab-Israeli War | 1956 Suez crisis |
| | 1963–73 US involvement in Vietnam War | 1957 Federation of Malaya independent | 1957 Ghana becomes independent, followed by other African states |
| 1961 Berlin Wall built: beginning of Cold War in Europe | 1968 Martin Luther King Jr, leader of the US Civil Rights Movement, is assassinated | 1962 Sino-Indian War | |
| | | 1967 Third Arab-Israeli War | 1960 Civil war follows independence in the Congo |
| 1968 USSR invades Czechoslovakia | 1969 Neil Armstrong becomes first man on the moon | 1971 East Pakistan becomes Bangladesh | 1962 Algeria gains independence from France |
| 1973 Britain, Eire and Denmark join EC (9 member states) | 1973 Political unrest in Chile culminates in a military coup | 1973 Fourth Arab-Israeli War | 1967–70 Civil war in Nigeria |
| | | 1974 Portuguese African colonies independent | |
| | | 1978 Fifth Arab-Israeli War | |
| 1975 Restoration of monarchy in Spain | 1974 Resignation of US President Nixon: Gerald Ford becomes US president | 1979 Soviet invasion of Afghanistan | 1979 General Amin flees from Uganda |
| | | Shah of Iran deposed: Islamic republic declared | |

| EUROPE | AMERICAS | ASIA | AFRICA |
|---|---|---|---|
| **1980** Polish Solidarity Trade Union, led by Lech Walesa, confronts the Polish Communist government | | **1980–88** Iran-Iraq War | **1980** Rhodesia, last British colony in Africa, becomes independent as Zimbabwe |
| **1981** Greece becomes 10th member of the EC | **1981** US hostages in Iran freed | **1984** Indian prime minister, Indira Gandhi, is assassinated | **1981** President Sadat of Egypt is assassinated |
| **1986** Prime Minister Palme of Sweden assassinated | **1982** Falklands War between Argentina and Britain: Britain retains Falklands | | |
| Spain and Portugal join the EC (12 member states) | **1983** US troops invade Grenada | **1986** Overthrow of Marcos regime in Philippines | **1985** Renewed unrest in South Africa |
| **1988** A bomb on board Pan Am Flight 103 causes the break-up of the plane over Lockerbie – 270 people are killed | **1986** US raid on Libya | **1987** Ongoing civil war in Lebanon | **1986** Ethiopia has worst famine in more than ten years |
| | Nuclear arms talks resume between USA and USSR | | |
| **1989** Berlin Wall dismantled | **1987** Falling dollar and Wall Street crash | **1990** Gulf War begins: Iran invades Kuwait | |
| **1991** Break up of the Soviet Union | **1989** US troops invade Panama | US and Allies send troops to Gulf region | **1990** Nelson Mandela, African National Congress (ANC) political prisoner, is freed in South Africa: process of dismantling apartheid begins |
| West and East Germany are united | | | |
| **1992** Bloody civil war in Yugoslavia: European Commission recognizes independence of Croatia and Slovenia | **1992** Bill Clinton is elected US president | **1994** Israel and PLO sign pact ending Israeli occupation of Gaza Strip and Jericho | |
| **1993** Czechoslovakia is split into Slovakia and the Czech Republic | | **1995** Israeli Prime Minister Yitzakh Rabin is assassinated | **1994** In South Africa ANC wins first multiracial election in Africa |
| **1994–96** First Russian-Chechen War | **1994** US troops invade Haiti to oust military government | **1997** Hong Kong returned to Chinese rule | Massacre of Tutsis by Hutus in Rwanda leaves estimated 500,000 dead and 1.5 million homeless |
| **1995** Dayton Peace Accords end civil war in Bosnia and Herzegovina | | **1999** King Hussein of Jordan dies: Prince Abdullah is king | |
| Austria, Finland and Sweden join the EC now the EU (15 member states) | | Allied jets attack missile sites in Iraq | **1997** End of civil war in Zaire and country is renamed as the Democratic Republic of Congo |
| **1997** Labour Party wins British general election: Tony Blair is prime minister | | Inhabitants of East Timor vote for independence from Indonesia: UN sends in an Australian peacekeeping force when Indonesian militia go on the rampage | |
| | **1999** Self-governing region of Nunavut in northwest Canada comes into being | | **1999** UN troops pull out of Angola |
| **1998** Good Friday Agreement in Northern Ireland | | | President Nelson Mandela of South Africa stands down from politics: Thabo Mbeki is new president |
| **1999** Entire European Commission resigns following a report on corruption | Lost Mayan city found at border of Mexico and Guatemala | Military coup ends civilian government in Pakistan | |

| EUROPE | AMERICAS | ASIA | AFRICA |
|---|---|---|---|
| **1999 –2002** Major combat in Second Russian-Chechen War | **2000** President Fuyimori of Peru decamps to Japan | **2000** Fijian government overthrown by armed coup | **2000** Devastating floods in Mozambique |
| **2000** Spain and Britain agree on administrative arrangements for Gibraltar | **2001** George W Bush becomes US president | Israel withdraws from South Lebanon | **2001** More devastating floods in Mozambique |
| **2001** Former Yugoslav president, Slobodan Milosevic, extradited to the Hague to stand trial for war crimes | IMF lends $8 billion to Argentina to stave off the country's financial collapse | **2001** Ongoing violence in Israeli-Palestinian conflict | Zimbabwe approves legislation for white-owned farms to be confiscated without compensation |
| **2001–02** Outbreak of foot and mouth disease rocks British agricultral industry | US is target of coordinated terrorist attacks on World Trade Center and the Pentagon: US Senate enacts anti-terrorism legislation | United Islamic Front for the Salvation of Afghanistan, with US and British air support, defeats the Taliban government | **2002** Mt Nyiragongo erupts in DR Congo |
| **2002** The euro, a single currency shared by 12 members of the EU, successfully launched | **2002** US slaps a heavy tariff on steel imports | **2002** East Timor recognised internationally as an independent state | Robert Mugabe re-elected as President of Zimbabwe |
| **2003** British prime minister Tony Blair supports coalition forces going into Iraq | **2003** NASA spacecraft breaks up on re-entry | **2003** US-led Coalition forces invade Iraq: US-led transitional authority is set up to oversee transference of rule to a civilian government | **2003** Nigerian peacekeeping force enters Liberia to stop civil war |
| Heatwave in Europe causes around 10,000 deaths among the elderly in France | US lifts much-criticized tariff on steel imports | | **2004** African National Congress wins South African general election with 70% of the vote |
| **2004** 10 more countries join the EU (25 member states) | Invasion of Iraq by US-led Coalition Forces | North Korea withdraws from Nuclear Non-Proliferation Treaty | In Sudan, the government and the People's Liberation Army agree to end the civil war: ongoing violence in the Darfur region |
| Swedish foreign minister, Anna Lindh, is stabbed to death in Stockholm | **2004** Haitian President Aristide resigns and goes into exile | **2004** Insurgency in Iraq reaches new heights of violence in a sustained suicide bombing campaign | |
| **2005** Suicide bombers in London underground trains and a bus kill 52 people and wound over 700: British born al-Qaeda activists are identified as responsible | NASA lands a mobile robot on Mars | Asian Tsunami devastates shoreline communities in Indonesia, Sri Lanka and India | A UN report states that life expectancy in 7 African countries has fallen below 40 |
| | Venezuela votes to keep President Hugo Chavez in office by 52% to 48% | **2005** Parliamentary elections held in Iraq: Shiites largest party but do not have majority vote | **2005** A forced 'slum clearance' by the government of Zimbabwe drives fringe town dwellers back into the countryside |
| Angela Merkel elected Chancellor of Germany | George W Bush re-elected as US president | Israel withdraws settlers from Gaza Strip | Ellen Johnson is elected President of Liberia: first woman president in Africa |
| | **2005** US continues its presence in Iraq | North Korea admits possession of nuclear weapons | |
| | Hurricane Katrina devastates US Gulf coast | | |
| | **2006** Space Shuttle Discovery is launched to the International Space Station. | | |

## EUROPE

- **2006** Montenegro declares independence
- **2007** Bulgaria and Romania join the EU
- **2008** Kosovo declares independence
- South Ossetia War takes place between Russia and Georgia
- **2009** Collapse of Icelandic banking system and government
- **2010** David Cameron's Conservatives win UK general election
- Greece in economic crisis
- European sovereign debt crisis declared
- **2011** Air travel in Northwestern Europe disrupted when Icelandic volcano erupts
- **2012** CERN announces the discovery of a new particle consistent with the Higgs boson
- Pope Benedict XVI resigns. Pope Francis becomes new pope
- **2013** Ukrainian president rejects trade deal with the EU. Hundreds of thousands protest in Kiev. Restrictive anti-protest laws are passed
- **2014** Protesters in Kiev killed by snipers. Crimea votes to become Russian state. Russian troops in Ukraine
- Croatia and Latvia join the EU
- **2015** The European migrant crisis escalates
- Greece accepts austerity measures and receives a third bailout package
- Co-ordinated terrorist attacks in Paris by ISIL

## AMERICAS

- **2007** The release of the first iPhone
- The US House of Representatives passes first gay rights bill, the Matthew Shepard Act
- **2008** Global economic recession is sparked by the US subprime mortgage crisis
- Barack Obama is first African-American President of US
- **2009** Peru's Supreme Court finds Alberto Fujimori guilty of authorizing death squads and sentences him to 25 years in prison
- **2010** Thirty-three miners are brought safely to the surface after being trapped deep underground for 69 days in the San José mine in Chile
- **2011** Mexican officials say nearly 13,000 people died in drug-related violence this year
- **2012** Hurrican Sandy claims 209 lives in the USA
- Terrorist attack at the Boston Marathon.
- Barack Obama is re-elected as president
- **2014** John Kovac and the team at Harvard Smithsonian Center for Astrophysics find evidence of the Big Bang theory.
- **2015** Cuba and America re-establish full diplomatic relations
- US and Mexico open first new rail link in more than a century

## ASIA

- **2006** North Korea carries out its first nuclear test underground
- **2007** Benazir Bhutto assasinated
- India's first commercial space rocket is launched
- **2008** The Gaza War of 2008–09 begins between Palestinians in the Gaza Strip and Israel
- 200 people killed and hundreds injured in a series of attacks by gunmen in Mumbai
- **2010** Malaysian Parliament celebrates the 50th anniversary of its formation
- **2011** Osama Bin Laden, leader of Al-Qaeda, is killed in a US operation
- Japanese tsunami kills 16,000 and causes meltdown of Fukushima nuclear plant
- Kim Jong-il of North Korea dies, son named as new leader
- **2013** Philippines struck by Typhoon Haiyan killing over 6000 people
- **2014** More Gaza–Israel conflict
- **2015** The growing terrorist threat in the Middle East from ISIS and civil war in Syria lead to hundreds of thousands of refugees seeking asylum in Europe
- Iran and 6 world powers reach a nuclear deal
- A 7.9 earthquake hits Nepal and kills more than 9,000 people

## AFRICA

- **2008** South Africa experiences a wave of xenophobic violence
- **2009** South African Parliament elects Jacob Zuma as president
- Lockerbie bomber Abdelbaset Ali al-Megrahi is freed by Scotland and returned to Libya
- **2010** Anti-government protests in Tunisia spark the Arab Spring
- **2011** Revolutions follow in Tunisia, Egypt, Libya and Yemen
- South Sudan Votes for independence
- Libyan leader Muammar Gaddafi is killed, ending the Libyan civil war
- UN Security Council votes to withdraw UN forces from Chad and the Central African Republic
- Civil war begins in Syria
- **2012** Conflict in Northern Mali, President Touré removed
- Egyptian president Mohamed Moursi deposed
- Sudan–South Sudan Border War
- **2013** Death of Nelson Mandela
- **2014** Islamic terrorist group Boko Haram kidnap around 200 girls from a school Chibok in Borno State, Nigeria
- Massacre in Bentiu South Sudan
- Ebola outbreak in West Africa
- **2015** A terrorist attack by al-Shabaab kills 148 students at Moi University in Garissa, Kenya

# The First Humans

Our closest relations in the animal world are chimpanzees and gorillas. By about 4 million years ago, the earliest human ancestors had evolved in Africa. They were called *Australopithecus* (which means 'southern ape'), but unlike apes they had the ability to walk upright. The first *Homo* (man) fossils which have been found date to 2 million years ago, but it was not until about 100,000 years ago that the first fully modern humans evolved in Africa. Over these millions of years of human evolution, the most noticeable development was in the size of the skull and the brain. As our ancestors' brains became larger, they developed other skills: the ability to make tools, to use language, to work together as a group, to create the first art.

During the cold phases of the last Ice Age, which lasted from about 2 million to 10,000 years ago, temperatures were, on average, 10–15°C lower than the present day. Humans were therefore forced to adapt to a hostile world. In cold climates, they learned to use fire, find or build shelters and make warm clothes. They became skilled at making tools and weapons, and were lethal hunters. By about 10,000 years ago modern humans had spread from Africa to the most remote corners of the globe. During cold periods, a great deal of water was locked up in the large ice sheets (glaciers) that covered much of the northern hemisphere. This caused sea levels to fall, revealing land 'bridges' that linked the continents, enabling our ancestors to cross from Asia into North America and from South East Asia into Australia.

When the ice finally retreated, large game, such as woolly mammoths, was increasingly scarce. Humans had to find new sources of food and began to experiment with the domestication of certain plants and animals – the agricultural revolution had begun.

### Homo Habilis

*Homo habilis (handy man) was so called because of his ability to make tools. Feet and hand fossils show some similarities to modern humans' feet and hands. They indicate that he would have had a strong grip and would have been able to manipulate tools effectively. He was probably a meat-eater – tools were needed to separate the flesh from the carcass.*

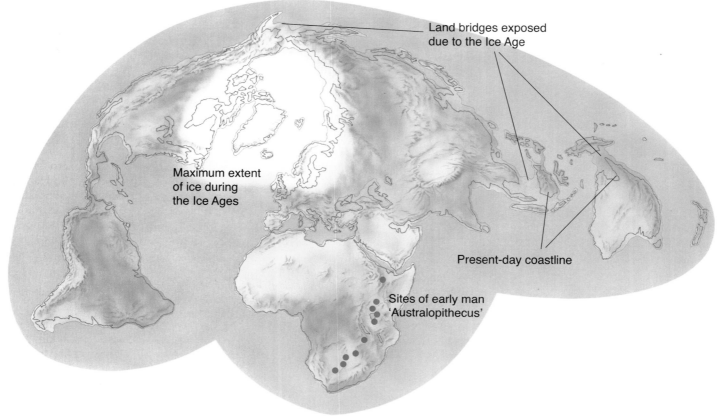

Land bridges exposed due to the Ice Age

Maximum extent of ice during the Ice Ages

Present-day coastline

Sites of early man 'Australopithecus'

# The First Civilizations 3500–1000 BC

The cultivation of plants, such as wheat and barley, and the domestication of animals, such as sheep, goats and cattle, began in the Near East in about 8500 BC. As people turned to farming, they began to live in fixed settlements, which became small towns. In about 5000 BC, farmers moved down into the fertile river valleys of Mesopotamia, and built dykes and ditches to irrigate the arid land. Their labours bore fruit; surplus food freed some of the population from farming. These people became merchants, craftsmen and priests. As the settlements grew into cities, they became more organized; laws were made, writing evolved, and religious and public buildings were built.

  Between 3500 and 1800 years ago, three great civilizations evolved in Mesopotamia, Egypt and the Indus valley of northern India. All three civilizations were located in the fertile valleys of great rivers. Each civilization was based on substantial cities, inhabited by several thousand people and containing imposing public buildings, such as temples and palaces. Each civilization had evolved a form of writing. All three civilizations show evidence of a strong, centralized administration or all-powerful rulers – in Mesopotamia, for example, rulers were buried with their sacrificed servants as well as a vast array of their worldly possessions.

## Egypt

The cities, tombs and temples of Ancient Egypt lined the banks of the River Nile. Every year the river flooded, depositing fertile mud along its banks – when the waters receded, these lands could be cultivated. During the Nile flood (August to October), the vast majority of the Egyptian population, who lived by farming, could work for the pharaoh, building temples, tombs and pyramids. During the Old Kingdom (c. 2685–2185 BC), when all of Egypt was under the rule of one pharaoh, the important centres were in the north, around Giza and Memphis. In the New Kingdom (c. 1552–1071), the main royal city was Thebes, in Middle Egypt.

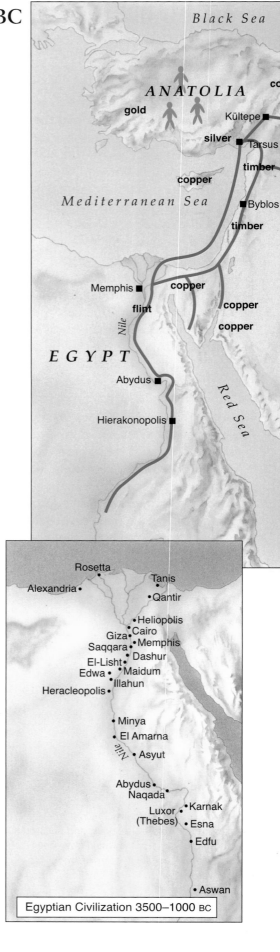

Egyptian Civilization 3500–1000 BC

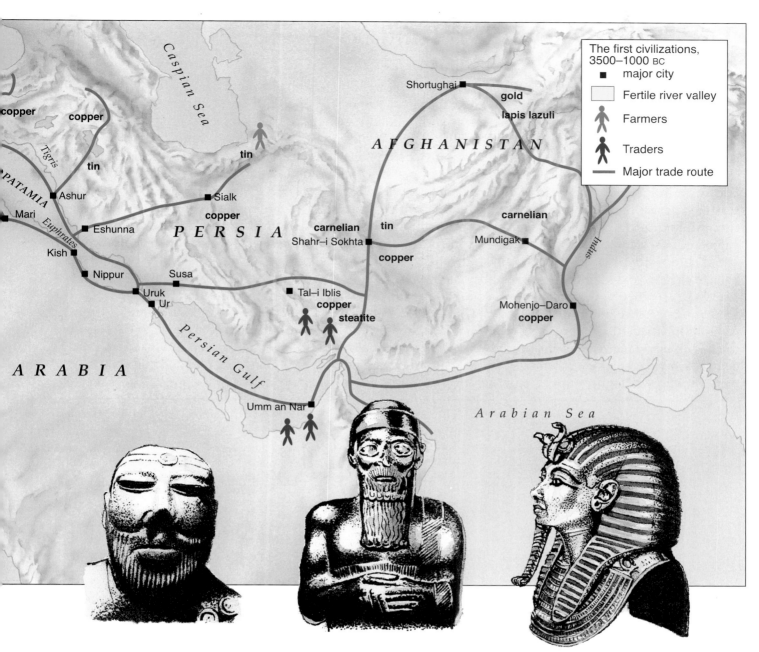

Shortughai

gold

lapis lazuli

AFGHANISTAN

Caspian Sea

copper

copper

tin

Tigris

tin

Ashur

Mari

Euphrates

Eshunna

Kish

Nippur

Uruk

Ur

Susa

Sialk

copper

PERSIA

carnelian

Shahr–i Sokhta

tin

copper

Tal–i Iblis

copper

steatite

carnelian

Mundigak

Indus

Mohenjo–Daro

copper

ARABIA

Persian Gulf

Umm an Nar

Arabian Sea

This head from the Indus valley
city of Mohenjo-Daro, c. 2100 BC, may
represent a priest-king.

Ishtup-Ilum, c. 2100 BC, was the ruler of
Mari, a city-state in northern
Mesopotamia.

The solid gold funeral mask of the Egyptian
pharaoh, Tutankhamun, c. 1340 BC.

### The Temple of Ur

The temple at the Mesopotamian city of Ur was
a ziggurat, comprising an ascending series of
terraces, made from mud bricks, and decorated
with mosaics. Each terrace would have been
planted with a 'hanging garden' of trees. The
temple was dedicated to the worship of the
city's patron deity, the moon-god, Nanna.
Surrounding the temple stood the houses of the
lower town, which contained 20,000 people at
its peak.

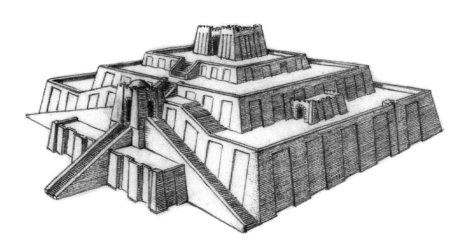

# The Bronze Age 2000–1000 BC

Metal-working first occurred in Turkey and Iran in about 6000 BC, when people began to smelt copper and lead. By 3000 BC, it was a flourishing craft in the city-states of Mesopotamia and it became increasingly specialized as craftsmen began to experiment with mixing together different metals to produce alloys. By adding a small quantity of tin to copper they produced bronze, a harder metal that could be used for making stronger weapons, with sharper cutting edges. By about 2500 BC, copper was in use over a region that stretched from the Iberian peninsula to Scandinavia and, within a thousand years, bronze was being used by craftsmen in Europe. At this time, much of Europe was still thickly forested, and people lived in widely scattered agricultural villages. Tin, a vital component of bronze, was a rare resource, found mainly along the Atlantic coast of Europe. It was transported along long-distance trade routes and exchanged for other highly valued goods, such as Baltic amber and salt. Control of these precious resources led to the rise of a wealthy social elite, who turned to metalsmiths to produce bronze regalia, symbolic of their rank. Costly daggers, bronze sheaths and helmets, and metal breastplates were buried with chieftains in 'barrow burials' – graves that were crowned with large mounds of earth or stone. As the European population grew, there was increasing pressure on limited resources. Conflict began to break out between communities, and people began to build fortified villages or fortresses, which could be defended against groups of marauders. In Crete and the Greek mainland, two sophisticated Bronze Age societies began to emerge between 2000 BC and 1500 BC, centred on palaces which ruled over an agricultural hinterland. The Minoans of Crete built substantial palaces, whose magnificent wall paintings depict young acrobats leaping over a bull's horns. The Cretans

### Trundholm Sun Chariot

Scandinavia flourished during the second millennium BC, growing rich on its trade in precious Baltic amber. Bronze-working was greatly valued. The sun was probably worshipped and sun symbolism was widespread. This bronze, wheeled model of a horse pulling a disk (the sun), was probably a revered religious object.

### Mask of Agamemnon

When the royal tombs of Mycenae in mainland Greece were excavated in the nineteenth century, gold death-masks, tiaras, bowls, daggers and wine cups were found. One of the gold masks was associated with Agamemnon, the Mycenaean warlord celebrated by the poet Homer in his epic works, the Iliad and the Odyssey.

were skilled craftsmen and traders, and examples of Minoan jewellery and pottery have been found in Egypt, Greece and Italy. It is thought that a massive volcanic eruption on the island of Santorini *c.* 1450 BC shattered Minoan civilization. On the Greek mainland, Mycenaean civilization was more warlike. Great Mycenaean cities, such as Mycenae and Pylos, were fortresses that ruled over the surrounding countryside, and Mycenaean traders dominated the eastern Mediterranean. But by 1000 BC internal conflict, or possibly foreign invasion, had brought about their downfall.

Meanwhile, in East Asia, the Shang state developed *c.* 1800 BC from earlier agricultural communities that had evolved on the Yellow River. It was a feudal society, ruled by the Shang Dynasty of kings who lived in elaborate, luxurious palaces. The Shang were fierce soldiers, who used ancestor worship and human sacrifice to assert their power. Ancestors were consulted through oracle bones – animal bones heated to produce cracks which were then interpreted. Elaborate bronze vessels were used by the king and his aristocrats to offer wine and food to the spirits of their ancestors. But Shang rule was not to last, and in about 1100 BC the dynasty collapsed and the era of Chou China began.

### Shang Bronze

Bronze halberds, with decorated hilts, were the main weapons of war in Shang China. Metalworking in China dates back to about 1800 BC, and bronze was widely used for everyday objects and weapons. More elaborate ritual vessels, cast from ceramic moulds, were decorated with vigorous animal motifs.

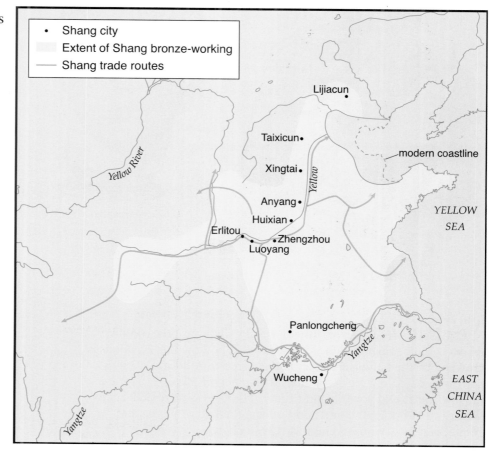

- • Shang city
- Extent of Shang bronze-working
- —— Shang trade routes

Yellow River
Lijiacun
Taixicun
Xingtai
Yellow
Anyang
Huixian
Erlitou
Zhengzhou
Luoyang
modern coastline
YELLOW SEA
Panlongcheng
Yangtze
Wucheng
EAST CHINA SEA
Yangtze

# Greece 750–150 BC

Europe's earliest advanced civilization flourished on the island of Crete from 2200 to 1400 BC. Minoan civilization, centred on palace-cities, prospered by trading goods such as olive oil and pottery within the Mediterranean. Meanwhile, on the Peloponnese peninsula, another Bronze Age civilization was emerging, based on fortified palace-cities such as Mycenae. This more warlike civilization collapsed in about 1200 BC. A period known as the 'dark ages' followed but, in about 800 BC, populations began to expand, and small city-states, consisting of a city surrounded by towns, villages and agricultural land, began to evolve. By about 500 BC, Athens had become the richest and most important city-state in Classical Greece, as well as the cultural and intellectual centre of the Greek world. Democracy was born in Athens: Athenian citizens (free men but not women) had the right to vote on all matters of govern-ment, and any citizen could serve for a year as a city magis-trate, paid by the state. But, in 404 BC, Athens was crushed by Sparta, a rival city-state, where a small elite ruled over their subject peoples with the help of a well-trained army. In the fourth century BC the Greeks were united under the Macedonian leader, Alexander, who conquered the mighty empire of Persia. Wherever he went, he founded cities, spread-ing Greek culture and language throughout the Middle East.

## Alexander the Great

*Alexander the Great, son of King Philip of Macedonia, conquered a vast area, stretching from Greece to the borders of India from 334–323 BC. He died when he was just 33.*

## Athens

Most Greek cities clustered around a rocky outcrop, or acropolis, which could be defended in times of crisis. The Athenian acropolis is crowned by the famous Parthenon, dedicated to Athena, the city's patron deity. Below the acropolis, lay the market place, or agora, and the law courts and government offices. The Greeks were dedicated to the health of both mind and body, so large public gymnasia and amphitheatres were found in most Greek cities.

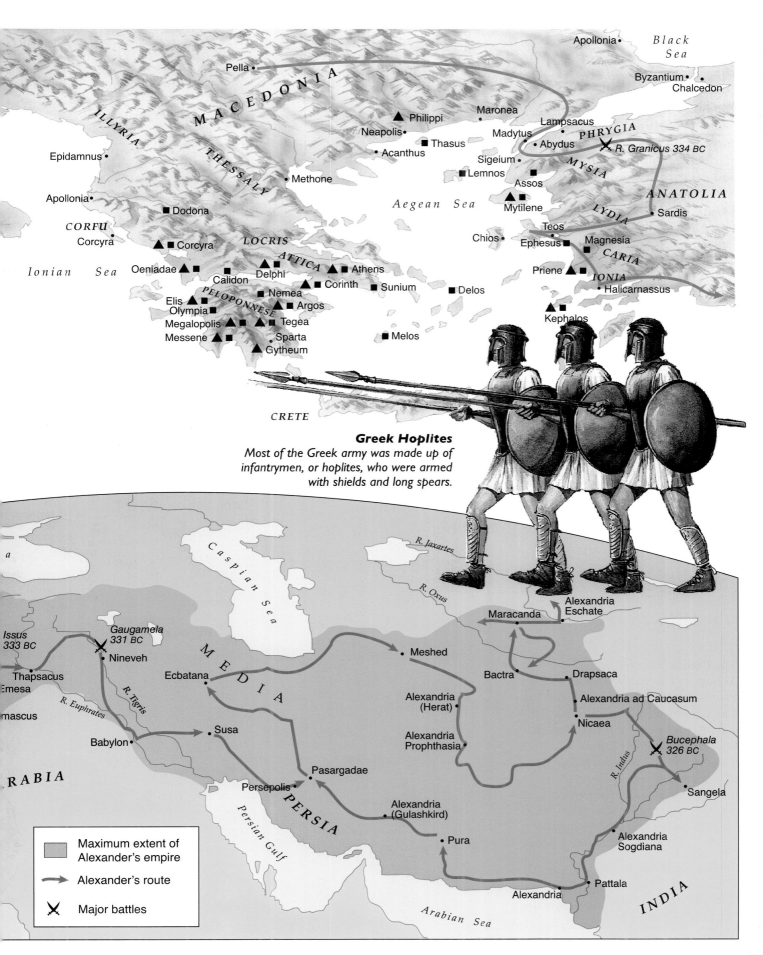

Apollonia •

Black Sea

Byzantium •
• Chalcedon

Pella •

MACEDONIA

ILLYRIA

Maronea
Lampsacus

Philippi ▲
Madytus

Neapolis •
Thasus ■

PHRYGIA

Abydus

✗ R. Granicus 334 BC

Epidamnus •

THESSALY

Acanthus •

Sigeium

MYSIA

Apollonia •

Methone •

Lemnos ■

Assos ■

ANATOLIA

CORFU

Dodona ■

Aegean Sea

Mytilene ▲■

LYDIA

Sardis •

Corcyra

Corcyra ▲■

LOCRIS

Teos •

Chios •

Ephesus ■

Magnesia ■

Ionian Sea

Oeniadae ▲■

ATTICA

Delphi ▲■

Athens ▲■

Priene ▲■

CARIA

Calidon •

Corinth ▲■

IONIA

Nemea ■

Sunium •

Delos •

Halicarnassus •

Elis ▲

Olympia •

Argos ▲■

Megalopolis ▲

Tegea ▲■

Melos ■

Kephalos ▲■

Messene ▲■

Sparta •

Gytheum ▲

CRETE

**Greek Hoplites**
*Most of the Greek army was made up of infantrymen, or hoplites, who were armed with shields and long spears.*

R. Jaxartes

Caspian Sea

R. Oxus

Alexandria Eschate

Maracanda

*Issus 333 BC*

*Gaugamela 331 BC*

Meshed

Thapsacus

✗ Nineveh

MEDIA

Bactra

Drapsaca

Emesa

R. Tigris

Ecbatana

Alexandria (Herat)

Alexandria ad Caucasum

mascus

R. Euphrates

Susa

Nicaea

Babylon •

Alexandria Prophthasia

*Bucephala 326 BC*

ARABIA

Pasargadae

R. Indus

Persepolis •

Alexandria (Gulashkird)

Sangela

PERSIA

Persian Gulf

Pura •

Alexandria Sogdiana

Maximum extent of Alexander's empire

Pattala •

Alexander's route

Alexandria

INDIA

✗ Major battles

Arabian Sea

57

# Rome 500 BC–AD 500

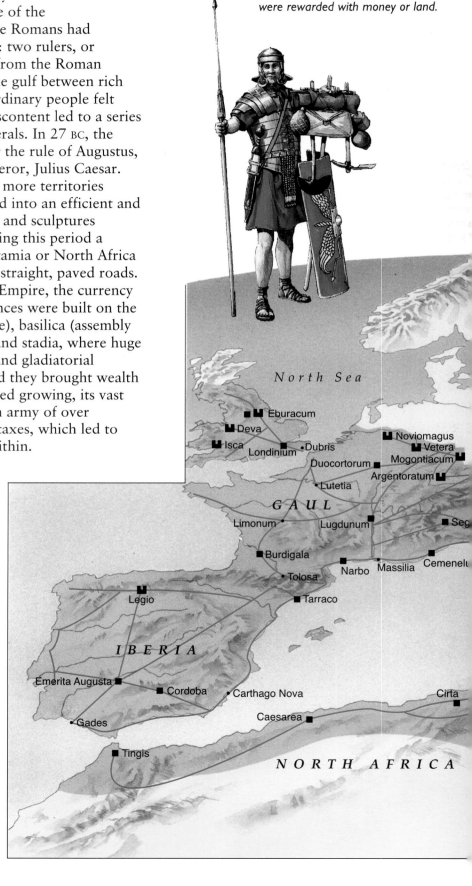

In 1000 BC Rome was no more than a collection of farming villages clustered around seven hills. Yet by 203 BC the Romans controlled the Italian peninsula, the whole of the Mediterranean Sea, Spain and Greece. The Romans had evolved a form of republican government: two rulers, or consuls, presided over the senate, drawn from the Roman aristocracy and rich landowners. But as the gulf between rich and poor within Rome grew wider, the ordinary people felt that they held none of the power. This discontent led to a series of bitter civil wars between powerful generals. In 27 BC, the Roman Republic became an empire under the rule of Augustus, the adopted son of the general and conqueror, Julius Caesar.

Under the rule of the Emperor Augustus more territories were conquered, the army was reorganized into an efficient and loyal fighting force, magnificent buildings and sculptures adorned all the empire's major cities. During this period a Roman citizen could travel from Mesopotamia or North Africa to the northern borders of England along straight, paved roads. Latin was spoken throughout the Roman Empire, the currency was universal. Even cities in distant provinces were built on the Roman model, with a forum (market place), basilica (assembly hall), temples, theatres, palaces, libraries and stadia, where huge crowds gathered to watch chariot racing and gladiatorial combat. As new provinces were conquered they brought wealth to the empire. But when the empire stopped growing, its vast size became a problem; the expenses of an army of over 300,000 men had to be met by increased taxes, which led to discontent, weakening the empire from within.

## The Roman Empire

As new provinces were added to the Roman Empire, the conquerors set about 'Romanizing' them. Towns and capital cities were built to follow the layout and design of Rome. Straight, paved roads and aqueducts linked these new settlements. In the countryside, land was cleared and irrigated so that it was ready for cultivation. A provincial governor was appointed to run the province and ensure that there were no revolts against Roman rule. Legions of the Roman army were sent to the provinces to help keep the peace and were often stationed in fortresses along the borders of the empire.

58

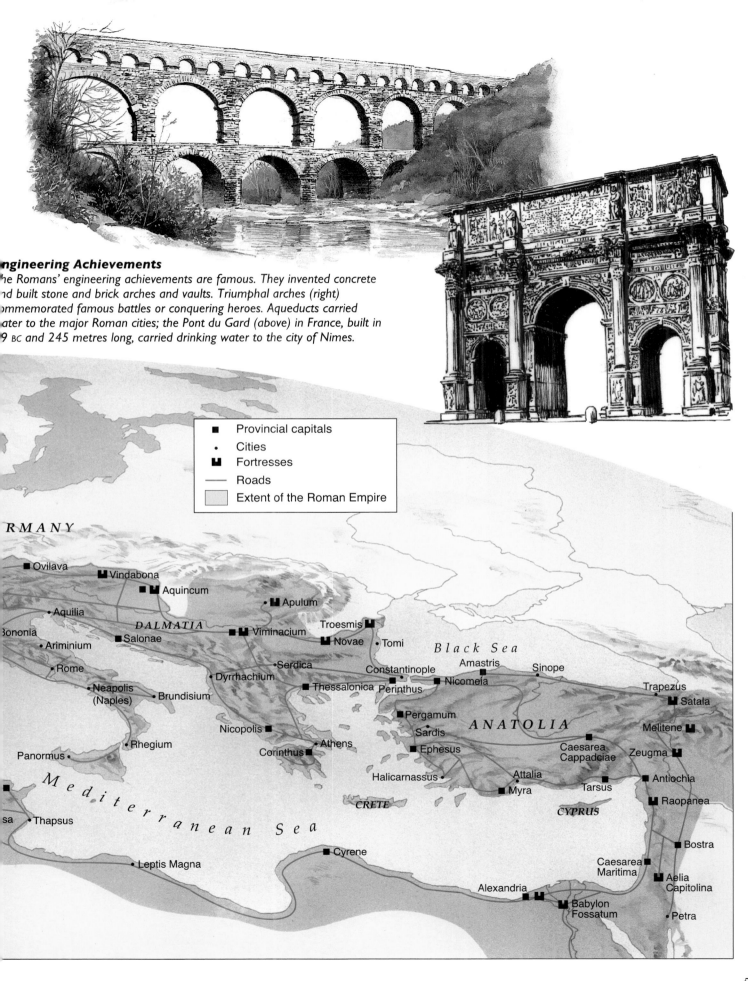

## Engineering Achievements

The Romans' engineering achievements are famous. They invented concrete and built stone and brick arches and vaults. Triumphal arches (right) commemorated famous battles or conquering heroes. Aqueducts carried water to the major Roman cities; the Pont du Gard (above) in France, built in 19 BC and 245 metres long, carried drinking water to the city of Nimes.

**Legend:**
- ■ Provincial capitals
- · Cities
- ⬛ Fortresses
- — Roads
- ▨ Extent of the Roman Empire

GERMANY

- ■ Ovilava
- ⬛ Vindabona
- ⬛⬛ Aquincum
- · Aquilia
- DALMATIA
- Bononia
- · Ariminium
- ■ Salonae
- · Rome
- ⬛⬛ Viminacium
- · Apulum
- Troesmis ⬛
- ⬛ Novae
- · Tomi
- Black Sea
- · Serdica
- Amastris
- · Sinope
- · Dyrrhachium
- Constantinople
- ■ Thessalonica
- Nicomeia
- Perinthus
- Trapezus
- Pergamum
- ⬛ Satala
- ■ Neapolis (Naples)
- · Brundisium
- Nicopolis ■
- ANATOLIA
- Melitene ⬛
- Sardis
- · Rhegium
- · Athens
- Ephesus
- Caesarea Cappadciae
- Zeugma ⬛
- Panormus ·
- Corinthus ■
- Halicarnassus ·
- Attalia
- Tarsus
- ■ Antiochia
- Myra
- Mediterranean Sea
- CRETE
- CYPRUS
- ■ Raopanea
- ·sa
- · Thapsus
- · Bostra
- Caesarea Maritima ■
- · Cyrene
- · Leptis Magna
- Alexandria
- Babylon Fossatum
- Aelia Capitolina
- · Petra

# Europe Attacked AD 600–1100

The success of the Roman Empire led to its downfall, its sheer size making administration increasingly difficult. In the third century the empire split into the Byzantine Empire and the Western Empire. Throughout the third century AD, nomadic tribes from central Asia, such as the Visigoths and Franks, had been pressing on Rome's northern frontiers. With the weakening of the empire, they broke through, sweeping south in search of new lands. These tribes were pastoralists; accompanied by their animal herds they travelled long distances, living in tented camps. With the collapse of the Western Roman Empire in the fifth century AD, one of the nomadic tribes, the Franks, became Europe's most powerful rulers. Under their great king, Charlemagne, the Frankish Carolingian Empire became known as the 'Holy Roman Empire' and extended from France to Italy.

**Charlemagne**
*A gold bust of Charlemagne (742–814), King of the Franks.*

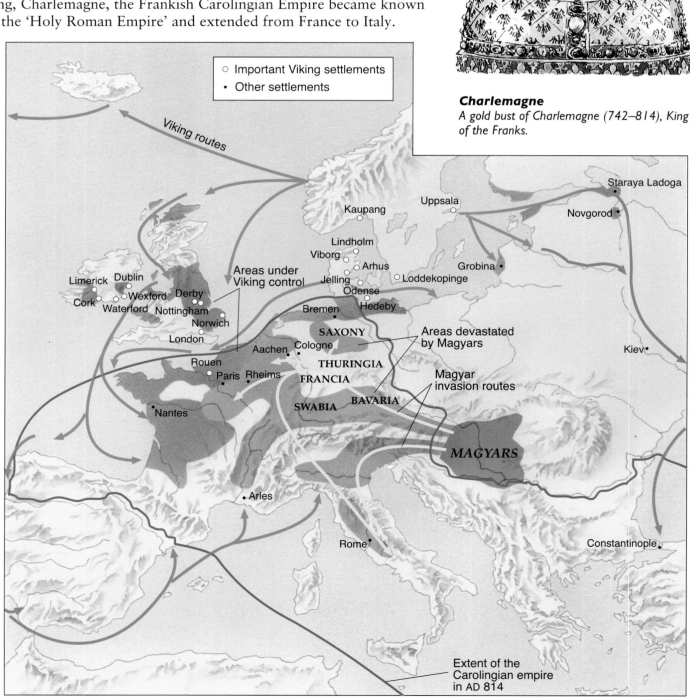

- ○ Important Viking settlements
- • Other settlements

Viking routes

Kaupang
Uppsala
Staraya Ladoga
Novgorod
Lindholm
Viborg
Arhus
Grobina
Jelling
Loddekopinge
Odense
Limerick
Dublin
Derby
Cork
Wexford
Waterford
Nottingham
Norwich
London
Bremen
Hedeby
**SAXONY**
Areas under Viking control
Aachen
Cologne
Rouen
Paris
Rheims
**THURINGIA**
**FRANCIA**
Areas devastated by Magyars
Kiev
**SWABIA**
**BAVARIA**
Magyar invasion routes
Nantes
**MAGYARS**
Arles
Rome
Constantinople

Extent of the Carolingian empire in AD 814

## The Vikings

In the eighth century, a seafaring people called the Vikings sailed in their longboats from Norway, Denmark and Sweden to find new lands to colonize. They raided coastal settlements, murdering and terrorizing the native populations and plundering their monasteries, returning to their homelands laden with treasure. In the mid-ninth century, instead of returning home, Viking raiders began to make permanent settlements. They were good farmers, adapting themselves to the culture of the peoples they conquered. Accomplished traders, they established trade routes throughout northwestern Europe. Some reached America. By crossing the Baltic Sea, Vikings entered the great river systems of European Russia, and *c.* 862 formed the first Russian state in Novgorod. Using the south-flowing rivers, they penetrated the forests and frozen wastes of Russia, establishing trading stations as far as the Black Sea and the Mediterranean. Though fearless warriors, the Vikings were also good craftsmen, producing fine swords and beautiful woodcarvings.

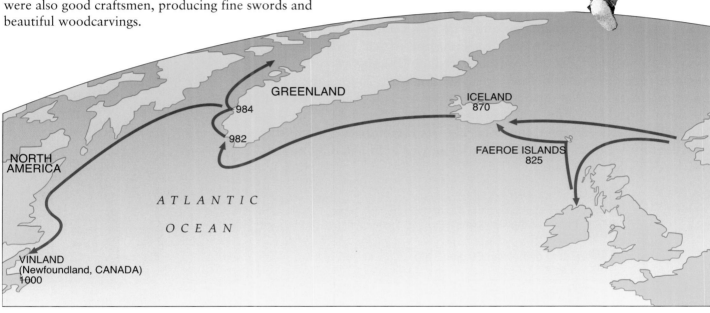

GREENLAND

ICELAND
870

984

982

FAEROE ISLANDS
825

NORTH
AMERICA

*ATLANTIC*

*OCEAN*

VINLAND
(Newfoundland, CANADA)
1000

### A Viking Settlement
*The Vikings established a trading centre at Hedeby in Denmark where several major trade routes intersected. Over the years, Hedeby became a major trading centre. To protect the town from hostile German tribes, an earth embankment topped with a timber palisade was built around it. The houses were constructed of wood and earth. The entire family slept, ate, worked and played together in one small room. The house of a more prosperous Viking might have two or three rooms. Their food came from fishing, hunting and from local farms.*

# Asian Empires 100 BC–AD 1300

China was first united under the short-lived Ch'in Dynasty in 221 BC. The succeeding Han Dynasty (202 BC–AD 220) ruled a united China for over four centuries. During this period, China grew prosperous, with an efficient administration, extensive road and canal network, and a growing number of large towns. Paper was invented. Chang'an (or Xi'an), the Han capital, stood at the beginning of the Silk Road, the great trade route across central Asia. Merchants travelled the road, their camels laden with silk. After a long period of decline, the Han Empire collapsed and for 400 years China was fragmented. Its unification, begun during the Sui Dynasty, was consolidated by the T'ang (618–907), one of the greatest periods in Chinese history. Chang'an became one of the world's largest cities. The T'ang were famed for their arts, literature and poetry. With the decline of the T'ang, a new dynasty, the Sung or Song (AD 960–1279), began. The Sung built a centrally controlled bureaucracy and army. Ocean-going junks laden with tea, silk and porcelain sailed for India and Africa. Urban centres grew and flourished. Printing was invented, developing later into movable type, 400 years before it reached the West. Among the Sung's finest products were its superb pottery and porcelain. The refinement of the Sung period lasted for 300 years until it was shattered by the Mongol invasion. In Japan, Imperial rule was established in about the fifth century AD. In the ninth century, Japan was dominated by military overlords, called shoguns.

Samarkand

Area under
Chinese military
control

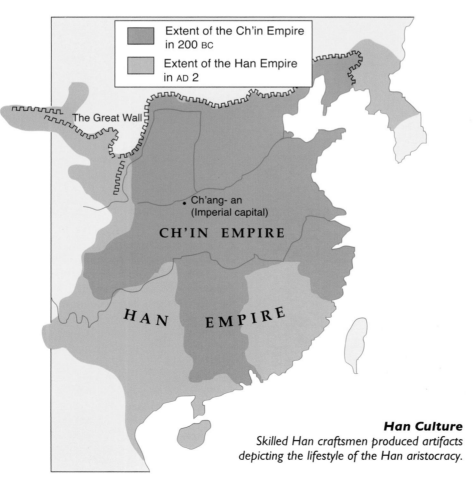

The Great Wall

Ch'ang- an
(Imperial capital)

**CH'IN EMPIRE**

**HAN EMPIRE**

Extent of the Ch'in Empire
in 200 BC

Extent of the Han Empire
in AD 2

**Model Army**
*In 221 BC Shi Huang Ti founded the Ch'in Dynasty. On his death he was buried with thousands of life-size pottery figures and horses.*

**Han Culture**
*Skilled Han craftsmen produced artifacts depicting the lifestyle of the Han aristocracy.*

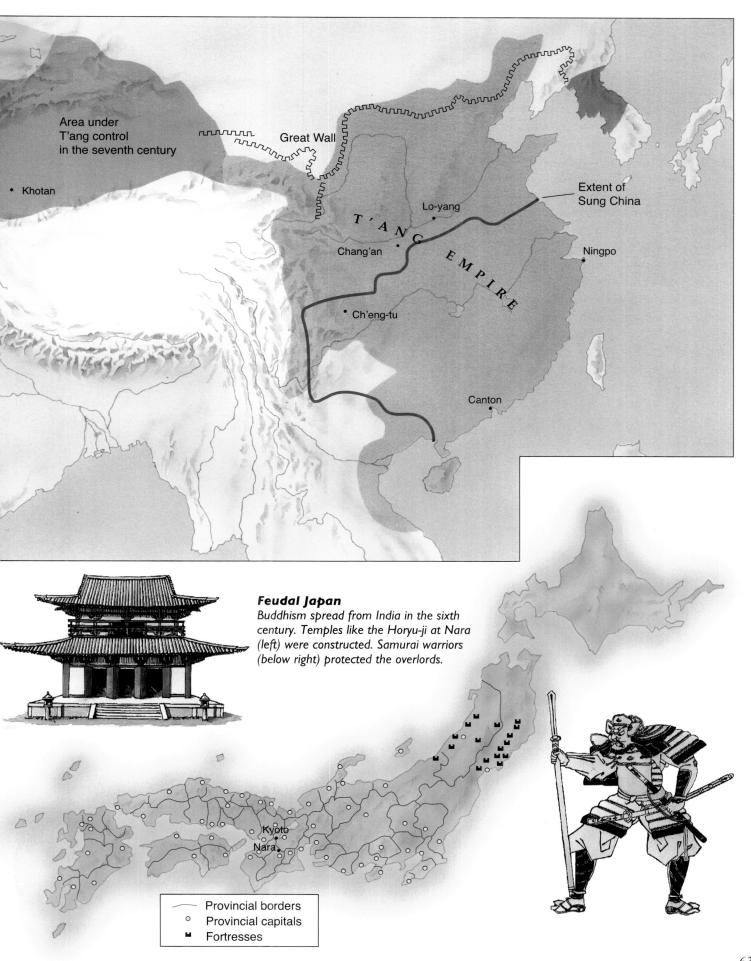

Area under
T'ang control
in the seventh century

• Khotan

Great Wall

Lo-yang

Extent of
Sung China

T´ANG

Chang'an

EMPIRE

Ningpo

• Ch'eng-tu

Canton

### Feudal Japan

Buddhism spread from India in the sixth
century. Temples like the Horyu-ji at Nara
(left) were constructed. Samurai warriors
(below right) protected the overlords.

Kyoto

Nara

——— Provincial borders
○  Provincial capitals
⚑  Fortresses

# The Rise of Islam AD 632

In the seventh century, the Prophet Muhammad founded the Islamic religion. Based on the simple message that there is no God but the one God, Allah, the religion united the warring nomadic tribes of the Arabian peninsula. Arab armies advanced east and west, engulfing the ancient world. By the time of the Prophet Muhammad's death in AD 632 the tide of conquest had spread from West Africa to the Far East. Today there are some 1.6 billion Muslims in the world.

While Western Europe struggled through the 'dark ages' (fifth–tenth century), the Arab world pushed forward the frontiers of learning in science, medicine, astronomy and mathematics. Arab merchants travelled the trade routes, carrying with them not only goods but a new and sophisticated culture. A prosperous Arab bathed in a 'Turkish' bath, strolled among the geometrically laid out paths and water courses of his garden, or went shopping in the great covered markets – or souks – where everything was for sale under one roof. He could even send his son to university, whereas it was to be three hundred years before such centres of learning existed in Europe. Islamic architects designed exquisite buildings that contained intricate mosaics, brilliantly coloured glazed tiles and splashing fountains.

**The Minaret**
The tall slender minaret of the Ahmad ibn Tulun Mosque towers above the rooftops of Cairo, capital of Egypt.

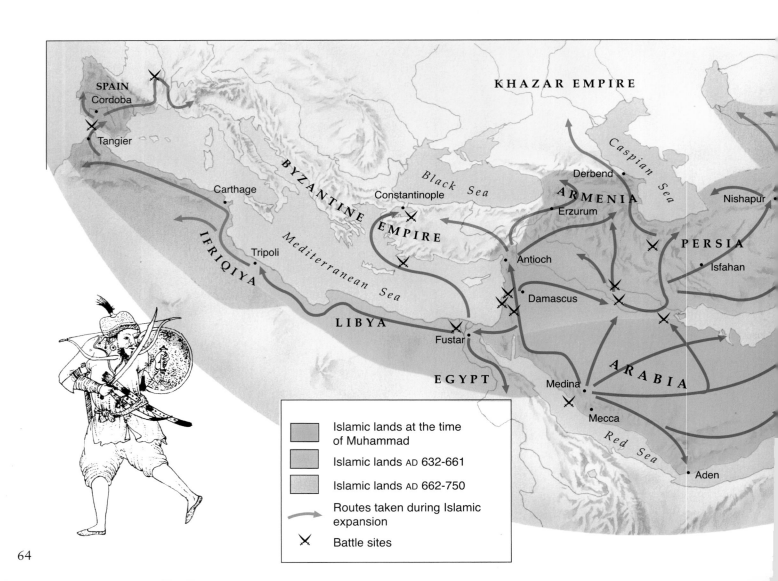

SPAIN
Cordoba
Tangier
KHAZAR EMPIRE
Carthage
BYZANTINE EMPIRE
Constantinople
Black Sea
Caspian Sea
Derbend
ARMENIA
Erzurum
Nishapur
IFRIQIYA
Tripoli
Mediterranean Sea
Antioch
PERSIA
Isfahan
LIBYA
Damascus
Fustar
EGYPT
Medina
ARABIA
Mecca
Red Sea
Aden

Islamic lands at the time of Muhammad

Islamic lands AD 632-661

Islamic lands AD 662-750

Routes taken during Islamic expansion

✕   Battle sites

## Islamic Religion

The Islamic religion is based on a series of revelations that Muslims (followers of Islam) believe were received directly from God by the Prophet Muhammad (*c.* 570–632). These revelations are contained in the Koran, the Holy Book of Islam. Islam means submission to the will of God, known as Allah to Muslims. The Koran lays down strict rules for every aspect of a Muslim's life. A devout Muslim should pray to Allah five times a day, either in a mosque or wherever he happens to be so long as he kneels facing towards Mecca, the birthplace of Muhammad and the holiest city of Islam. The Koran also decrees that once in a lifetime every Muslim should make a pilgrimage to Mecca to worship at the Ka'aba, the holy shrine of Islam. It is also a Muslim's duty to fast during the daylight hours of the holy month of Ramadan.

**Dome of the Rock**
*The magnificent Dome of the Rock in Jerusalem is one of the holiest places of Islam.*

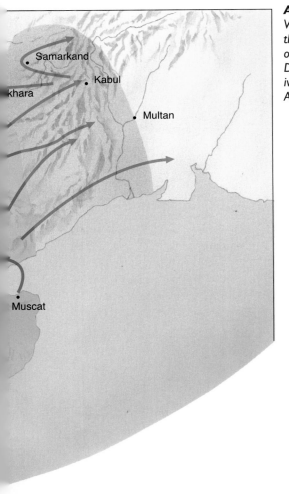

## Arab Trade

With the coming of Islam to North Africa in the eleventh century, Arab merchants opened up trade routes across the Sahara Desert. Their camel caravans carried salt, ivory, African slaves and gold from West Africa to the Mediterranean lands. Dates and grain were stored in pottery jars, like the one below from Syria. From the Arab markets, travelling merchants traded spices along the trade routes of Asia, returning with silk from China.

Samarkand

Kabul

khara

Multan

Muscat

# Europe in the Middle Ages 1100–1300

By the mid-tenth century, the invasions of the northern tribes, like the Vikings, had been halted. Western Europe was divided into kingdoms, ruled by kings or lords. Society was organized under a system called the feudal system whereby the king or lord gave land to nobles who in return swore an oath of loyalty and provided soldiers, or knights, for his protection. Throughout Europe these rulers built castles in strategic positions as defences against their potential enemies. Peasants were owned by the lord; they farmed his land for nothing but in return were given strips of land of their own and protected by his soldiers. Trade expanded during the Middle Ages, and towns developed into cities. As Christianity spread, the church played an increasingly important part in people's lives. Religious communities called monasteries were founded, where monks devoted their lives to prayer. As centres of pilgrimage, learning and medical care, they became an integral part of medieval life. The most powerful ruler in Western Europe was the pope, head of the Roman Catholic Church. The church owned vast amounts of land and grew rich on the payment of taxes.

## Christianity

The Christian religion is based on the teachings of Jesus Christ whom Christians believe was the son of God. It began in Palestine, and after its adoption by the Romans in the fourth century, spread throughout Europe. Churches and cathedrals, like Santiago de Compostela in Spain, shown below, were built for worship and to glorify God.

### Daily Life
Most people lived as farmers, cultivating crops, such as wheat, barley and beans, and grazing livestock. The wool trade flourished in the Middle Ages, especially in England.

### Craftsmen
Craftsmen, such as the carpenter below, tended to live in towns. They were independent of the feudal system and were paid for their work.

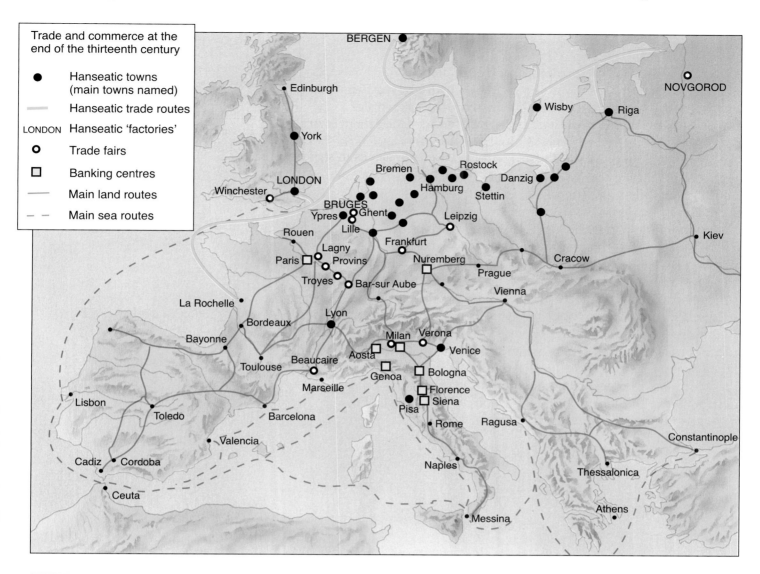

**Trade and commerce at the end of the thirteenth century**

- ● Hanseatic towns (main towns named)
- ▬ Hanseatic trade routes
- LONDON Hanseatic 'factories'
- ○ Trade fairs
- □ Banking centres
- ── Main land routes
- --- Main sea routes

BERGEN

NOVGOROD

Edinburgh

Wisby

Riga

York

Bremen · Rostock · Danzig

LONDON · Hamburg · Stettin

Winchester

BRUGES · Ghent · Leipzig

Ypres · Lille · Kiev

Rouen · Frankfurt

Lagny · Nuremberg · Cracow

Paris · Provins · Prague

Troyes · Bar-sur Aube · Vienna

La Rochelle

Bordeaux · Lyon · Milan · Verona

Bayonne · Aosta · Venice

Toulouse · Beaucaire · Genoa · Bologna

Marseille · Florence · Siena

Lisbon · Pisa · Rome · Ragusa

Toledo · Barcelona · Constantinople

Valencia · Naples · Thessalonica

Cadiz · Cordoba

Ceuta · Messina · Athens

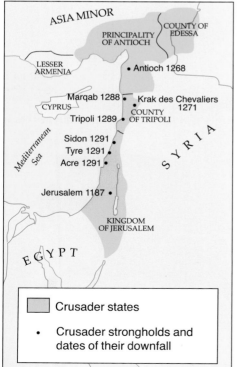

ASIA MINOR

PRINCIPALITY OF ANTIOCH

COUNTY OF EDESSA

LESSER ARMENIA

Antioch 1268

Marqab 1288

CYPRUS · Krak des Chevaliers 1271

Tripoli 1289 · COUNTY OF TRIPOLI

Sidon 1291

Tyre 1291 · SYRIA

Acre 1291

Mediterranean Sea

Jerusalem 1187

KINGDOM OF JERUSALEM

EGYPT

- ▨ Crusader states
- • Crusader strongholds and dates of their downfall

***The Hansa***
*In northern Europe an association of trading towns, the Hansa, regulated commerce. Banking originated in the city states of medieval Italy. See above.*

## The Crusades

With the spread of Christianity, pilgrims journeyed to Palestine (or the Holy Land) to worship at the Christian holy places. When Seljuk Turks conquered Palestine in 1071, these pilgrimages were forbidden. This sparked off the Crusades, a series of military campaigns fought by Christians against Muslims for control of the holy places. The Crusaders built magnificent castles, like Krak des Chevaliers in Syria (below), to protect the pilgrim routes.

# The Mongol Empire 1200–1405

Covering a vast area of northern Asia are the steppes – windswept grasslands inhabited by tribes of pastoral nomads grazing their sheep and horses. In the early thirteenth century the Mongol tribes were united under Genghis Khan (c. 1162–1227) who welded them into a formidable fighting force. The Mongols' first target was China. Despite the Great Wall, built by the Chinese in the third century BC to repel northern barbarians, the Mongol hordes invaded China, occupying it until driven out by the Ming Dynasty in 1368. In 1219 Genghis Khan's armies swept westwards, overrunning central Asia, Russia, entering Hungary and Poland and continuing their conquests until they reached the Black Sea. The Mongols then withdrew into central Asia, but within a few years a fresh onslaught began. Total domination of Europe and Muslim Asia was probably prevented only by the defeat of a Mongol army near Baghdad and by disputes between Genghis Khan's successors. Attempts to invade Java and Japan were also unsuccessful. In the late fourteenth century one of Genghis Khan's greatest successors, Tamerlane, led campaigns south of the Caspian Sea and as far as northern India. At its height, the Mongol Empire was the largest the world had ever seen. Though the hordes left a trail of death and destruction in their wake, once the empire was established it was followed by a period of peace and consolidation.

**Yurt**
*The Mongols lived in tents, or yurts, which were perfectly adapted to their nomadic way of life. Greased animal skins or textiles were stretched over a wooden frame, then covered with handwoven rugs which helped to keep out the bitter winter cold. Inside the floor was covered with felt, skin or rugs. The yurt could be quickly dismantled and loaded onto a pony.*

Liegnitz

**EUROPE**

Craco

Gran

*1242*

Ragusa

Constantinople

**AFRICA**

Ain Jalut

## Mongol Horsemen
Superb horsemen, the Mongols rode ponies that could travel immense distances without tiring. The Mongols could fire their arrows from the saddle at full gallop. Their manoeuverability was aided by stirrups, such as those above, which were reputedly made for Genghis Khan himself. It was their speed, mobility and firepower that gave the Mongols their military superiority.

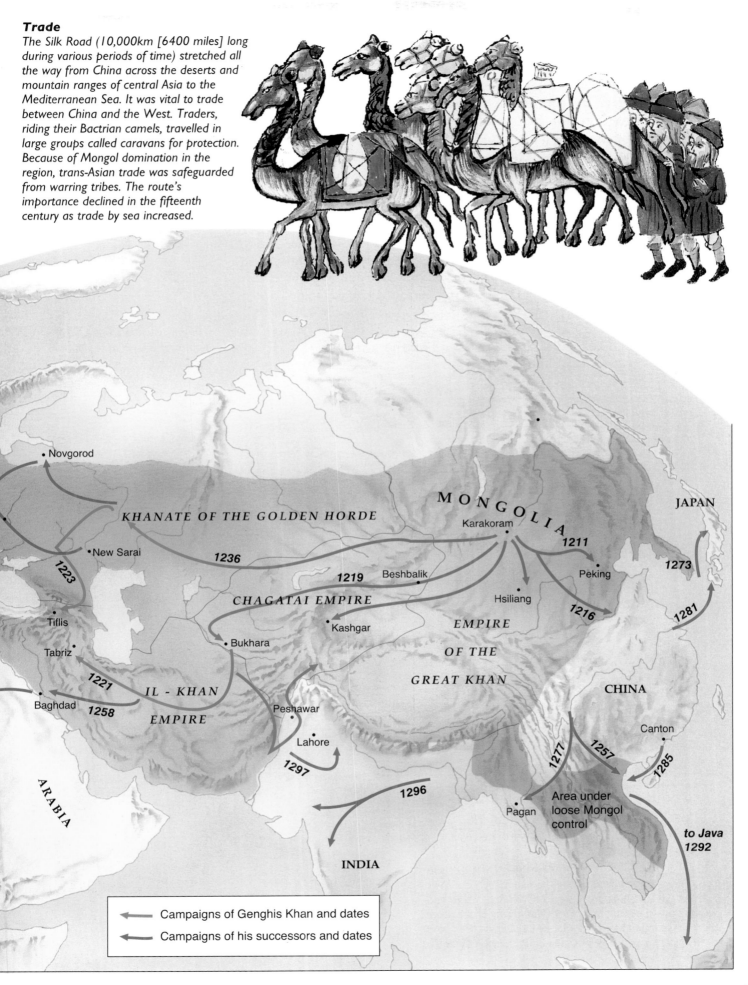

## Trade

The Silk Road (10,000km [6400 miles] long
during various periods of time) stretched all
the way from China across the deserts and
mountain ranges of central Asia to the
Mediterranean Sea. It was vital to trade
between China and the West. Traders,
riding their Bactrian camels, travelled in
large groups called caravans for protection.
Because of Mongol domination in the
region, trans-Asian trade was safeguarded
from warring tribes. The route's
importance declined in the fifteenth
century as trade by sea increased.

Novgorod

KHANATE OF THE GOLDEN HORDE

MONGOLIA

Karakoram

JAPAN

New Sarai

1236

1211

1273

1223

1219

Beshbalik

Peking

1281

CHAGATAI EMPIRE

Hsiliang

1216

Tiflis

Kashgar

EMPIRE

Tabriz

OF THE

1221

Bukhara

GREAT KHAN

IL - KHAN

CHINA

Baghdad

1258

Peshawar

EMPIRE

Canton

Lahore

1277

1257

1285

1297

ARABIA

1296

to Java
1292

Pagan

Area under
loose Mongol
control

INDIA

| | Campaigns of Genghis Khan and dates |
| --- | --- |
| | Campaigns of his successors and dates |

69

# Europe in Crisis 1300–1400

In the early fourteenth century Europe suffered from a number of disasters. A change in the climate caused harvests to fail, resulting in widespread famine. This was followed by a pandemic plague (called 'the Black Death'), and the beginning of the Hundred Years' War between England and France. This war was not one continuous conflict but a series of attempts by English kings to dominate France, which began with Edward III's claim to the French throne. The English armies won battles at Sluys, Crécy, Calais and Poitiers, but these were countered by later French victories, and by 1377 France had recovered most of its lost territories. War was renewed by Henry V of England who won a crushing victory over the French at Agincourt in 1415 and then went on to conquer much of Normandy. France's recovery was begun by Joan of Arc who led an army against the English at Orleans in 1429. By the mid-fifteenth century Calais was the only English possession left in France. The misery caused by war, famine, plague and high taxes led to popular uprisings, like the Peasants' Revolt in England in 1381.

**Knights**
*Medieval knights went into battle wearing plate armour over a layer of chain mail.*

Legend:
- English domains in 1339
- English domains after Peace of Bretigny (1360)
- ○ English bases in 1380

× Sluys
○ Calais • Brussels
× Agincourt
× Crécy
Cherbourg
• Paris
○ Brest
**BRITTANY**
× Orléans
**FRANCE**
× Poitiers
Lyon
Bordeaux
Bayonne
Carcassonne

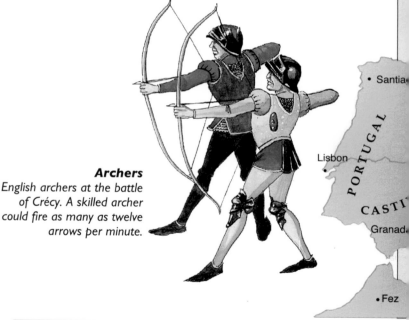

**Archers**
*English archers at the battle of Crécy. A skilled archer could fire as many as twelve arrows per minute.*

• Santia
**PORTUGAL**
Lisbon
**CASTI**
Granada
• Fez

**Changes in Warfare**
*The various conflicts during the Hundred Years' War were dominated by sieges of fortified castles and towns. An assault began with the mining of the outer walls and bombardment by cannon, as seen here in the siege of Rouen by the English in 1419.*

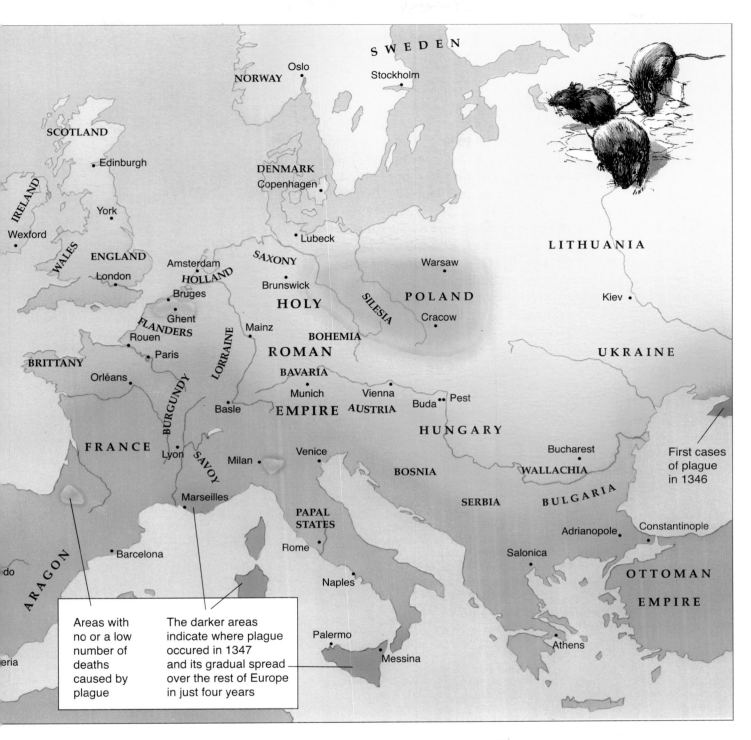

Areas with no or a low number of deaths caused by plague

The darker areas indicate where plague occured in 1347 and its gradual spread over the rest of Europe in just four years

First cases of plague in 1346

## Black Death

In the fourteenth century, Western Europe was ravaged by a terrible scourge called the Black Death. Carried by infected fleas on rats, it made its first appearance in the Crimea in 1346, probably brought by ships from Asia. Victims were covered by black swellings that oozed blood and were incredibly painful. Few people who contracted the plague survived. Its effect on the populations of Europe was devastating: some towns and villages were left virtually uninhabited. The dead had to be buried in mass graves. It is estimated that some 20 million Europeans died.

# The Ottoman Empire 1300–1500

Until the late thirteenth century, the Ottoman Turks were nomadic tribesmen who patrolled the eastern borders of the Byzantine Empire. United by a strong leader – Othman or Osman I – in the early fourteenth century, they began their conquest of Eastern Europe, extending as far west as Hungary and the Balkans. In 1453, after a prolonged siege, the Ottomans captured Constantinople (now Istanbul), thus bringing to an end the Christian Byzantine Empire which had lasted some six hundred years.

Constantinople became the empire's cultural and administrative centre, and the residence of the sultan. In the Topkapi Palace overlooking the city, the sultan ruled his empire, surrounded by his family and protected by his personal bodyguard, the janissaries – Christians who had been captured by the Turks, converted to Islam and given a rigorous military training. No sultan could rise to power or maintain it without their support.

Under Suleiman I, further expansion into Europe began, but with the failure of the siege of Vienna in 1529, westward expansion by land halted. In their shipyards in Constantinople the Ottomans built a magnificent fleet of galleys with which they ravaged the coasts of Spain, Italy and Greece. But in 1571 they were defeated in a great sea battle at Lepanto, off the coast of Greece. This defeat meant further expansion was only possible to the east. Expansion continued until 1680 when the empire's slow decline began.

**Turkish Janissaries**
*Turkish janissaries served the sultan, both as soldiers and administrators, with unquestioning obedience.*

**Hagia Sophia**
*Influenced by both Muslim and Byzantine architecture, the Ottomans developed a style of their own. Magnificent mosques, surmounted by several domes and often with as many as six minarets, pierced the city skylines. St Sophia in Constantinople began life as a Christian church but was converted into an Islamic mosque when the city fell to the Turks in 1453.*

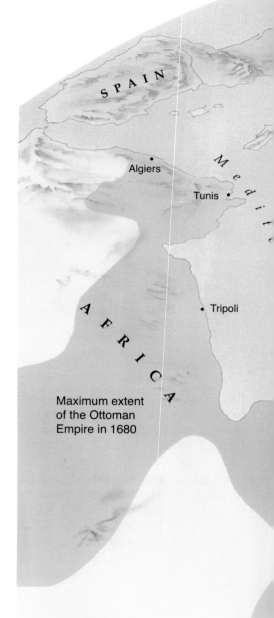

SPAIN

Algiers

Tunis

Mediterra

AFRICA

Tripoli

Maximum extent
of the Ottoman
Empire in 1680

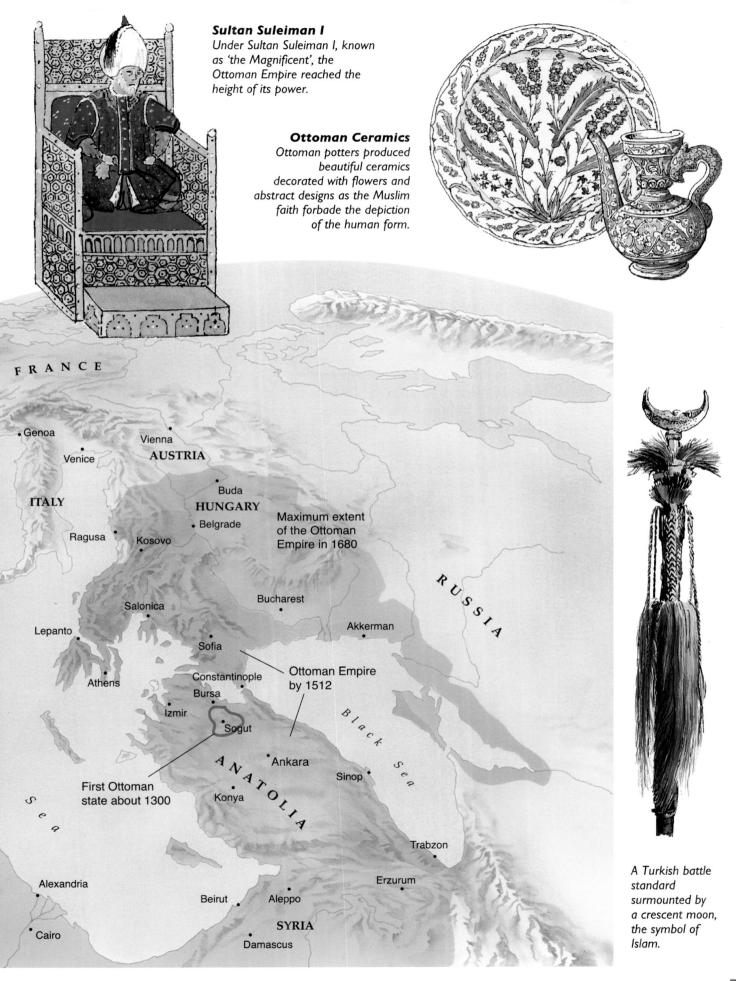

**Sultan Suleiman I**

Under Sultan Suleiman I, known as 'the Magnificent', the Ottoman Empire reached the height of its power.

**Ottoman Ceramics**

Ottoman potters produced beautiful ceramics decorated with flowers and abstract designs as the Muslim faith forbade the depiction of the human form.

FRANCE

Genoa

Vienna

Venice

AUSTRIA

ITALY

Buda

HUNGARY

Belgrade

Maximum extent of the Ottoman Empire in 1680

Ragusa

Kosovo

RUSSIA

Salonica

Bucharest

Lepanto

Akkerman

Athens

Sofia

Ottoman Empire by 1512

Constantinople

Bursa

Izmir

Black Sea

Sogut

ANATOLIA

Ankara

Sinop

First Ottoman state about 1300

Konya

Sea

Trabzon

Alexandria

Erzurum

Beirut

Aleppo

SYRIA

Cairo

Damascus

A Turkish battle standard surmounted by a crescent moon, the symbol of Islam.

73

# The Americas from the Eve of Conquest to 1519

Sometime between 40,000 and 25,000 years ago, hunters from Asia migrated to North America by crossing the Bering Strait. Living as hunter-gatherers, they gradually spread throughout the continent. Their descendants moved southwards, reaching Mexico in *c.* 20,000 BC. There they settled and became farmers, cultivating crops of maize and beans. Two warrior societies rose to power, first the Olmecs and then the Toltecs. The Olmecs are known for their huge helmeted stone heads and small jade axes, while the Toltecs erected temples and monumental stone warriors in their city at Tula. In the thirteenth century, the Toltecs were succeeded by the warlike Aztecs, who established a power-ful empire centred on their capital, Tenochtitlán, built on an island in Lake Texcoco – the site of Mexico City today. Believing that their gods required to be fed on human blood, the Aztecs waged continuous war on their neighbours, sacrificing their prisoners to the gods.

Further south, in the tropical rain forests of Guatemala and Belize, a sophisticated civilization called the Maya had been in existence since AD 300. Great builders, their huge temple complexes and spectacular pyramids can still be seen in the jungles of Yucatán. In Peru another great civilization, the Inca, had established its empire in the Cuzco valley in the twelfth century. The Inca and the Aztec were conquered by the Spanish conquistadors in the early sixteenth century.

**Murder of Atahualpa**
*At its height, the Inca Empire stretched for 3218km (2000 miles) along the Andes. In 1532 Spaniards, led by the conquistador Pizarro, invaded Peru, murdered the Inca leader, Atahualpa, (see left) and brought the empire to an end.*

**Totem Pole**
*Tribes who settled along the Pacific coast of North America erected painted wooden totem poles on which were carved symbolic animals and spirits.*

**Machu Picchu**
In 1911, some four centuries after it was built, archaeologists discovered a remarkable Inca town high in the Andes. Extensive buildings and great terraces clung to the bare hillsides, evidence of a thriving community. Although only 70km (43 miles) from the Inca capi-tal at Cuzco, Machu Picchu was never discovered by the Spanish conquistadors.

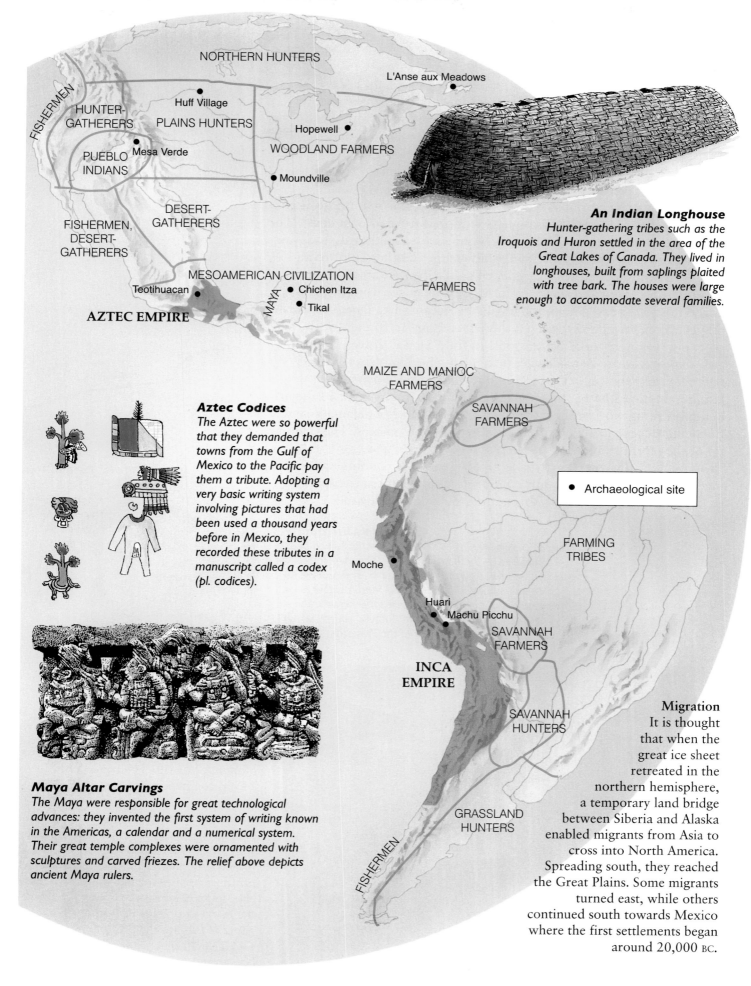

NORTHERN HUNTERS

L'Anse aux Meadows

FISHERMEN

HUNTER-GATHERERS

Huff Village

PLAINS HUNTERS

Hopewell

WOODLAND FARMERS

PUEBLO INDIANS

Mesa Verde

Moundville

FISHERMEN, DESERT-GATHERERS

DESERT-GATHERERS

MESOAMERICAN CIVILIZATION

Teotihuacan

MAYA

Chichen Itza

Tikal

AZTEC EMPIRE

FARMERS

MAIZE AND MANIOC FARMERS

SAVANNAH FARMERS

FARMING TRIBES

Moche

Huari

Machu Picchu

SAVANNAH FARMERS

INCA EMPIRE

SAVANNAH HUNTERS

GRASSLAND HUNTERS

FISHERMEN

● Archaeological site

### An Indian Longhouse
Hunter-gathering tribes such as the Iroquois and Huron settled in the area of the Great Lakes of Canada. They lived in longhouses, built from saplings plaited with tree bark. The houses were large enough to accommodate several families.

### Aztec Codices
The Aztec were so powerful that they demanded that towns from the Gulf of Mexico to the Pacific pay them a tribute. Adopting a very basic writing system involving pictures that had been used a thousand years before in Mexico, they recorded these tributes in a manuscript called a codex (pl. codices).

### Maya Altar Carvings
The Maya were responsible for great technological advances: they invented the first system of writing known in the Americas, a calendar and a numerical system. Their great temple complexes were ornamented with sculptures and carved friezes. The relief above depicts ancient Maya rulers.

### Migration
It is thought that when the great ice sheet retreated in the northern hemisphere, a temporary land bridge between Siberia and Alaska enabled migrants from Asia to cross into North America. Spreading south, they reached the Great Plains. Some migrants turned east, while others continued south towards Mexico where the first settlements began around 20,000 BC.

# Europe: The Expansion of Knowledge 1400–1600

In the fifteenth century the great age of discovery began. Europeans sailed the seven seas in search of knowledge, goods to trade and new lands to conquer. Vasco da Gama's ships buffeted their way around the Cape of Good Hope, continuing east until they reached India. Christopher Columbus stumbled upon the Americas. Amerigo Vespucci gave his name to the American continent after his journeys along the coasts of what are now Brazil and Guiana. Ferdinand Magellan achieved the first circumnavigation of the world; the Spanish invaded Mexico and Peru; and the Portuguese explored Africa's west coast. The world began to take shape and maps began to look as they do today. These great voyagers returned with knowledge of other cultures and with their ships loaded with cargoes of gold, silver and tobacco from the Americas, ivory and slaves from Africa and spices from Indonesia. Trade routes formed a network across the oceans. The Dutch, Spanish, English, French and Portuguese founded colonies in foreign lands that grew into vast territorial possessions. In Italy a great flowering of the arts – known as the Renaissance, or rebirth – began. New forms of architecture, painting, music and literature evolved. Powerful families and wealthy members of the church became patrons of the arts, commissioning work from artists like Raphael and Michelangelo and financing the construction of great cathedrals and palaces. The opening up of the world stimulated an interest in geography and cartography. Advances were made in navigation, astronomy and medicine, while the development of printing accelerated the spread of knowledge and new ideas throughout Europe and beyond.

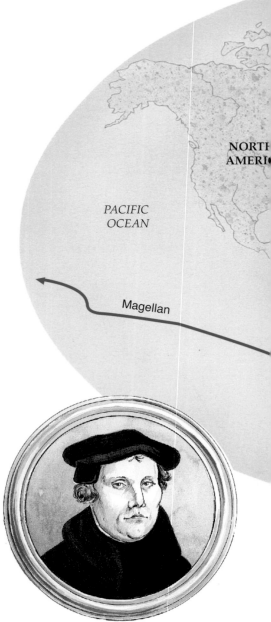

**NORTH AMERICA**

*PACIFIC OCEAN*

Magellan

### European Christianity
*From its early beginnings, European Christianity had been dominated by the Roman Catholic Church – so-called because it was ruled by the pope in Rome. In the sixteenth century a German priest called Martin Luther led a movement of protest – later called the Reformation – against the corruption of the Catholic Church, which resulted in the establishment of the Protestant Church.*

### The Printing Press
Until the mid-fifteenth century, information was communicated by word of mouth or written by hand. In the 1450s, communication was revolutionized by the printing press, invented by Johannes Gutenberg. The first book to be printed was the Bible. Individual letters were made which could be moved and reused – movable type. The interior of a printing shop on the left shows two men choosing the letters required to compose the manuscript page in front of them; paper is fed into the printing press and as each printed sheet comes off the press, a boy arranges it in order.

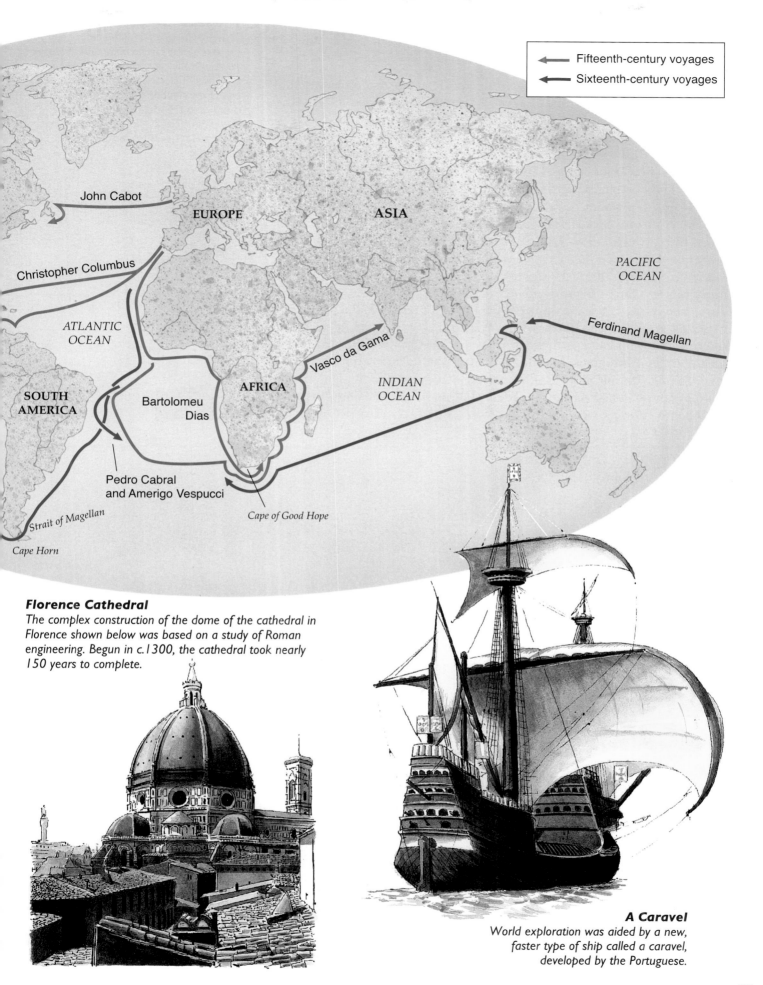

| | Fifteenth-century voyages |
|---|---|
| | Sixteenth-century voyages |

John Cabot

EUROPE

ASIA

PACIFIC
OCEAN

Christopher Columbus

ATLANTIC
OCEAN

Ferdinand Magellan

Vasco da Gama

SOUTH
AMERICA

AFRICA

INDIAN
OCEAN

Bartolomeu
Dias

Pedro Cabral
and Amerigo Vespucci

*Cape of Good Hope*

*Strait of Magellan*

*Cape Horn*

### Florence Cathedral

*The complex construction of the dome of the cathedral in Florence shown below was based on a study of Roman engineering. Begun in c.1300, the cathedral took nearly 150 years to complete.*

### A Caravel

*World exploration was aided by a new, faster type of ship called a caravel, developed by the Portuguese.*

# Colonial Expansion 1500–1700

The great voyages of discovery had defined the areas of interest for the seafaring and trading nations of Western Europe. In the sixteenth and seventeenth centuries they began to expand their settlements into colonies and their colonies into empires. In the Americas the Spanish consolidated their empire in Mexico, extending it throughout Central America to the Caribbean and southwards from Peru to Chile and beyond. The Portuguese settled in Brazil. The success of these overseas empires was dependent on forced labour by the native populations – as in Mexico – or by Africans who were shipped from Africa to be sold as slaves. In North America, French fur traders penetrated along the St Lawrence River deep into Canada; the Dutch settled along the Hudson Valley; in 1607 the English established a colony at Jamestown, Virginia. Trade was not the only motive for conquest and colonization; religion too played its part, some colonizers fleeing from religious persecution. In 1620 a group, later known as the 'Pilgrim Fathers', left England for America and founded a settlement at Plymouth. On the other side of the globe, the Portuguese founded a colony at Goa and set up slave-trading stations along the East African coast, while the Dutch established control of the spice trade in Indonesia. By the end of the seventeenth century, only Oceania remained undiscovered by the Europeans.

***The Slave Trade***
*Between the mid-fifteenth century and the end of the seventeenth century, some 10 million Africans were crammed into the holds of slave ships and transported across the Atlantic to work the sugar, cotton and tobacco plantations of the European colonies. In the picture below sugar cane is crushed in a Spanish sugar mill.*

*A Benin brass statue of a Portuguese soldier.*

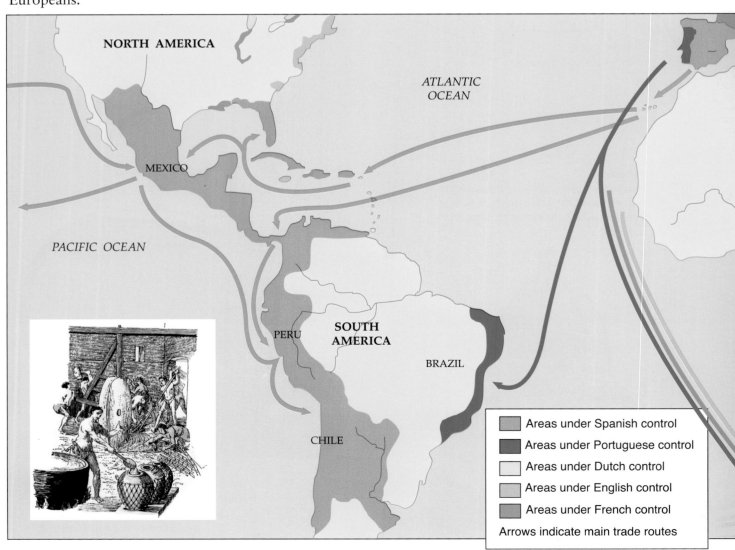

Areas under Spanish control
Areas under Portuguese control
Areas under Dutch control
Areas under English control
Areas under French control
Arrows indicate main trade routes

**New York**

New York began as a Dutch trading post on Manhattan Island at the mouth of the Hudson River, originally named New Amsterdam. Its fine natural harbour attracted a flourishing trade, especially in furs. Here ships enter the Great Dock. It was renamed New York in 1664, after the Duke of York (later James II of England) in whose name the English had captured it. The Dutch gave up their claim in exchange for control of the Spice Islands.

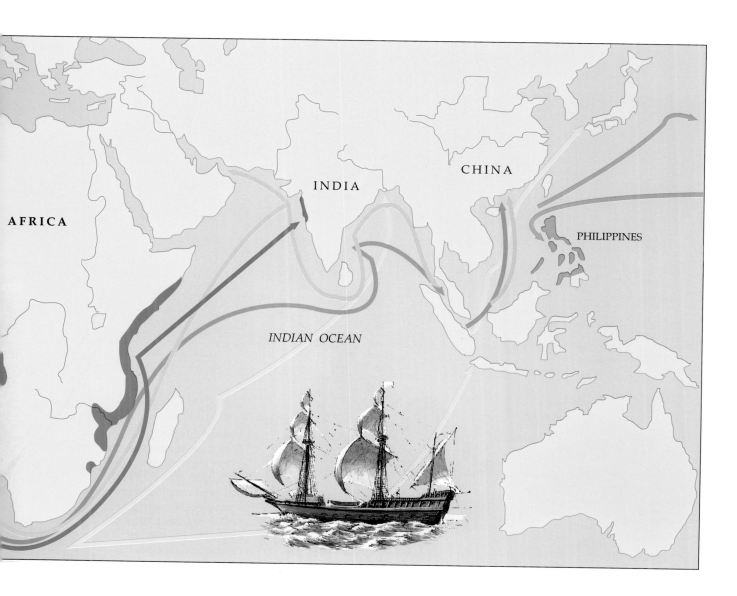

# Asian Empires 1300–1700

Although Europeans had established trading ports in South East Asia, the continent remained largely unaffected by the European quest for colonization. Only the Indian subcontinent, invaded in the early sixteenth century by the Mughals, was radically altered by an alien culture. Of mixed Mongol and Turkish descent, the Mughals brought the Islamic religion to India. A series of remarkable rulers extended the empire and introduced the distinctive Islamic style of architecture which changed the face of Indian cities forever.

China was ruled by an equally successful dynasty, the Ming, which brought peace and stability to a population twice the size of all Europe. The arts flourished, especially the production of silk and pottery. But, threatened from without by Japan and a tribe from Manchuria called the Manchus, the Ming dynasty was ended in 1644 when the Manchus seized power and founded a new Imperial dynasty – the Ch'ing. During Ch'ing rule, the Chinese Empire reached its greatest extent, developed a successful economy and improved cultivation, especially of rice, the staple diet. Trade with Western nations, except Russia, was not permitted.

Throughout the 1400s and 1500s Japan had been torn by civil strife, but in the late sixteenth century a series of powerful warriors broke the power of the feudal overlords and restored peace and prosperity. In 1639 all foreigners were expelled from Japan and for the next 200 years it existed in virtual isolation from the rest of the world.

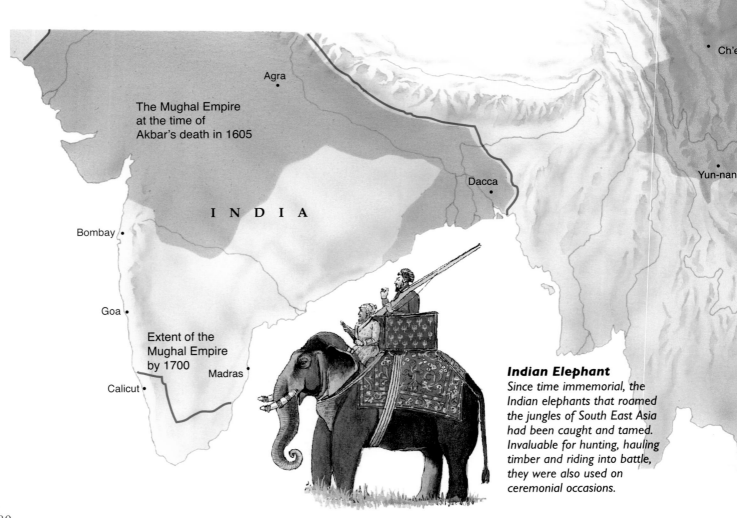

Great Wall

Ch'eng

Agra

The Mughal Empire
at the time of
Akbar's death in 1605

Dacca

Yun-nan

I N D I A

Bombay

Goa

Extent of the
Mughal Empire
by 1700

Madras

Calicut

**Indian Elephant**
*Since time immemorial, the Indian elephants that roamed the jungles of South East Asia had been caught and tamed. Invaluable for hunting, hauling timber and riding into battle, they were also used on ceremonial occasions.*

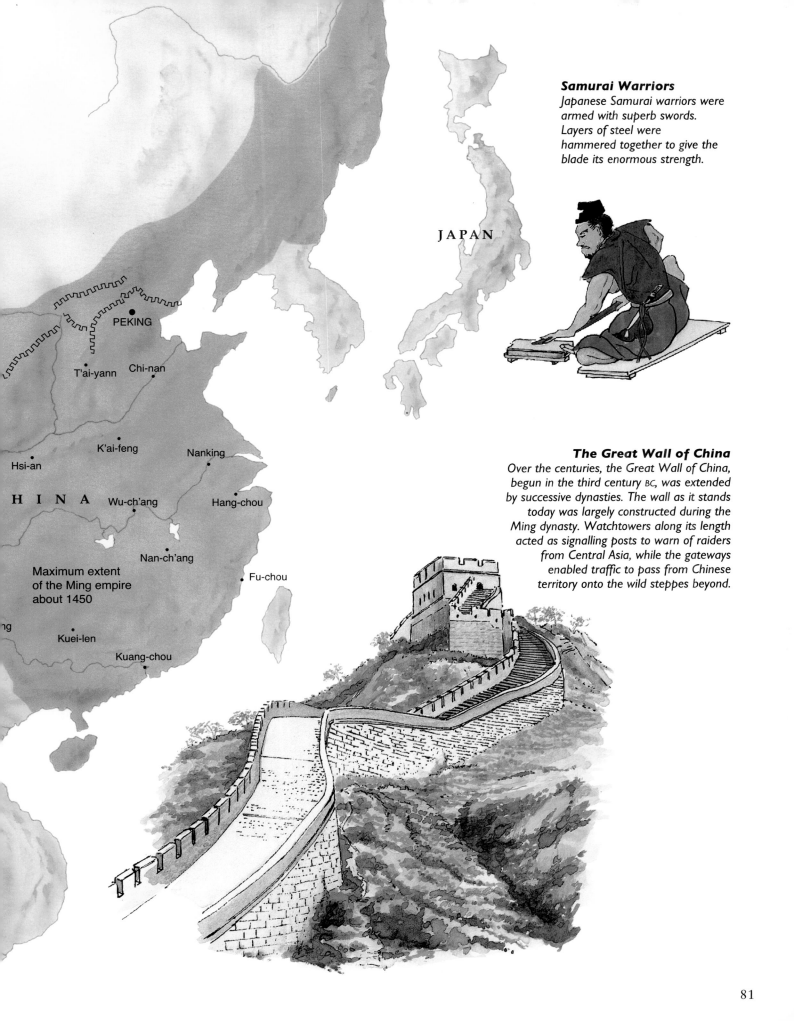

**JAPAN**

## Samurai Warriors
Japanese Samurai warriors were armed with superb swords. Layers of steel were hammered together to give the blade its enormous strength.

PEKING

T'ai-yann
Chi-nan

K'ai-feng
Nanking

Hsi-an

H I N A
Wu-ch'ang
Hang-chou

Nan-ch'ang
Fu-chou

Maximum extent of the Ming empire about 1450

ng

Kuei-len
Kuang-chou

## The Great Wall of China
Over the centuries, the Great Wall of China, begun in the third century BC, was extended by successive dynasties. The wall as it stands today was largely constructed during the Ming dynasty. Watchtowers along its length acted as signalling posts to warn of raiders from Central Asia, while the gateways enabled traffic to pass from Chinese territory onto the wild steppes beyond.

# Europe: Nations and Conflict 1600–1715

In the fifteenth and sixteenth centuries Europe was divided into a number of small states, but in the seventeenth century these states were absorbed into strong nations, larger and fewer in number, and ruled by powerful kings and emperors. The nations began to compete with one another for political supremacy in Europe. A nation's strength depended on its wealth, administration, military and naval forces and on its agriculture – 90% of Europe's population still derived its living from the land. Conflicts which had previously been largely religious now became territorial. To maintain a balance of power in Europe, nations formed alliances with each other.

An illustrated drill manual of 1607 shows how soldiers in the Dutch army used their muskets.

### The Thirty Years' War (1618–48)

This began as a religious war between the Catholic Habsburg emperors and their Protestant subjects in the Holy Roman Empire, but evolved into a major conflict involving the majority of the European states of the time. The war devastated central Europe, especially large areas of Germany, which was left with its economy in ruins and its population greatly reduced. The war was ended by the Peace of Westphalia in 1648.

*A musketeer of the English Civil War period with his flintlock musket. Over his shoulder he carries his bandolier in which he kept his cartridge pouches.*

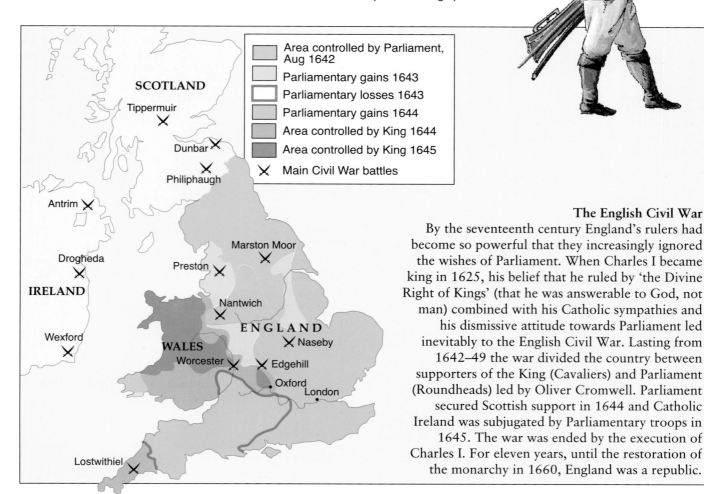

| | |
|---|---|
| | Area controlled by Parliament, Aug 1642 |
| | Parliamentary gains 1643 |
| | Parliamentary losses 1643 |
| | Parliamentary gains 1644 |
| | Area controlled by King 1644 |
| | Area controlled by King 1645 |
| ✕ | Main Civil War battles |

SCOTLAND
Tippermuir ✕
Dunbar ✕
Philiphaugh ✕
Antrim ✕
Drogheda ✕
IRELAND
Wexford ✕
Marston Moor ✕
Preston ✕
Nantwich ✕
ENGLAND
WALES
Worcester ✕
Oxford
London
Naseby ✕
Edgehill ✕
Lostwithiel ✕

### The English Civil War

By the seventeenth century England's rulers had become so powerful that they increasingly ignored the wishes of Parliament. When Charles I became king in 1625, his belief that he ruled by 'the Divine Right of Kings' (that he was answerable to God, not man) combined with his Catholic sympathies and his dismissive attitude towards Parliament led inevitably to the English Civil War. Lasting from 1642–49 the war divided the country between supporters of the King (Cavaliers) and Parliament (Roundheads) led by Oliver Cromwell. Parliament secured Scottish support in 1644 and Catholic Ireland was subjugated by Parliamentary troops in 1645. The war was ended by the execution of Charles I. For eleven years, until the restoration of the monarchy in 1660, England was a republic.

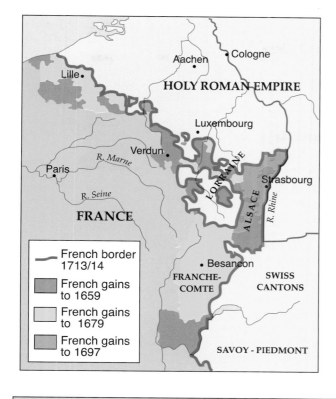

## Louis XIV's France

King of France from 1643 to 1715, Louis XIV was a prime example of an absolute monarch. Aided by a few brilliant ministers, he ruled France almost single-handedly, dispensing with the French version of parliament, the Estates General. During his reign France's frontiers were extended and French culture became the envy of all Europe. But France's ascendancy was bought at a price: the country was crippled by the taxes required to finance the wars that Louis waged throughout his reign.

### French border
French border 1713/14
French gains to 1659
French gains to 1679
French gains to 1697

### Louis XIV
*Louis XIV's reign was the golden age of French art and literature. In his splendid palace at Versailles the 'Sun King' surrounded himself with the aristocracy.*

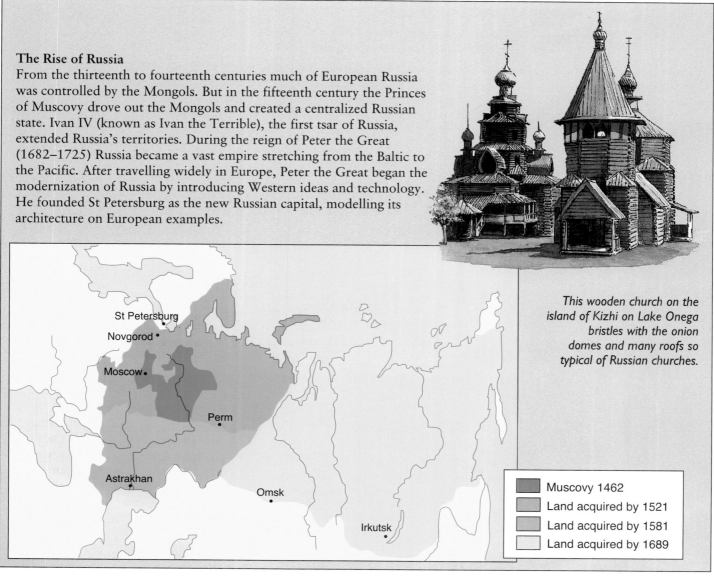

## The Rise of Russia

From the thirteenth to fourteenth centuries much of European Russia was controlled by the Mongols. But in the fifteenth century the Princes of Muscovy drove out the Mongols and created a centralized Russian state. Ivan IV (known as Ivan the Terrible), the first tsar of Russia, extended Russia's territories. During the reign of Peter the Great (1682–1725) Russia became a vast empire stretching from the Baltic to the Pacific. After travelling widely in Europe, Peter the Great began the modernization of Russia by introducing Western ideas and technology. He founded St Petersburg as the new Russian capital, modelling its architecture on European examples.

*This wooden church on the island of Kizhi on Lake Onega bristles with the onion domes and many roofs so typical of Russian churches.*

Muscovy 1462
Land acquired by 1521
Land acquired by 1581
Land acquired by 1689

# The Age of Revolution 1770–1815

The eighteenth century was an age of prosperity, elegance and new ways of thinking. It witnessed the beginning of the Industrial Revolution, the rise of the press, the novel and the publication of the first encyclopedias. The population of Europe doubled, and people moved increasingly from the country to the town. It was also the age of absolute monarchy. Western Europe was ruled by monarchs who presided over their subjects from magnificent palaces which became centres of art and fashion. In the latter part of the century, minor upheavals erupted in many parts of the Western hemisphere, but these were overshadowed by major revolutions in France and America. The French Revolution sent shock waves throughout Europe, changing for ever the relationship between the rulers and the ruled, and precipitating over twenty years of conflict which devastated Europe.

**George Washington**
*George Washington commanded the colonial forces which expelled the British from America.*

*The Stamp Act*
*A British tax collector (below) is tarred and feathered by an angry mob of American colonists protesting against the Stamp Act imposed on them by the British Parliament. The colonists argued that they could not be legally taxed since they were not represented in Parliament.*

### The American War of Independence
Having defeated the French at Québec in 1759, Britain became the dominant power in North America. The original settlements – known as the Thirteen Colonies – now extended along the Atlantic coast. Increased resentment among the colonials against British rule led to war. In 1776 the Thirteen Colonies proclaimed the Declaration of Independence. With the defeat of British forces at Yorktown in 1781, America became independent.

*Soldiers of the American War of Independence*
*The British 'redcoats' (left) were well-trained professional soldiers. The American volunteers (far left) were largely untrained and often ill-equipped.*

**Maximilien Robespierre**
*Robespierre was one of the most influential members of the French National Assembly, formed by the Third Estate to challenge the power of the aristocracy and the church.*

**Marie Antoinette**
*Louis XVI's Austrian queen, Marie Antoinette, went to her death on the scaffold nine months after her husband.*

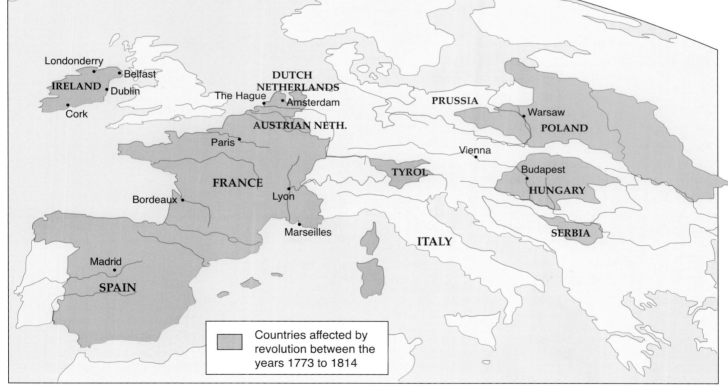

Londonderry
• Belfast
IRELAND • Dublin
Cork
DUTCH
NETHERLANDS
The Hague • Amsterdam
PRUSSIA
Warsaw
POLAND
AUSTRIAN NETH.
Paris •
Vienna
FRANCE
TYROL
Budapest
HUNGARY
Bordeaux •
Lyon •
Marseilles •
ITALY
SERBIA
Madrid •
SPAIN

Countries affected by revolution between the years 1773 to 1814

### The French Revolution

While the French aristocracy lived in luxury, the peasants, who made up over 90% of the population, existed in a state of abject poverty. Opposition to the old order grew, erupting into full-scale revolution when a Paris mob stormed the Bastille prison. The monarchy was overthrown, the king executed and a republic established.

These cataclysmic events were followed by the Terror, in which some 40,000 people were guillotined. For the first time in history, the middle and lower classes had taken power into their own hands. In the picture on the right, French citizens of the Revolution march through Paris with a banner proclaiming 'Liberty or Death'.

# The Napoleonic Years 1799–1815

Alarmed by the Revolution in France and the execution of Louis XVI, neighbouring states, including Britain, formed a coalition against France. The French then mobilized an army of some 750,000 men and went on the offensive. Led by Napoleon, the French forces defeated one European state after another but failed to drive the British out of Egypt. The first coalition broke up, leaving Britain as Napoleon's only opponent. A second coalition was formed, this time including Russia. In 1799, Napoleon seized control of the French government and appointed himself First Consul. After a brief period of peace, war was renewed in 1803. A year later Napoleon crowned himself Emperor of France. The French armies continued their inexorable progress, and by 1810 Napoleon was at the peak of his power. Only Britain continued to withstand his ambitions to dominate the whole of Europe. In 1805 the British navy confirmed its superiority at sea by defeating the French at Trafalgar, thus frustrating Napoleon's plans for invasion. When French forces invaded Spain, Britain sent an army commanded by Wellington to confront them. After six years of conflict, the Peninsular Wars ended in a French withdrawal. In 1812 Napoleon made the fatal decision to invade Russia. The French army's subsequent retreat from Moscow, and its crushing defeat by the allies at Leipzig, forced Napoleon's abdication and exile to Elba. But he escaped, gathered up an army and confronted the British and Prussians, commanded by his old enemy, Wellington, at Waterloo. The French were defeated. Napoleon again abdicated and was exiled to St Helena where he died in 1821. The French monarchy was restored, and Louis XVI's brother was crowned Louis XVIII. After nearly 23 years of war, the victorious powers met at the Congress of Vienna and began the task of reorganizing Europe.

## Napoleon Bonaparte

*Napoleon Bonaparte (1769–1821), a man of magnetic personality and vaunting ambition, was a military genius. A brilliant general and a skilful administrator, he introduced reforms that shaped modern France. The Code Napoléon reorganized the French legal system and is still used by a large part of the world today.*

## Napoleon's Invasion of Russia, 1812

Napoleon's invasion of Russia in 1812 was the turning point in his fortunes. Prophesying a quick victorious campaign, he marched his armies over the frontier. After one of the bloodiest battles of the Napoleonic Wars, at Borodino, the Russians withdrew towards Moscow, luring the French deeper into Russian territory. When Napoleon reached Moscow, he found it almost deserted. A day later, the Russian holy city was virtually destroyed by fire. Napoleon, with his goal in ruins, his supply lines threatened and the terrible Russian winter approaching, retreated.

The retreat became a disaster: short of food, transport and adequate clothing, and hounded by the Russians, the exhausted troops struggled through deep snow and icy winds towards the frontier. Of the 400,000 French soldiers who entered Russia, only 25,000 survived. For Napoleon, it was the beginning of the end of his empire.

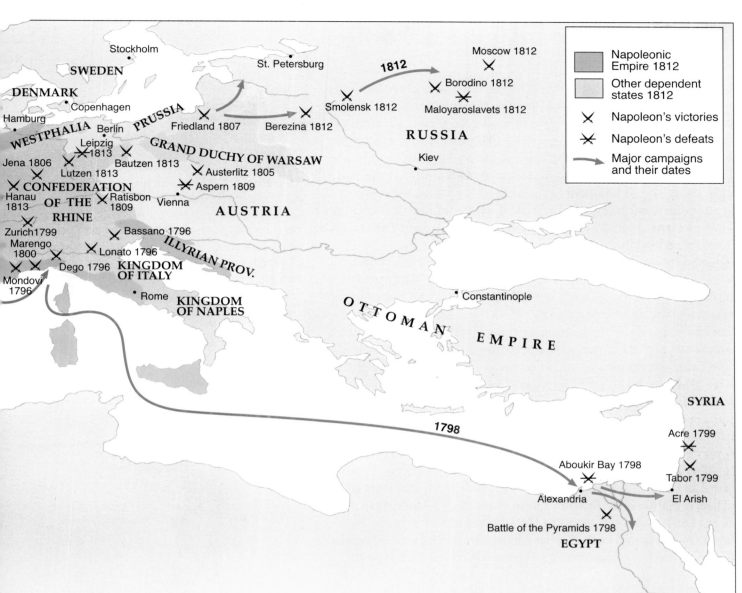

Stockholm

SWEDEN

St. Petersburg

**1812**

Moscow 1812 ✕

DENMARK

Copenhagen

PRUSSIA

Borodino 1812 ✕

Hamburg

WESTPHALIA

Berlin

Friedland 1807 ✕

Berezina 1812 ✕

Smolensk 1812 ✕

Maloyaroslavets 1812 ✕

RUSSIA

Leipzig 1813

GRAND DUCHY OF WARSAW

Jena 1806 ✕

Bautzen 1813

Lutzen 1813

CONFEDERATION

Austerlitz 1805 ✕

Kiev

Hanau 1813

OF THE

Ratisbon 1809

Aspern 1809 ✕

RHINE

Vienna

AUSTRIA

Zurich 1799 ✕

Bassano 1796 ✕

Marengo 1800 ✕

Lonato 1796 ✕

ILLYRIAN PROV.

Dego 1796 ✕

KINGDOM OF ITALY

Mondovi 1796 ✕

Rome

KINGDOM OF NAPLES

Constantinople

OTTOMAN EMPIRE

SYRIA

**1798**

Acre 1799 ✕

Aboukir Bay 1798 ✕

Tabor 1799 ✕

Alexandria

El Arish

Battle of the Pyramids 1798 ✕

EGYPT

| | Napoleonic Empire 1812 |
| --- | --- |
| | Other dependent states 1812 |
| ✕ | Napoleon's victories |
| ✕ | Napoleon's defeats |
| → | Major campaigns and their dates |

# The Making of America 1800–1900

During the nineteenth century, the United States grew from the thirteen colonies strung out along the North Atlantic coast to become the world's most powerful and prosperous nation, stretching 'from sea to shining sea'. The push westwards began with the sale of Louisiana by the French to America. It cost the US government $15 million and immediately doubled the country in size. The opening up of the far west was a more gradual process: hunters in search of game, and settlers seeking land to farm, drifted ever deeper into the interior of the country. This relentless progression was disastrous for the Native American population, whose ancestral lands were overrun by settlers, miners and cattlemen, and whose game – particularly the buffalo – were slaughtered. Some Native American tribes fiercely resisted these incursions, but by 1890 they had been confined to reservations. The construction of the railway did much to open up the west, the gleaming rails penetrating the wilderness until by 1869 the east coast was joined to the west by 85,000km of track. The Midwest was largely populated by immigrants from Europe in search of a new life and freedom from political or religious persecution; many also found work in the industrial cities of the north. Further west, from Texas to Montana, the plains became home to the cowboy and the cattle barons, who sent countless head of cattle by train to feed the growing populations of cities like Chicago. In the Deep South slaves worked the cotton and tobacco plantations. Despite the horrors of the American Civil War (1861–65), by the end of the nineteenth century the 48 separate states in North America had become the United States of America, with a population of 76 million.

## American Civil War

The disparity between the rich industrial states in the north and the poverty of much of the population in the south was one of the main causes of the American Civil War. So too was the north's hatred of slavery, and its fear that it would be extended into the western states of America. When Abraham Lincoln became president in 1860, his declared opposition to slavery led to the withdrawal of eleven southern states (the Confederacy) from the Union. The war, which began in 1861, raged from Pennsylvania to Mississippi. It ended with the Confederacy's defeat in 1865; slavery was abolished. More Americans died in the American Civil War than in all the country's other wars combined.

*A Union soldier in regulation dress.*

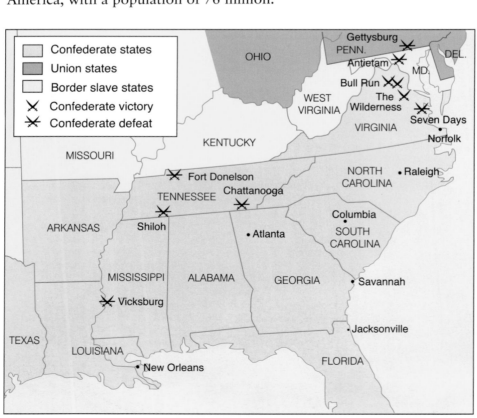

Legend:
- Confederate states
- Union states
- Border slave states
- ✗ Confederate victory
- ✗ Confederate defeat

*A Confederate soldier in battle dress.*

## Settlers

Pioneers returned from the far west with tales of limitless fertile land to be had for the taking. Families loaded their possessions into covered wagons and set off on the long hazardous journey. As the trails became established, forts (see map below) were built as staging posts and to provide refuge from hostile Native Americans.

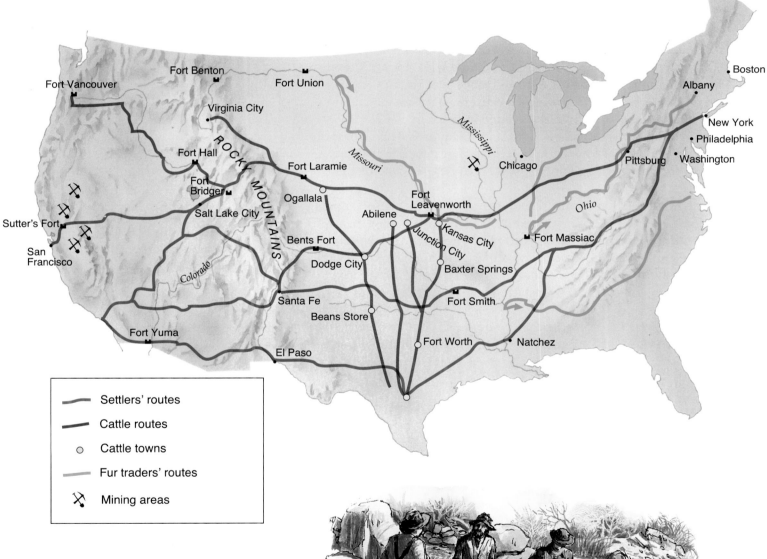

**Settlers' routes**

**Cattle routes**

○ Cattle towns

**Fur traders' routes**

⚒ Mining areas

### Gold Rush

*In 1848 a settler found a lump of gold in a stream in California. As news spread, gold-hungry adventurers from all over America and the world converged on California. In five years, half a billion dollars of gold were dug from the Californian mud. In 1850 the state became part of the Union.*

# Canada: The Creation of a Nation 1600–1880

Humans have inhabited the land now known as Canada for perhaps 20,000 years. It is thought that animals and humans may have travelled from Asia to North America over a land bridge that joined the North American and Asian landmasses where the Bering Straits now are. These humans are believed to be the ancestors of the people we now know as Canada's Aboriginal peoples (who include the First Nations, Inuit and Métis peoples). They adapted to the varied climates of a vast country.

Fishing brought contact between Canada's indigenous population and Europeans. The first Europeans to come to Canada were the Vikings in the eleventh century, meeting with First Nations peoples in Newfoundland. Later, fishermen ventured from Portugal, Spain, France and England to North America. However, it was men searching for a westward sea route to China who 'found' Canada. The first colonists were Portuguese. France sent the first large group of settlers in the seventeenth century, but Canada came to be dominated by the British until its independence in 1867.

The country's name was given to it by Jacques Cartier, who, on hearing the First Nations people in the St Lawrence River area refer to their villages as 'kanata', took it to be the name of their country.

Demand in Europe for fur drove explorers further into Canada. The First Nations people were astute traders and, at first, peaceful trade with European immigrants strengthened their societies. However, European diseases – as well as guns and alcohol – were introduced into a population that did not have any immunity against them and this had devastating consequences for the indigenous peoples of the time.

In 1604, French colonists began to establish settlements in the east, first in Acadia (the name given to a territory in northeastern

## Canada's Aboriginal Peoples

Canada's Aboriginal peoples include First Nations, Inuit and Métis peoples. Historians have tended to group First Nations in Canada according to the six main geographic areas of the country as it exists today: Woodland First Nations; Iroquoian First Nations; Plains First Nations; Plateau First Nations; Pacific Coast First Nations; and the First Nations of the Mackenzie and Yukon River Basins. Within each of these six areas, First Nations had similar cultures.

The Inuit people in the north of the country perfected a way of life that suited their icy, hostile environment – hunting, whaling and fishing, and using their prey for food, tools and clothes (like the furs pictured here).

The Métis people are indigenous North Americans of mixed race. The term Métis historically described all mixed-race people of First Nations and other ancestry. In the nineteenth century and particularly in central and western Canada, a distinct Métis culture developed and the Métis homeland today includes regions scattered across Canada. They are now recognized as an Aboriginal people, with formal recognition equal to that given to the Inuit and First Nations peoples.

**Distribution of Indigenous Peoples, Shown by Language, c. 1823**

| | Legend |
|---|---|
| | Eskimo Aleut/Inuit |
| | Na-dene/Athabaskan |
| | Algic/Algonquian |
| | Tsimshianic |
| | Wakashan |
| | Salishan |
| | Chimakuan |
| | Chinookan |
| | Plateau Penutian/Shahapwailutan |
| | Kalapuyan |
| | Alsean |
| | Coosan |
| | Siouan-Catawban |
| | Caddoan |
| | Iroquoian |
| | Others |

**Canadian Bison**
*Almost 200,000 bison once roamed the north but by the early 1900s there were fewer than 300 left. A recovery programme brought their numbers up to approximately 4500.*

North America that includes parts of eastern Quebec), then in Quebec City in 1608, to exploit the fishing and fur trade. Over the next 150 years, the region of Acadia expanded to reach the St Lawrence River, the Great Lakes and the Mississippi Valley. The British waged a series of wars defeating France. By 1763, France had lost all its North American colonies except for the islands of Saint-Pierre and Miquelon.

Following the American Revolution of 1775, British North America (Newfoundland, Nova Scotia, Prince Edward Island and Quebec) still remained part of the British Empire.

Following the Treaty of Paris of 1783, which ended the American Revolutionary War, the international border between the colonies, that would divide the United States and British North America, was established. In 1791, the British divided Quebec into two provinces: Lower Canada and Upper Canada.

In the late eighteenth century, the western coast began to be populated by immigrants, as Europeans, mostly Scots who worked for the North West Company, crossed the Rocky Mountains and reached the coast.

In 1812 the United States invaded British North America. While this war ended in stalemate, a greater sense of nationhood had emerged that would lead towards the emergence of Canada as a nation. From 1837–1838, rebellions led by William Lyon Mackenzie and Louis Joseph Papineau against British control took place. These rebellions were defeated, however, but they prompted the British government to allow elected local assemblies in 1841. This was a step towards Canadian self-government. However, this electorate did not include the indigenous peoples.

After the rebellions, the colonies of Lower and Upper Canada were united under one government, the Province of Canada, with the 1840 Act of Union. This act failed to assimilate the French Canadians. The Charlottetown Conference and Quebec Conference, in 1864, were held to work out the details of a federal union.

On July 1, 1867, with the passing of the British North America Act, three colonies of British North America (the Province of Canada, New Brunswick and Nova Scotia) became a confederation called the Dominion of Canada, composed of four provinces: Ontario, Quebec, New Brunswick and Nova Scotia.

By 1880, Canada included all the areas it has now, including Arctic lands, except for Newfoundland and Labrador, which joined in 1949. In 1982, Canada broke the last legal link of subordination with the United Kingdom. However, Canada has continued to be an independent constitutional monarchy and a member of the British Commonwealth.

**Canada before Confederation**

RUSSIAN AMERICA

NORTH-WESTERN TERRITORY (British)

NEWFOUNDLAND AND LABRADOR COAST

OREGON TERRITORY (Britain, USA)

RUPERT'S LAND (HBC)

LOWER CANADA

PRINCE EDWARD ISLAND

NEW BRUNSWICK

UPPER CANADA

NOVA SCOTIA

UNITED STATES OF AMERICA

MEXICO

# Age of Empire 1800–1914

Until the early nineteenth century, European imperialism had been motivated by trade. But the Industrial Revolution, which began in Britain in the mid-nineteenth century and spread throughout Europe, required cheap raw materials to feed its hungry machines. Countries like China and Japan, which had been closed to outsiders, now opened their doors to European trade.

Britain, which had retained trading posts at strategic points around the world, such as the Cape of Good Hope and Ceylon, now added others in the Far East, such as Hong Kong and Singapore, which became thriving British colonies. The opening of the French-built Suez Canal in 1869 gave Britain the justification for adding Egypt to its empire. Britain also laid claim to Australia and New Zealand. Since the establishment of the East India Company in the seventeenth century, British power in India had grown until it dominated the subcontinent.

**Mexican Independence**
The people of Mexico, resentful of Spanish rule and inspired by the ideals of the French Revolution, demanded their independence. Their struggle went on till 1821 when Spain granted Mexico its independence.

## COLONIAL EMPIRES IN 1914

- British
- French
- Dutch
- German
- Belgian
- Portuguese
- Italian
- Spanish
- Ottoman
- Russian

—— Main sea routes

***Trade Routes***
*By the end of the nineteenth century, a network of trade routes had been established around the globe. The opening of the Suez Canal saved ships from making the hazardous journey around the Cape. Mid-ocean islands, like Mauritius and the Seychelles, became important strategic footholds for the nations that possessed them.*

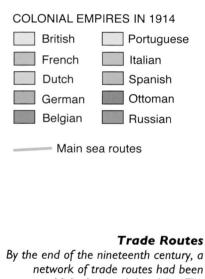

CANADA

UNITED STATES OF AMERICA

BRITISH HONDURAS

JAMAICA

BRITISH GUIANA
DUTCH GUIANA
FRENCH GUIANA

NETHERL
BELGI
GREAT
BRITAIN
FRAN
PORTUGAL SPAIN
MOROCCO
RIO DE ORO
FREN
WES
AFRI
GAMBIA
PORTUGUESE GUINEA
SIERRA LEONE
LIBERIA
GOLD COAST
TO

Many of Britain's acquisitions were to protect its trade with India, its most prized possession, but in the late nineteenth century a fever for acquiring new territory gripped the European powers as each one tried to outdo the other in the size of its empire. It was Africa that bore the full brunt of this imperialism. Earlier in the nineteenth century, explorers and missionaries had penetrated deeper and deeper into the 'dark continent', establishing routes that could be used for trade. From the Cape to Cairo, the continent was carved up by the European nations. Their culture and religion were imposed upon the conquered peoples and borders were established across tribal areas. Britain was foremost among the nations involved in the scramble for Africa and, with her other colonial conquests, by 1914 had built up the world's largest empire covering one quarter of the world's land surface.

## Anglo-Boer War

In 1814 the British took control of South Africa from the original Dutch settlers, who were known as 'Boers' (farmers). Determined to maintain their independence from Britain, the Boers trekked into the interior and founded two republics, the Orange Free State and the Transvaal. When gold and diamonds were discovered in Boer territory, the massive influx of prospectors, and Britain's refusal to withdraw its troops from the Transvaal, led to war. Although British forces were superior in numbers, they were steadily out-fought by the brilliant guerilla tactics of the Boers. But the arrival of British reinforcements forced a Boer surrender in 1902.

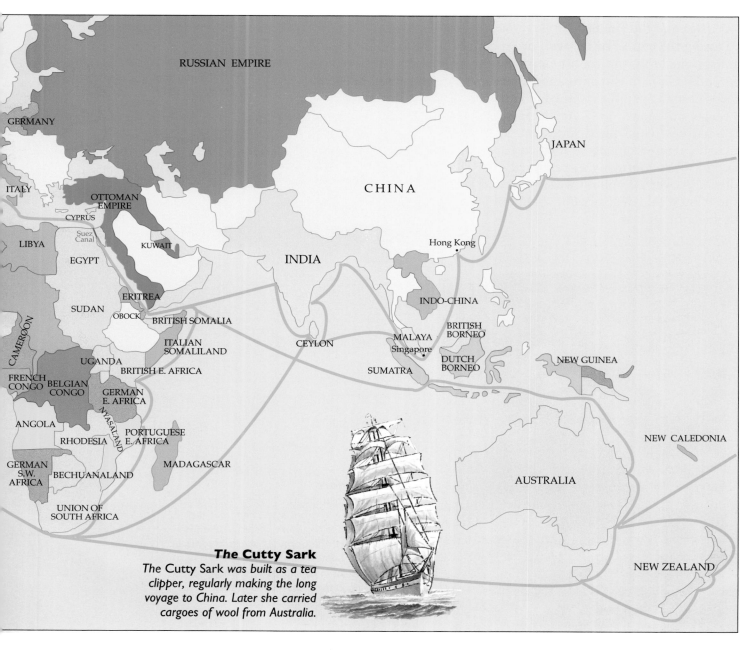

### The Cutty Sark
The Cutty Sark was built as a tea clipper, regularly making the long voyage to China. Later she carried cargoes of wool from Australia.

# The First World War 1914–1918

By 1900, Germany had become the most powerful industrial power in Europe. Fearing Germany's ambitions to increase its colonial empire, and alarmed by its formidable army and navy, France, Britain and Russia formed an alliance (Allied forces), while Germany allied itself with Austria (Central forces). In an atmosphere of mutual suspicion, an arms race developed. But it was increased tension in the Balkans – which had long been a centre of conflict – that precipitated matters. Serbia's emergence as the strongest state threatened the collapse of Austria's shaky empire in the region, which would isolate Germany in Europe. When the heir to the Austrian throne was assassinated in June 1914 at Sarajevo, Austria blamed Serbia and declared war. By August, all the European powers had mobilized and war was inevitable. Most of the fighting took place in Europe, but campaigns were fought as far afield as Mesopotamia (today's Iraq), the Middle East and in Germany's colonies in Africa and the Pacific.

During the course of the war, other countries, such as Greece and Italy, joined the war against Germany. At sea, the British navy was faced by German warships and submarines, which caused havoc to ships carrying supplies to the embattled French and British armies in France. In January 1917 American ships were sunk by German submarines. The United States entered the war, bringing massive reinforcements of men and arms to the aid of Britain and its allies. Germany surrendered in 1918: 10 million people had died and over 20 million were wounded. For future generations the First World War became a symbol of the futility and senseless destruction of war.

North Sea

GREAT BRITAIN

London

NETHERLAN
Amsterdam

Trench line
in the West, 1914

BELGIUM
• Brussels

Amiens •

LUX

Farthest German
advance in the West, 1914

Paris •

Armistice line
in the West,
November 1918

FRANCE

SW

SPAIN

### Trench Warfare
In Western Europe the war took the form of two lines of opposing trenches stretching from the English Channel to the Swiss border. The British and French faced the Germans across an area of neutral territory, known as 'no-man's land'. Both sides fought in conditions of unbearable squalor. Living in the trenches, up to their knees in mud, their quarters infested by rats, they were shelled and gassed.

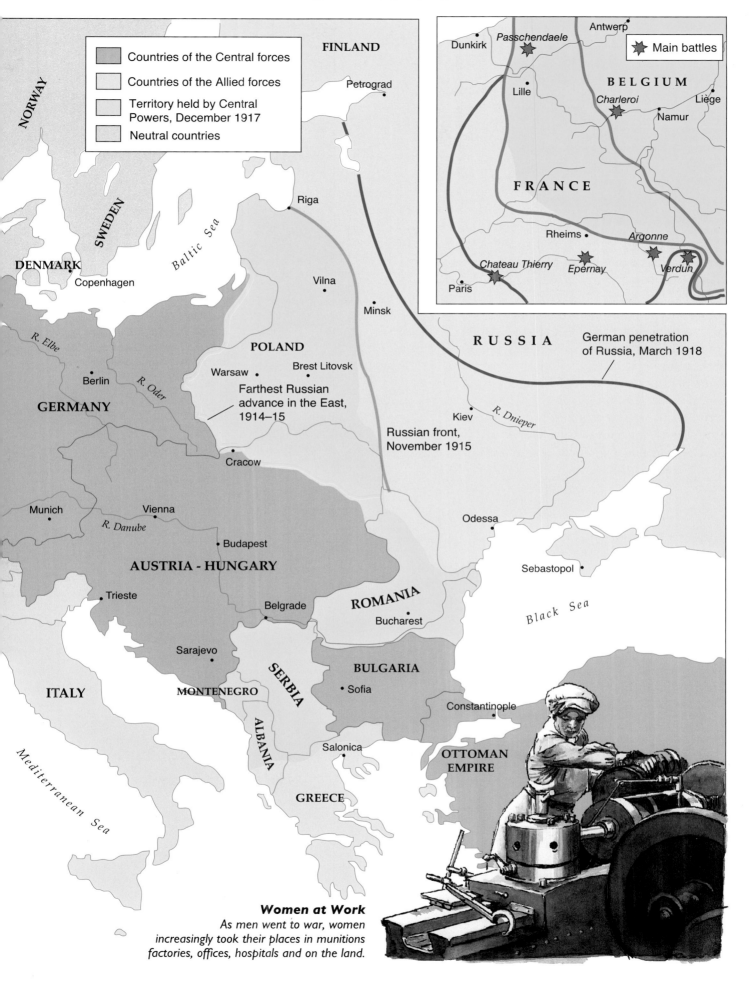

## Main map legend

Countries of the Central forces
Countries of the Allied forces
Territory held by Central Powers, December 1917
Neutral countries

NORWAY

FINLAND

Petrograd

SWEDEN

Baltic Sea

Riga

DENMARK
Copenhagen

Vilna

Minsk

RUSSIA

German penetration of Russia, March 1918

R. Elbe

Berlin

R. Oder

GERMANY

POLAND

Warsaw

Brest Litovsk

Farthest Russian advance in the East, 1914–15

Russian front, November 1915

Cracow

Kiev

R. Dnieper

Munich

Vienna

R. Danube

Budapest

AUSTRIA - HUNGARY

Odessa

Sebastopol

Trieste

Belgrade

ROMANIA

Bucharest

Black Sea

ITALY

Sarajevo

MONTENEGRO

SERBIA

BULGARIA

Sofia

ALBANIA

Salonica

Constantinople

OTTOMAN EMPIRE

Mediterranean Sea

GREECE

### Inset map (top right)

Dunkirk
Passchendaele
Antwerp

★ Main battles

Lille

BELGIUM

Charleroi

Liège

Namur

FRANCE

Rheims

Argonne

Chateau Thierry

Epernay

Verdun

Paris

### Women at Work

As men went to war, women increasingly took their places in munitions factories, offices, hospitals and on the land.

# Between the Wars 1919–1939

In 1919, a shattered Europe, crippled by the cost of the First World War, began the struggle toward recovery. The thirty victorious states met at Versailles (1919) to work out peace conditions. Germany was blamed for the war and made to pay huge reparations, which led to inflation, high unemployment and resentment against the European powers. In America a loss of confidence in the economy caused the collapse of the New York Stock Exchange in 1929: banks closed and thousands were thrown out of work. The American Depression sent shock waves round the world. Unemployment in America rose to 6 million by the end of 1930, while world unemployment doubled. The Great Depression had political repercussions: with promises of a 'New Deal' which would get people back to work, FD Roosevelt became US president. In Germany, mounting unemployment and fear of social chaos created support for the National Socialist (or Nazi) Party, led by Adolf Hitler. The Nazis created jobs in the armed forces and munitions factories. Nationalism swept through Europe. In Italy, the Fascist dictator, Mussolini, rose to power, pledging to increase Italy's prestige in Europe. In Spain, a conflict erupted between Republicans and Nationalists (the latter supported by Italy and Germany) which developed into three years of civil war. The failure of Britain and France to aid the Republicans in Spain encouraged Italian and German expansion in Europe. In the Far East, Japanese economic growth threatened the region's stability. The stage was set for the Second World War.

***Wall Street Crash 1929***
*Thousands of panic-stricken investors thronged Wall Street after the collapse of the New York Stock Exchange in 1929. In the next three years, 5000 American banks closed and thousands lost their savings.*

Legend:
- Area occupied by Japan, 1933
- Japanese-sponsored puppet state
- Area under control of Nationalist government, 1928
- Area subsequently under Nationalist control, 1929-37
- → Route of the long march

Mukden

Peking

KOREA

Yenan

C H I N A

Nanking

Tsunyi

Jui-chin

TAIWAN

**The Chinese Revolution (1911–1949)**
With the end of Imperial rule, provincial warlords controlled China. The misery they caused precipitated an upsurge of nationalism.

Chiang Kai-shek united much of China, ruling from Nanking with his Nationalist Party. But his Republic of China collapsed in the face of the Japanese invasion of Manchuria and civil war with Chinese Communists.

Led by Mao Tse-tung, the remnants of the Communist forces set off on 'the long march', gathering widespread support as they journeyed north. After a brief truce, civil war resumed. The Nationalists were defeated and the People's Republic of China was proclaimed in 1949.

### Adolf Hitler

*To the German people, suffering the aftermath of the First World War, Hitler's promises of a return to prosperity ensured his rise to power. Hitler believed that the Germans were a 'master race' and that people who were not members of the master race, such as the Jews, must be eliminated.*

### The Russian Revolution (1917–21)

The First World War brought great hardship to the Russian people, and a loss of confidence in the government. In 1917, there was an uprising in St Petersburg and Tsar Nicholas II was forced to abdicate. A provisional government was formed, but the Bolsheviks (communists), led by Lenin, seized power, declared Russia a Soviet republic and made peace with Germany. The Revolution was followed by a conflict between anti-communist forces (the Whites), supported by certain Western powers, and the communists (the Reds). The conflict became widespread. The Whites were defeated. In 1921 the new Soviet Union was established.

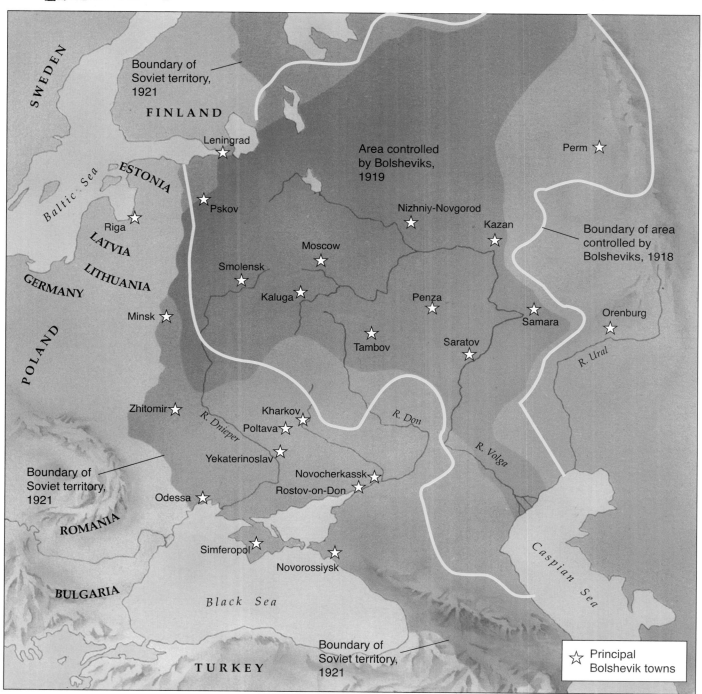

# The Second World War 1939–1945

The Second World War was primarily fought between two large alliances: the Axis Powers – a group of countries led by Germany and Japan and including Italy – and the Allies – Britain, France, the Soviet Union and the USA. Adolf Hitler's ambitions for a Greater Germany had been demonstrated by his annexation of Austria in March 1938, followed by the seizure of Czechoslovakia. British and French attempts to curb German aggression by negotiation (the Munich agreement) had failed. Fearful that Germany would overrun central Europe, Britain and France guaranteed to protect Greece, Poland and Romania. When Germany invaded Poland, Britain and France declared war. Surprised but undeterred, Hitler invaded Denmark, Norway and the Low Countries. The French, British and Belgian forces were forced to retreat into northern France and to evacuate their armies from Dunkirk. The Germans pressed inexorably into France. Italy joined Germany in the war and France surrendered. By June 1940, with little cost in either men or equipment, Germany dominated Western Europe. Only Britain remained at war with Germany. Hitler's attempt to bomb Britain into a surrender in August–September 1940 failed. The war now spread farther east; Yugoslavia fell and Italy attacked Greece. In June 1941, confident of victory, Hitler invaded Russia. Instead of yielding to German aggression, the Russians resisted fiercely and in December 1941 began a counter-offensive.

**Tank Warfare**
*The Germans were masters of tank warfare: fast-moving tanks and mobile infantry, supported by dive bombers, were used to great effect in Poland, France and Greece. But by 1942 the Allies were better equipped, winning decisive tank battles in the deserts of North Africa. In 1943, the Russians successfully stemmed the tide of German invasion in a massive tank battle at Kursk.*

Axis territory Sept. 1939

Axis satellites

Axis-occupied

Soviet occupied 1939–40

British Empire

Neutral countries

German advances

At the end of 1941 an event took place that altered the course of the war: Japan bombed the US naval base at Pearl Harbor in the Pacific. The US had been reluctant to become involved but Japan's unprovoked attack was a decisive factor and the US entered the war. A series of crucial battles in late 1942 and 1943 gave the initiative to the Allies on land and at sea. In June 1944, the Allies invaded France and liberated Western Europe, while Russia advanced on the eastern front. War in Europe ended on 8 May 1945.

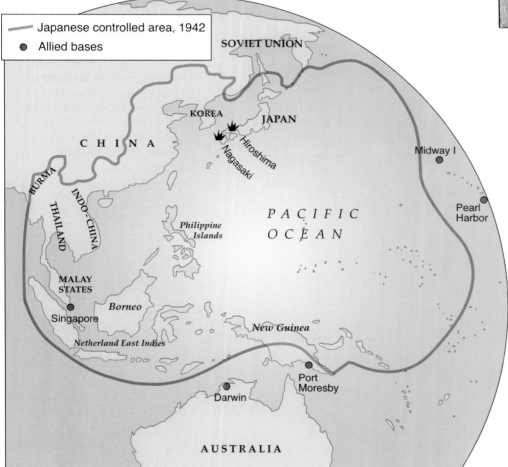

### War in the Pacific

With the collapse of European empires in the Far East, Japan saw its chance for expansion. In 1941, it bombed Pearl Harbor and overran much of South East Asia. War in the Pacific now became inevitable. At Midway in 1942, Japanese naval power was shattered by the US fleet. Japanese land forces, however, fought on. In 1945, fearing Japanese resistance would continue indefinitely, the Allies dropped atomic bombs (above) on Hiroshima and Nagasaki, causing the death of 155,000 people in Hiroshima alone. Japan surrendered in August 1945.

### *Civilian Populations in the Second World War*

*In no previous conflict had civilian populations become so deeply involved. The bombing of Europe's cities took the war into people's homes. In the first four months of the German air raids on London – the Blitz – over 30,000 people were killed or injured. Hitler's persecution of the Jews and other civilians caused the death of more than 6 million people in German concentration camps.*

# The Postwar World

At the end of the Second World War much of Europe lay in ruins. Germany was divided into four zones, controlled by the victorious nations. Berlin, the pre-war German capital, was also divided into four zones. Under the dictator Stalin, the Soviet Union (USSR) took control of the eastern part of Germany and regained much of the territory it had lost at the end of the First World War. Repressive one-party (communist) regimes replaced the previous democracies. Fears that the Soviet Union would extend its control into the West accelerated the division of the continent into two armed camps, divided by the so-called 'Iron Curtain'. Mutual suspicion was aggravated by the formation in the West of the North Atlantic Treaty Organization (NATO) – which included the US – and the Warsaw Pact in the East. What became known as the Cold War developed between the two opposing blocs. The Western economies, stimulated by American aid, began to recover. In 1957 a number of them became founding members of the European Economic Community. But recovery in Eastern Europe was painfully slow. Harsh conditions led to widespread strikes and unrest. Uprisings in Hungary (1956) and Czechoslovakia (1968) were brutally suppressed by Soviet troops.

**Nuclear Weapons**
*After the Second World War, the Soviet Union rapidly increased its hold on Eastern Europe and extended its control into the Baltic states. In the arms race between the US and the Soviet Union, each side stockpiled nuclear weapons like the Atlas missile above.*

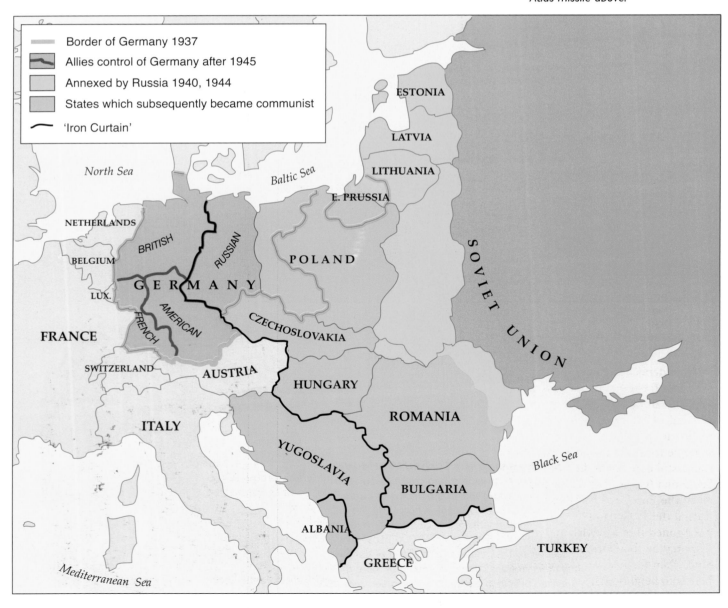

The West's fear of the spread of communism caused a series of confrontations around the world. In the civil war between communist North Vietnam and non-communist South Vietnam, America became involved on the side of the South, while China and the USSR supported the North. After enormous losses, America withdrew in 1975. When Gorbachev became leader of the USSR in 1985, a new era in East–West relations began. With the USSR on the verge of economic collapse, it could no longer afford to maintain its place in the arms race, and agreements were reached between the USSR and the US to reduce nuclear weapons. Discontented with communist rule, the republics within the USSR began to demand independence, and in 1991 the USSR officially ceased to exist. In the Far East, China had experienced two major upheavals: Mao Tse-tung's reforms, embodied in the Great Leap Forward (1958–59), met with opposition that Mao sought to suppress with the Cultural Revolution. A decade of chaos and political unrest followed, during which millions of Chinese died.

**War in Vietnam**
*The retreat from empire caused conflict in both the Middle East and South East Asia. In Asia, the withdrawal of French colonists led to a communist takeover in North Vietnam. The US's involvement in the conflict, despite a huge injection of men and arms, ultimately led to their withdrawal and humiliation.*

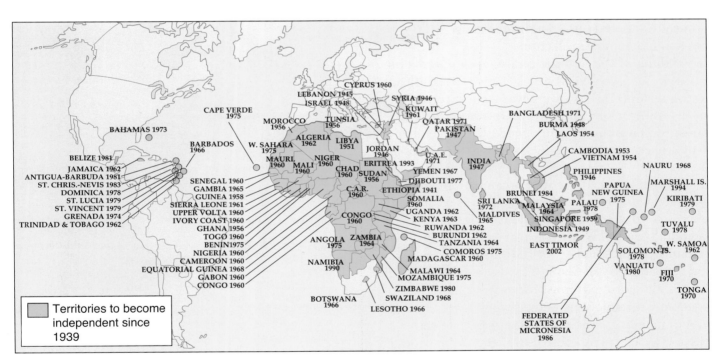

Territories to become independent since 1939

**Independence for Many**
Within a few years of the end of the Second World War, virtually all of Europe's empires had collapsed. France lost Indo-China and Algeria; Indonesia regained the territories previously under Dutch control. India's long struggle for independence from Britain came to a successful conclusion in 1947. Independence for Burma, Sri Lanka (Ceylon) and Singapore followed. In Africa, all of the European colonies won independence mainly during the 1950s and 60s. In 1947, when Palestine was partitioned into a Jewish and an Arab state, the plan was disputed by the Palestinians and war broke out in 1948. Since then further wars have erupted between Israel and her Arab neighbours.

**Civil War and Famine**
*For some African nations, independence brought new and terrible problems. Old tribal enmities, suppressed by colonial rule, resurfaced and boiled over into civil wars. In Ethiopia, civil war caused an appalling famine in 1984–1985 which shocked the world.*

# The World in Conflict

With the fall of the Berlin Wall in 1989, the Cold War era came to an end, and a new world order began to emerge. The USSR was broken into separate republics and former communist states in Europe gained their independence. In some regions, this fragmentation led to civil war, especially when it was fuelled by ethnic nationalism as in Yugoslavia. In the Middle East, disputes between Israel and her Arab neighbours remained unresolved, and Palestinians continued their violent struggle to eject Israeli settlers from the Autonomous Palestinian Territories. Islamic fundamentalism in Iran fuelled the tension, while Saddam Hussein, the dictator of Iraq, turned his attention to oil-rich Kuwait, igniting the Gulf War of 1991, when a US-led coalition of 29 states launched air and ground attacks against the Iraqis. In South Africa, political protest led to the breakdown of apartheid, with the first democratic elections held in 1994. The rest of the continent did not fare so well, however; ethnic warfare in east and central Africa led to the displacement of millions, and brutal genocide in Rwanda; in northeast Africa, Islamic fundamentalism continues to cause severe tension. On September 11 2001, terrorists belonging to an Islamic group called al-Qaeda hijacked passenger airliners and used them as bombs to attack the World Trade Center in New York City and the Pentagon in Washington, DC. This attack unleashed a 'War on Terror' by the US. In 2001, US troops invaded Afghanistan, ruled by the aggressively Islamic Taliban, and installed a democratic government. In 2003 they turned their attention to Iraq, and led a coalition of international forces into the country. They captured Saddam Hussein and eventually sponsored democratic elections.

The killing of the founder of al-Qaeda, Osama bin Laden, by US Navy SEALs in 2011 was a significant victory in America's ongoing war against terrorism but it was to be several more years before the US war in Afghanistan officially ended (28 December 2014). There is still a small US military presence in Afghanistan.

The rise of another terrorist organization which once pledged allegiance to al-Qaeda was a cause for concern in many countries. The Islamic State of Iraq and Syria (ISIS), also known as the Islamic State of Iraq and the Levant (ISIL), the Islamic State of Iraq and ash-Sham (Daesh) or Islamic State, is a jihadist extremist militant group and self-proclaimed Islamic state and caliphate, which is led by, and mainly composed of, Sunni Arabs from Iraq and Syria. It has control over the country now

## Terrorism

*Terrorists are people who are prepared to risk their own lives for a cause, whether it is to attack a hated target or an individual, or to destroy whole communities. Terrorist outrages are happening all over the world.*

Civil wars/wars of secession/atrocities by a state are shown irrespective of their length during the period

## US-led Intervention

*Since September 2001, the US has been a leader in the 'War on Terror'. It has led international coalitions into Afghanistan, Iraq and Syria, using a wide variety of economic and other sanctions to pressure states into abandoning their support of terrorism. The price is high, however, and many coalition troops have lost their lives overseas.*

### Osama bin Laden

*Osama bin Laden was implicated in a string of deadly attacks against the United States and its allies. He was the chief suspect behind the World Trade Center attacks of 2001. He was killed in Pakistan by US Navy SEALs in 2011.*

Daily, we read, hear and see a world still very much in conflict.

We see a world in fear of terrorist and cyber attacks. We read of civil war in Syria; civil war in Iraq; continuing Israeli-Palestinian conflict; violence in Eastern Ukraine, Nigeria, Mexico, Central African Republic, Eastern Democratic Republic of Congo, Myanmar, Bangladesh, South Sudan, Turkey and Lebanon; conflict between Armenia and Azerbaijan and conflict in Somalia. There are rising security threats in Pakistan and Indo-Pakistani military confrontations. Instability continues in many parts of the world. Mali has been destabilized and there are difficult relations with North Korea and a strengthening of al-Qaeda in the Arabian Peninsula.

Refugees fleeing from civil wars are streaming across European borders seeking asylum and a massive migration across the Mediterranean grows.

The first-century Temple of Bel, one of the most culturally significant pieces of architecture in the world, the centre of religious life in Palmyra, Syria, for over 2000 years, was destroyed in August 2015 by ISIS. The most brutal terrorist group to emerge in modern times, ISIS is highly fanatical, killing Shia Muslims and Christians whenever possible and choosing to demolish irreplaceable ancient sites and antiquities because they consider pre-Islamic religious objects or structures to be sacrilegious.

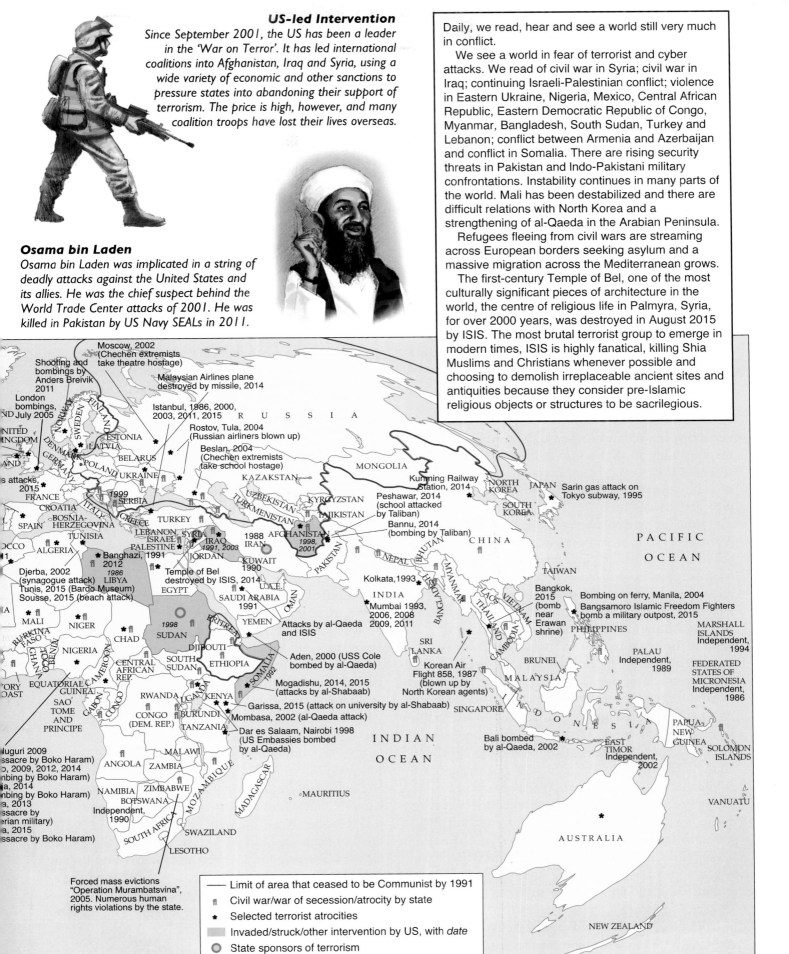

— Limit of area that ceased to be Communist by 1991

⚑ Civil war/war of secession/atrocity by state

✴ Selected terrorist atrocities

▨ Invaded/struck/other intervention by US, with *date*

◯ State sponsors of terrorism

# The World in Conflict (ctd)

occupied by ten million people in Iraq and Syria, as well as IS affiliate presence now in Algeria, Libya, Egypt, Nigeria, Saudi Arabia, Yemen, Chechnya, Afghanistan and Pakistan. The group also operates or has affiliates in other parts of the world, including South Asia. The group has been designated as a terrorist organization by the United Nations, the European Union, the United Kingdom, the United States, India, Indonesia, Turkey, Saudi Arabia, Syria and other governments. Over 60 countries are directly or indirectly waging war against ISIS and many have been at the receiving end of their terrorist attacks.

Boko Haram in Nigeria is an Islamic extremist group that initially had links to al-Qaeda before pledging formal allegiance to Islamic State in 2015. Based in northeastern Nigeria it has also been active in Chad, Niger and northern Cameroon. Boko Haram has killed more than 17,000 people since 2009, including over 10,000 in 2014, in attacks occurring mainly in northeast Nigeria. They claimed responsibility for kidnapping some 276 female students from a girls' secondary school in the town of Chibok in Borno State, Nigeria – many of the girls are still missing.

In Somalia, where there has been an ongoing civil war since 1991, an important feature of the past two decades has been the emergence of a variety of Islamist movements, most notably al-Shabaab, seeking to establish an Islamic state in Somalia. Al-Shabaab has been fighting the Somali government and the African Union peacekeeping force for control of the country. In October 2011 Kenyan troops entered southern Somalia to assist the Somali military in a joint operation against al-Shabaab and to establish a temporary buffer zone inside Somalia. As a probable consequence of this action, Kenya saw an upsurge in violent terrorist attacks from late 2011 – according to Kenyan government officials many of the murders and attack were carried out by al-Shabaab. In 2015, a particularly shocking shooting rampage by al-Shabaab in Moi University in the northern town of Garissa in Kenya left 148 students dead. Al-Shabaab has also been suspected of having links with al-Qaeda in the Islamic Maghreb, which aims to overthrow the Algerian government and institute an Islamic state, and with Boko Haram.

A series of anti-government uprisings that arose independently and spread across the Arab world in 2011 became known as the 'Arab Spring'. The movement originated in Tunisia in December 2010

and quickly took hold in Egypt, Libya, Syria, Yemen, Bahrain, Saudi Arabia, and Jordan. By the end of February 2012, rulers had been forced from power in Tunisia, Egypt, Libya and Yemen; civil uprisings had erupted in Bahrain and Syria; major protests had broken out in Algeria, Iraq, Jordan, Kuwait, Morocco and Sudan and minor protests had occurred in Mauritania, Oman, Saudi Arabia, Djibouti, Western Sahara and Palestine. Weapons and Tuareg fighters returning from the Libyan Civil War helped a simmering conflict in Mali that has been described as 'fallout' from the Arab Spring in North Africa. The civil war in Syria, which began with pro-democracy protests, has resulted in one of the largest refugee exoduses in recent history. Almost 4.7 million people have fled Syria since the start of the conflict.

In many countries in Asia diversities within the worlds of Islam and Buddhism or Islam and Christianity have led to violent conflict in places such as the Philippines, Sri Lanka, Myanmar and Thailand – conflicts derived from deeply rooted religious and ethnic differences. Until June 2014 Buddhist Arakanese and Muslim Rohingyas lived side by side in the capital of Rakhine state in Myanmar but following several rounds of violence, the Buddhist majority has emptied the capital of its Muslim population. The Rohingya victims now scrape by in squalid refugee camps beyond the city boundaries. The best that most of them can hope for is to escape on an overloaded fishing boat to Malaysia. Many of them die trying.

In Europe there has been a cooling of relations between Russia and the West which hasn't been seen since the Cold War ended. This is mainly in reaction to Russia's dealings with Ukraine. Mass protests were initially sparked in Ukraine in 2013 when its president announced the abandonment of a trade agreement with the EU for closer ties with Russia. Protests by pro-Russian and anti-revolution activists began in the largely Russophone region of Crimea. These were followed by demonstrations in cities across eastern and southern Ukraine, including Donetsk, Luhansk, Kharkiv, and Odessa. As protests gripped Crimea, pro-Russian armed men gradually began to take over the peninsula and, on 18 March 2014, Russia annexed Crimea. Subsequently, unrest in Donetsk and Luhansk oblasts of Ukraine evolved into a war between the post-revolutionary Ukrainian government and pro-Russian insurgents. A peace agreement is in place but it has not led to a complete ceasefire.

# MAPS OF THE WORLD

## Symbols for maps:
### 8-22, 27-38, 40-54, 60-62

Inhabitants

More than 5 million     **Los Angeles**

1 000 000 - 5 000 000     **Seattle**

250 000 - 1 000 000     **Mexicali**

100 000 - 250 000     **Ensenada**

25 000 - 100 000     Sparks

Less than 25 000     Rockport

National capital (UPPERCASE)     **OTTAWA**

State capital     **Boise**

International boundary

Disputed international boundary

State boundary

Disputed state boundary

Major road

Other road

Road under construction

Seasonal road

Railway

Canal

Highest peak in continent     ▲ McKinley

Highest peak in country     △ Logan

Height in feet     ▲ 17000ft

Depth in feet     ▽ 185ft

Coral reef

Dam     | Kainji Dam

Waterfall     | Niagara Falls

Pass     )(

International airport     ⊕

National airport     ✈

Historical site     ⚏

Scientific site     ⚐

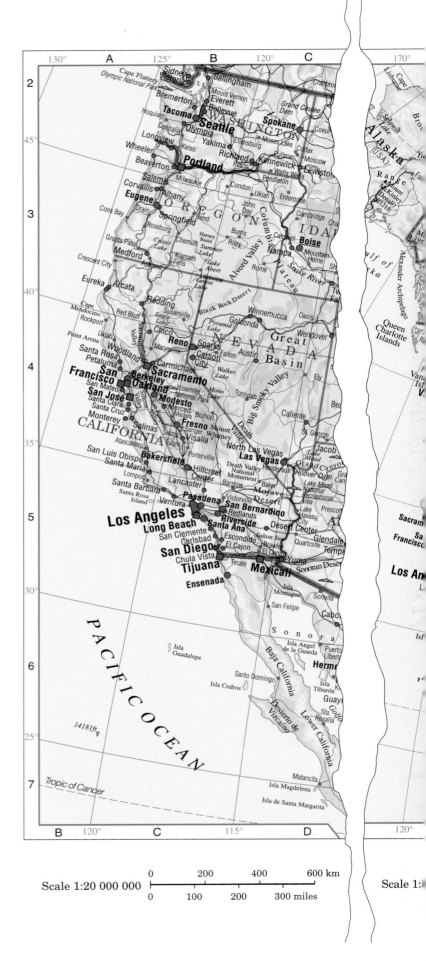

Scale 1:20 000 000

| 0 | 200 | 400 | 600 km |

| 0 | 100 | 200 | 300 miles |

Scale 1:

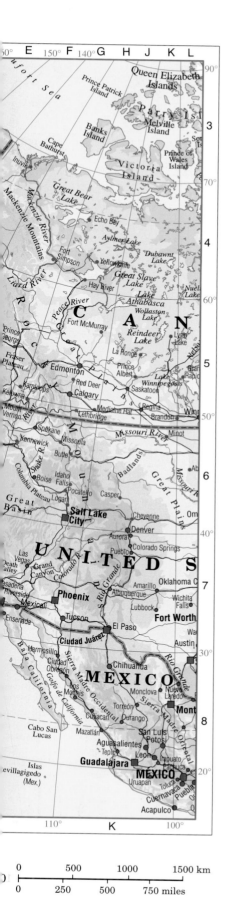

## Symbols for maps:
### 7, 24-25, 56-59

| | |
|---|---|
| | **Inhabitants** |
| **Los Angeles** | More than 5 million |
| **Seattle** | 1 000 000 - 5 000 000 |
| Mexicali | 250 000 - 1 000 000 |
| Hermosillo | 100 000 - 250 000 |
| Casper | Less than 100 000 |
| **MÉXICO** | National capital (UPPERCASE) |
| <u>Sacramento</u> | State capital |
| | International boundary |
| | Disputed international boundary |
| | Major road |
| | Road under construction |
| | Major railway |
| | Canal |
| McKinley | Highest peak in continent |
| Logan | Highest peak in country |
| 17000ft | Heights in feet |
| 185ft | Depths in feet |
| | Coral reef |
| | Scientific station |
| | Territorial claims in Antarctica |
| | Disputed territorial claims in Antarctica |
| Grand Coulee Dam | Dam |
| Virginia Falls | Waterfall |

## Colour Key for Contours

| | |
|---|---|
| | Glacier/ice cap |
| | 6000m |
| | 5000m |
| | 4000m |
| | 3000m |
| | 2000m |
| | 1000m |
| | 500m |
| | 200m |
| | 0m |
| | Marshland |
| | Salt lake |
| | Seasonal lake |
| | Salt desert |

## Symbols for Political maps:
### 6, 23, 26, 39, 55

| | |
|---|---|
| | **Inhabitants** |
| **Lagos** | More than 5 million |
| **Ibadan** | 1 000 000 - 5 000 000 |
| Kano | 250 000 - 1 000 000 |
| Gashua | 100 000 - 250 000 |
| Maradi | Less than 100 000 |
| | National Capital |
| | State Capital |
| | International boundary |
| | Disputed International boundary |
| | State boundary |
| | Railway |

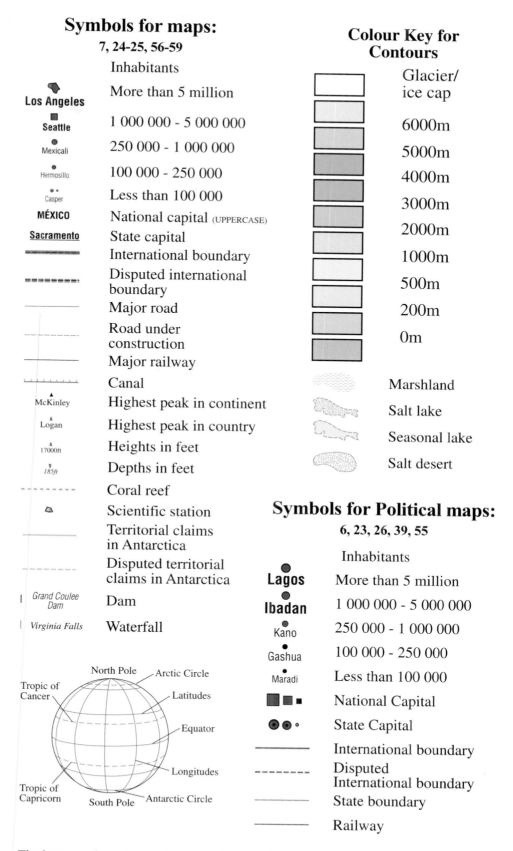

The letters and numbers in the map edges are there to help you find names. Look for London in the index: **29** D4. Turn to map 29 and look top or bottom for number 4 and left or right for letter D. In this blue grid square you will find the city of London.

Scale 1:50 000 000 means that a distance on the map is 50 000 000 times longer on the Earth's surface e.g. 1cm on the map represents 500km on the surface and 1 inch on the map represents 800 miles.

RUSSIA

Alaska
(U.S.A.)

*Arctic Circle*

Kalaallit Nunaat
(Greenland)
(Den.)

Jan Mayen
(Nor.)

Reykjavik   **ICELAND**

**PACIFIC**

**OCEAN**

*C  A  N  A  D  A*

Ottawa

**UNITE
KINGD**

Dublin
**IRELAND**

Lo

*N  O  R  T  H*

**FRA**

**UNITED
STATES OF
AMERICA**

Washington, D.C.

Bermuda
(U.K.)

*A  T  L  A  N  T  I  C*

**PORTUGAL**

**S**

*Tropic of Cancer*

Guadalupe
(Mex.)

*Hawai'ian
Islands
(U.S.A.)*

Islas Revillagigedo
(Mex.)

**MEXICO**

Mexico

La Habana
Nassau

**CUBA**
**THE BAHAMAS**

**DOMINICAN
REPUBLIC**
**HAITI**

Santo
Domingo

Lisboa
Azores
(Port.)

Canary Islands
(Sp.)

Rabat
Western
Sahara

*O  C  E  A  N*

M

**A**

**MOR**

**ST KITTS & NEVIS**
**ANTIGUA & BARBUDA**
**DOMINICA**
**ST LUCIA**
**BARBADOS**
**ST VINCENT**
**GRENADA**
**TRINIDAD & TOBAGO**

**CAPE VERDE**

**MAURITANIA**
Nouakchott

**SENEGAL**
Dakar
Praia

**THE GAMBIA**
**GUINEA-BISSAU** Bissau

**GUINEA**
Conakry
Freetown

**SIERRA LEONE**

**BUR**

Bamako

**GUATEMALA**
Guatemala
**EL SALVADOR**
San José
**NICARAGUA**
**COSTA RICA**
**PANAMA**

**BELIZE**
**HONDURAS**
Tegucigalpa
Managua

**JAMAICA**

Caracas

Panama
Bogota

**VENE-
ZUELA**

Georgetown
Paramaribo
Fr. Guiana (Fr.)

**LIBERIA**
Monrovia
Yamoussoukro

**CÔTE D'IVOIRE**

*Equator*

**TUVALU**
Funafuti

**KIRIBATI**

Islas Galápagos
(Ecu.)

Quito

**ECUADOR**

**COLOMBIA**

**GUYANA**
**SURINAME**

Ascension
(U.K)

**SAMOA**
Apia
American
Samoa
(U.S.A.)

Lima

**PERU**

**BRAZIL**

Brasília

St Helena
(U.K)

**VANUATU**
Port
Vila  Suva

**FIJI
ISLANDS**

**TONGA**
Nuku'alofa

Cook
Islands
(N.Z.)

*French
Polynesia
(Fr.)*

La Paz
Sucre

**BOLIVIA**

Trindade
(Braz.)

*Tropic of Capricorn*

Pitcairn
Islands
(U.K.)

Isla
Sala-y-Gómez
(Chile)
Isla de Pascua
(Easter Island)
(Chile)

Asunción

**PARAGUAY**

*S  O  U  T  H*

*A  T  L  A  N  T  I*

**NEW
ZEALAND**

Wellington

*PACIFIC

OCEAN*

Santiago

**CHILE**

**ARGENTINA**

Buenos
Aires

**URUGUAY**
Montevideo

Tristan da Cunha (U.K.)

*O  C  E  A  N*

Falkland Is.
(U.K.)

South Georgia
(U.K.)

• National capital

— International boundary

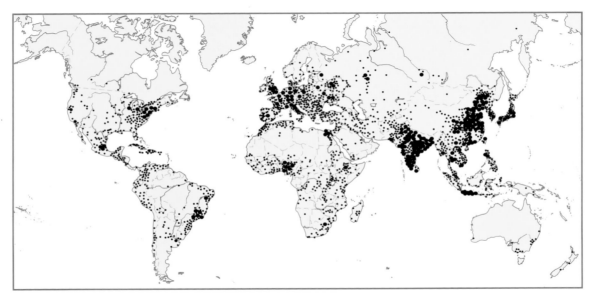

POPULATION

• 10 million inhabitants
· 1 million inhabitants

The density of population
varies over the Earth's lan
surface. Some parts are
sparsely populated becau
of geographical condition
high mountains, hot dese
or cold tundra. Compare
maps 8–9, 10–11. Some
parts are densely populat
due to good living conditi
economically or physicall
convenient for the big citi
as well as other reasons
such as religion or ethnic
grouping. Population gro
is mainly centred on the
already densely populate
areas.

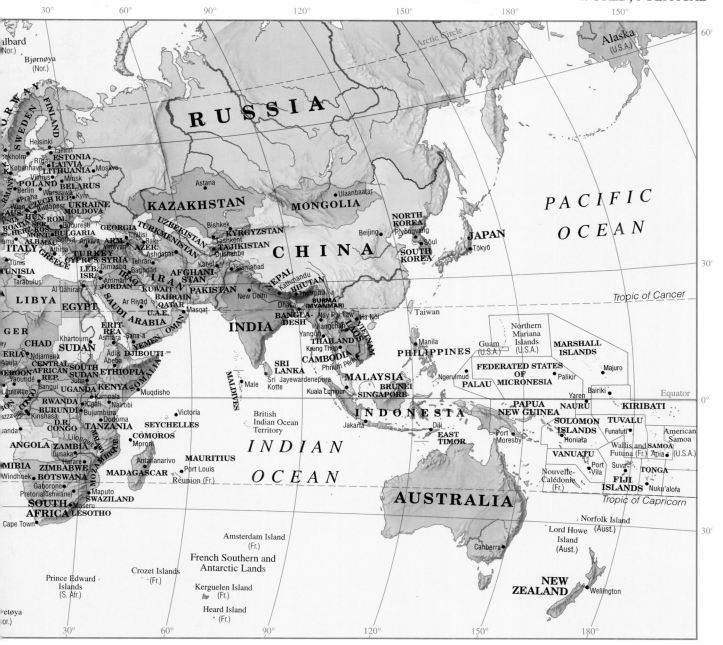

TIME ZONES

The Earth spins around its axis anticlockwise and completes one turn every 24 hours. As the world rotates it is day on the part facing the Sun and night on the side in shadow. As shown on this map, we have divided the Earth into 24 standard time zones. They are based upon lines of longitude at 25 degree intervals but mainly follow country or state boundaries. You can compare times around the world by using the map. For example: when it is 12 noon in London it is 5 hours earlier in New York or 7 am.

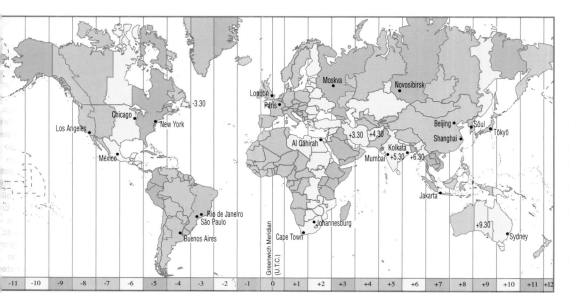

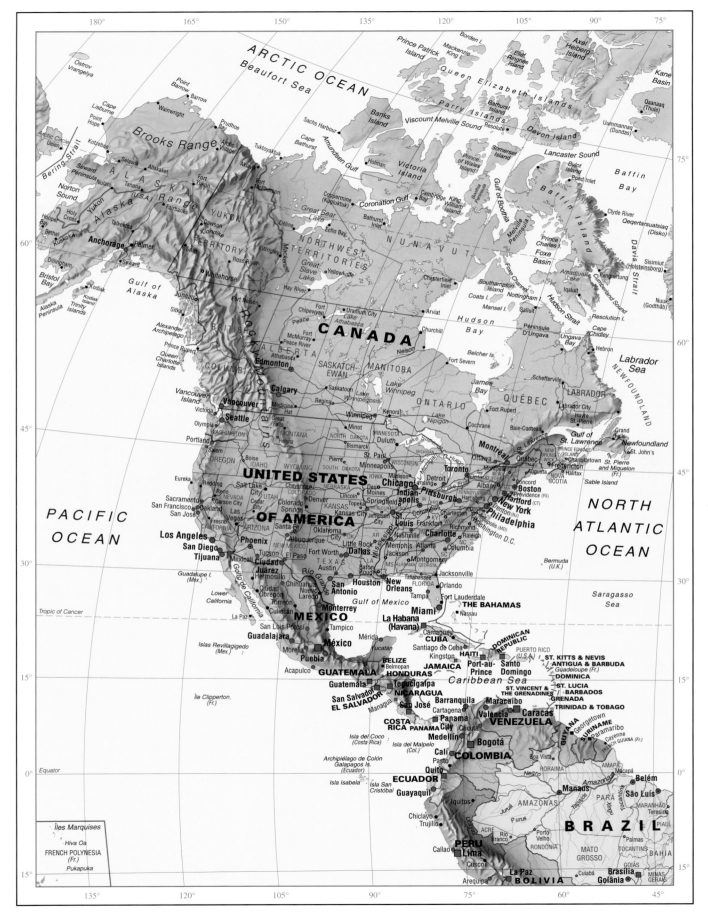

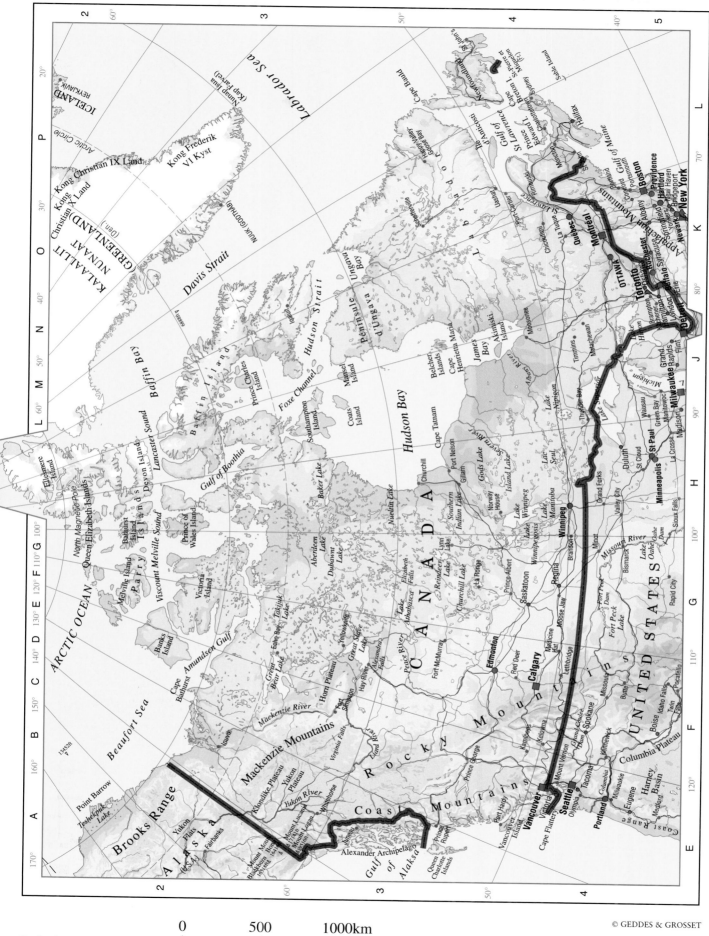

Scale 1: 24 414 000

| 0 | 500 | 1000km |
|---|---|---|

| 0 | 300 | 600miles |
|---|---|---|

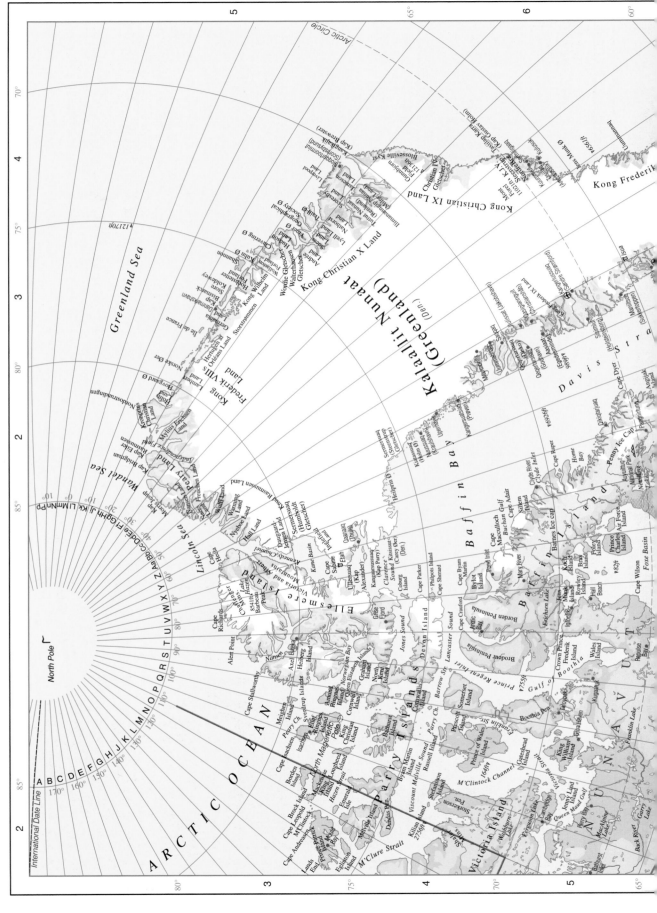

Scale 1: 15 625 000

| 0 | 250 | 500km |
|---|---|---|

| 0 | 150 | 300miles |
|---|---|---|

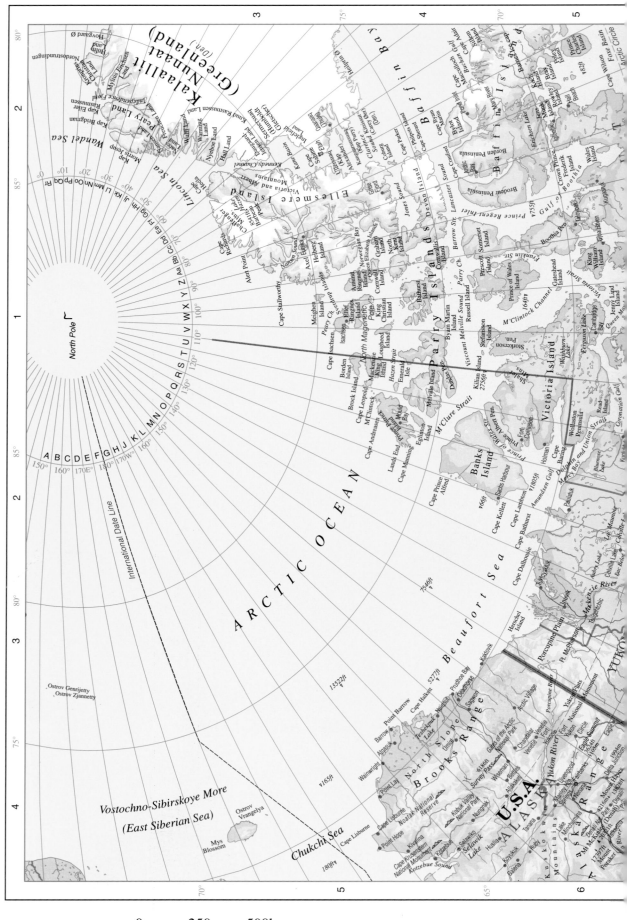

ARCTIC OCEAN

North Pole

Kalaallit Nunaat (Greenland) (Den.)

Wandel Sea

Lincoln Sea

Ellesmere Island

Baffin Bay

Parry Islands

Banks Island

Victoria Island

Beaufort Sea

Vostochno-Sibirskoye More (East Siberian Sea)

Chukchi Sea

Brooks Range

North Slope

U.S.A.

ALASKA

YUKON

International Date Line

Scale 1: 15 625 000

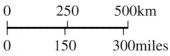

| 0 | 250 | 500km |
|---|-----|-------|
| 0 | 150 | 300miles |

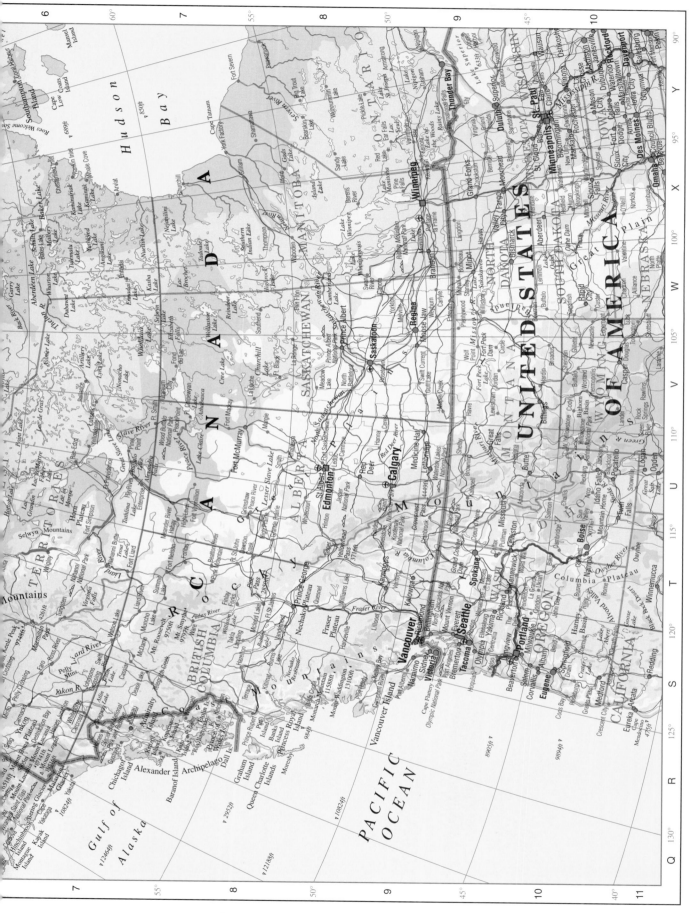

Scale 1: 15 024 000

| 0 | 200 | 400 | 600 | 800 | 1000km |
|---|---|---|---|---|---|

| 0 | 100 | 200 | 300 | 400 | 500 | 600miles |
|---|---|---|---|---|---|---|

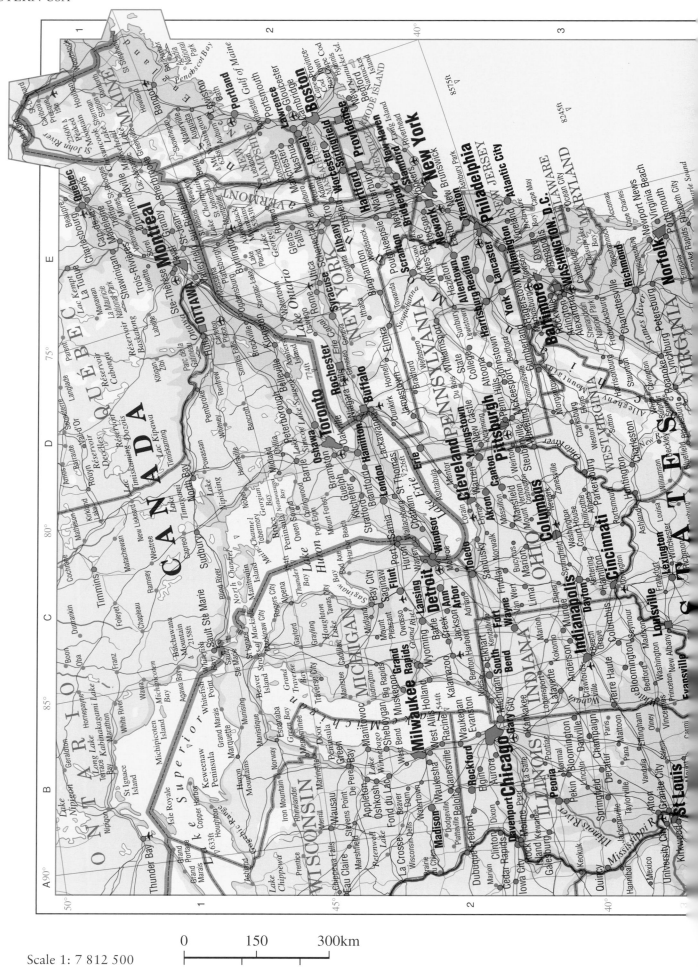

Scale 1: 7 812 500

0    150    300km

0    75    150miles

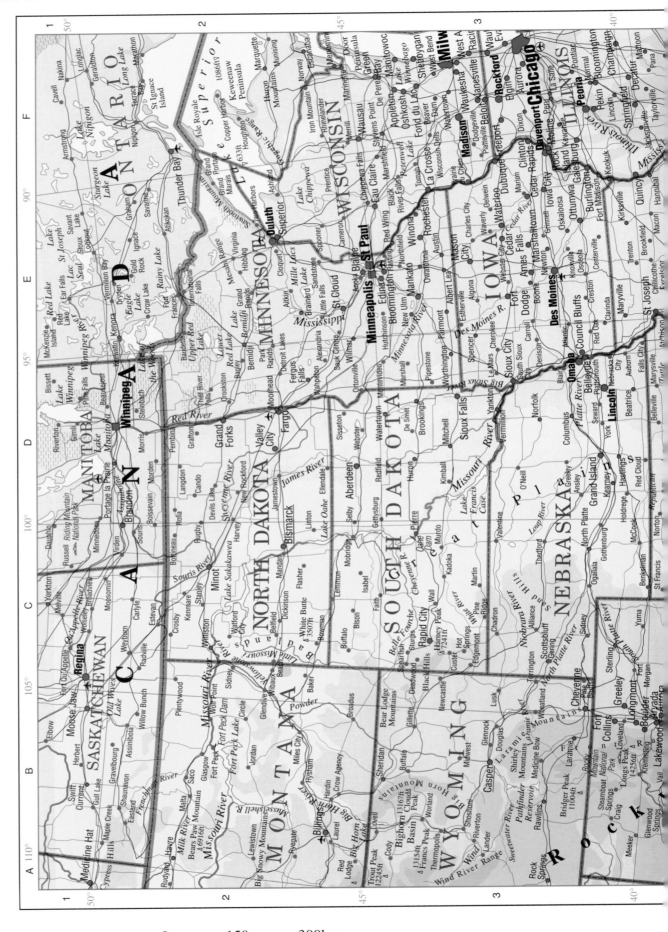

Scale 1: 7 812 500

| 0 | 150 | 300km |

| 0 | 75 | 150miles |

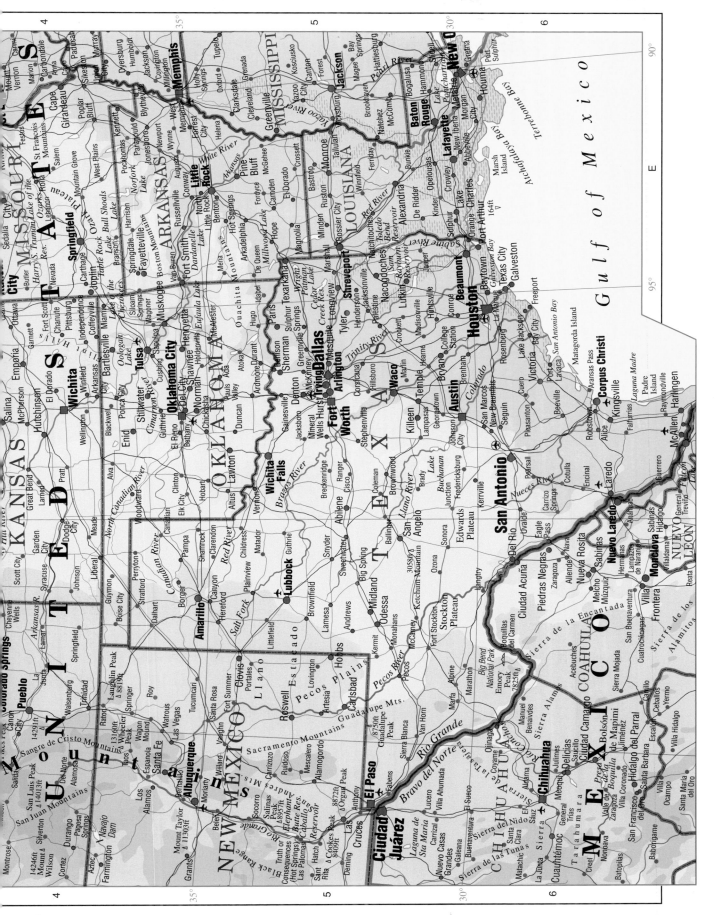

Scale 1: 7 812 500

| 0 | 150 | 300km |
|---|-----|-------|

| 0 | 75 | 150miles |
|---|-----|---------|

Scale 1: 10 000 000

0    200    400km

0    100    200miles

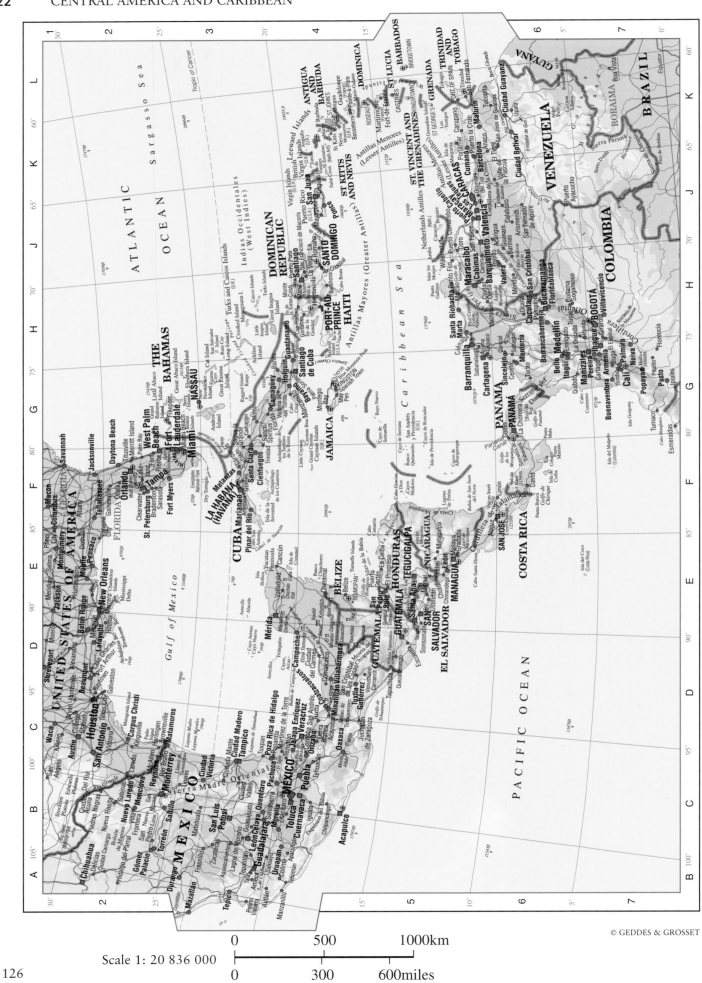

Scale 1: 20 836 000

© GEDDES & GROSSET

Yucatán
BELIZE
Belmopan
Kingston
HAITI
DOMINICAN
REPUBLIC
PUERTO RICO
(U.S.A.)
ST. KITTS & NEVIS
ANTIGUA & BARBUDA
JAMAICA
Port-au-
Prince
Santo
Domingo
Guadeloupe (Fr.)
HONDURAS
Cerro las Minas 2827m
DOMINICA
Tegucigalpa
*Caribbean Sea*
ST. VINCENT &
THE GRENADINES
ST. LUCIA
BARBADOS
NICARAGUA
Picó Cristóbal
Colón
Managua
Barranquilla
Maracaibo
GRENADA
San José
Cartagena
TRINIDAD & TOBAGO
COSTA
RICA
Chirripó
3820m
Panama
City
Valencia
Caracas
Georgetown
Cúcuta
VENEZUELA
GUYANA
Paramaribo
PANAMA
Isla del Coco
(Costa Rica)
Medellín
Pico Bolívar
5007m
Mount
Roraima
2810m
Cayenne
FRENCH GUIANA (Fr.)
Isla del Malpelo
(Col.)
Bogotá
Penedos de
São Pedro & São Paulo
(Brazil)
Cali
COLOMBIA
Juliana Top
1230m
Pasto
Boa Vista
RORAIMA
AMAPÁ
Arquipélago de
Fernando de
Noronha
(Brazil)
*Equator*
Pico da
Neblina
3014m
Macapá
Isla San
Cristóbal
Quito
*Negro*
ECUADOR
Chimborazo
6310m
*Amazonas*
Belém
São Luís
Guayaquil
Manaus
PARÁ
Fortaleza
RIO GRANDE
DO NORTE
Iquitos
*Juruá*
AMAZONAS
Teresina
CEARÁ
Natal
Chiclayo
*Purus*
*Tapajós*
*Xingu*
MARANHÃO
João Pessoa
PARAÍBA
Trujillo
Nevado de
Huascaran
6768m
*Ucayali*
Rio
Branco
ACRE
Porto
Velho
PIAUÍ
PERNAMBUCO
Recife
B R A Z I L
Maceió
PERU
RONDÔNIA
Palmas
ALAGOAS
Callao
Lima
MATO
GROSSO
TOCANTINS
SERGIPE
Aracaju
Cusco
BAHIA
Salvador
GOIÁS
*Tropic of Capricorn*
Arequipa
La Paz
BOLIVIA
Cuiabá
Brasília
Belmonte
Nevado Sajama
6542m
Sucre
Santa Cruz
Goiânia
MINAS GERAIS
Caravelas
Potosí
Uberlândia
Belo
Horizonte
ESPÍRITO
SANTO
Tocopilla
Campo Grande
MATO GROSSO
DO SUL
SÃO PAULO
Vitória
Trindade
(Braz.)
Volcán Llullaillaco
6723m
*Paraguay*
Campos
Nova Iguaçu
RIO DE JANEIRO
Antofagasta
PARAGUAY
PARANÁ
Rio de Janeiro
Chañaral
San Miguel
de Tucumán
Asunción
Curitiba
São
Paulo
San Félix
(Chile)
*Paraná*
SANTA CATARINA
San Ambrosio
(Chile)
La Serena
RIO GRANDE
Porto Alegre
Córdoba
Salto
DO SUL
Pelotas
Cerro Aconcagua
6960m
Rosario
Santa Fé
URUGUAY
Islas
Juan Fernández
(Chile)
Valparaíso
Mendoza
Mirador Nacional
501m
Santiago
Buenos Aires
Montevideo
La Plata
Concepción
ARGENTINA
Mar del Plata
CHILE
Bahía Blanca
PACIFIC
Puerto Montt
*Golfo San Matías*
SOUTH
OCEAN
Isla de Chiloé
Punta Delgada
ATLANTIC
Archipiélago
de los
Chonos
Comodoro Rivadavia
OCEAN
Deseado
Isla
Wellington
*Patagonia*
Falkland Islands
(Islas Malvinas)
(U.K.)
Puerto
Santa Cruz
West
Falkland
Stanley
South
Georgia
(U.K.)
Puerto Natáles
East Falkland
Punta Arenas
*Strait of Magellan*
Isla Grande de
Tierra del Fuego
Ushuaia
Isla de los Estados
*Cabo de Hornos*
*(Cape Horn)*

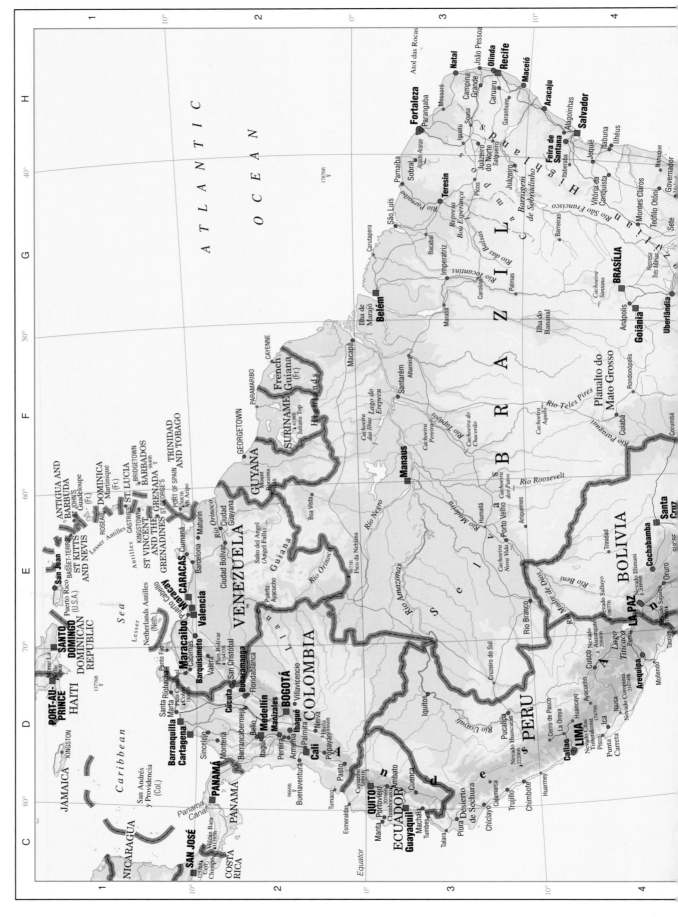

Scale 1: 24 414 000

| 0 | | 500 | 1000km |
|---|---|---|---|

| 0 | 250 | 500miles |
|---|---|---|

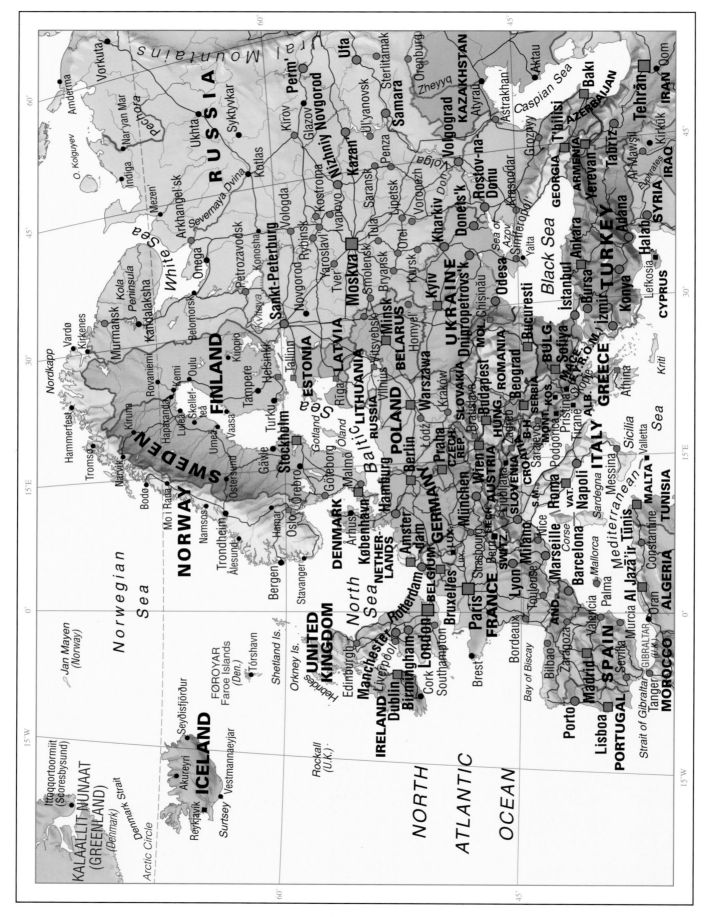

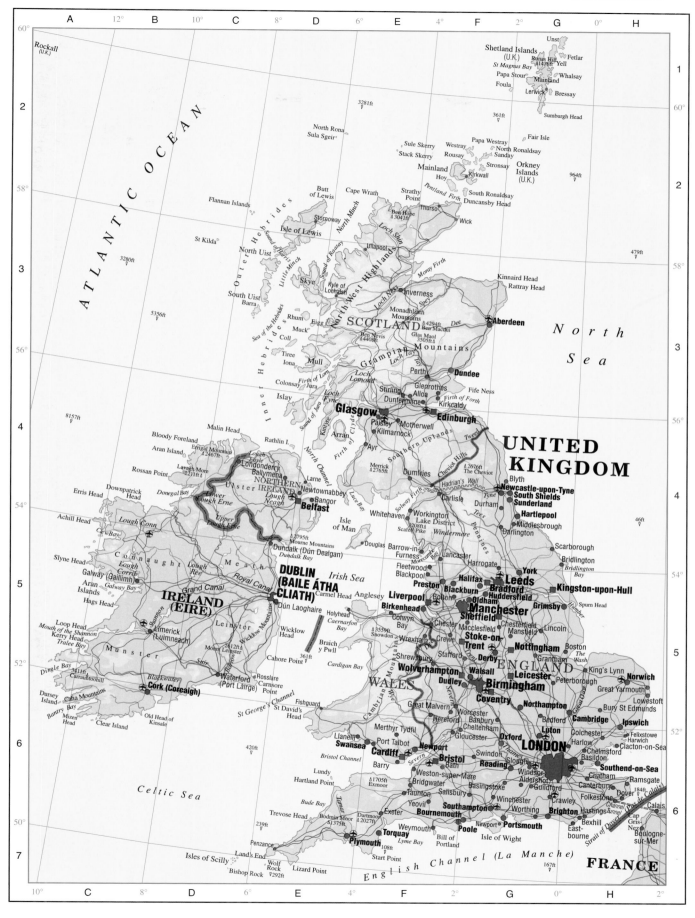

Scale 1: 5 211 000

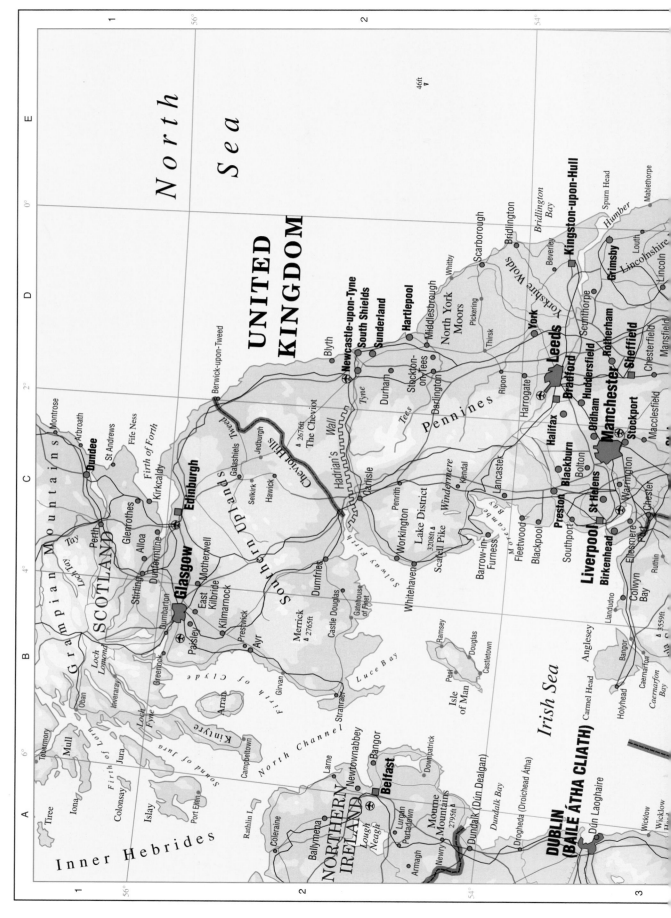

Scale 1: 2 605 000

| 0 | | 50 | | 100km |
|---|---|---|---|---|

| 0 | 25 | | 50miles |
|---|---|---|---|

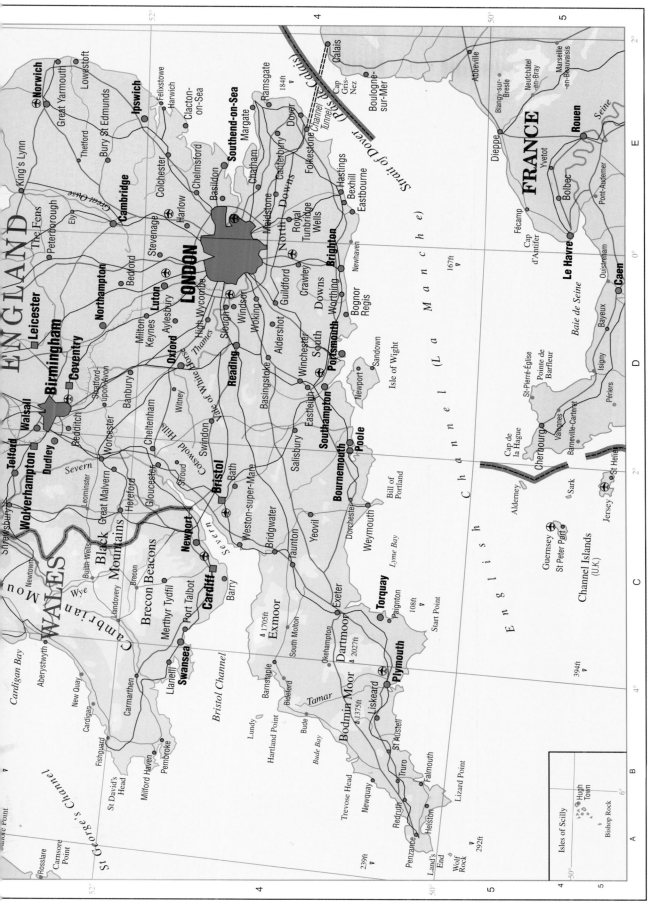

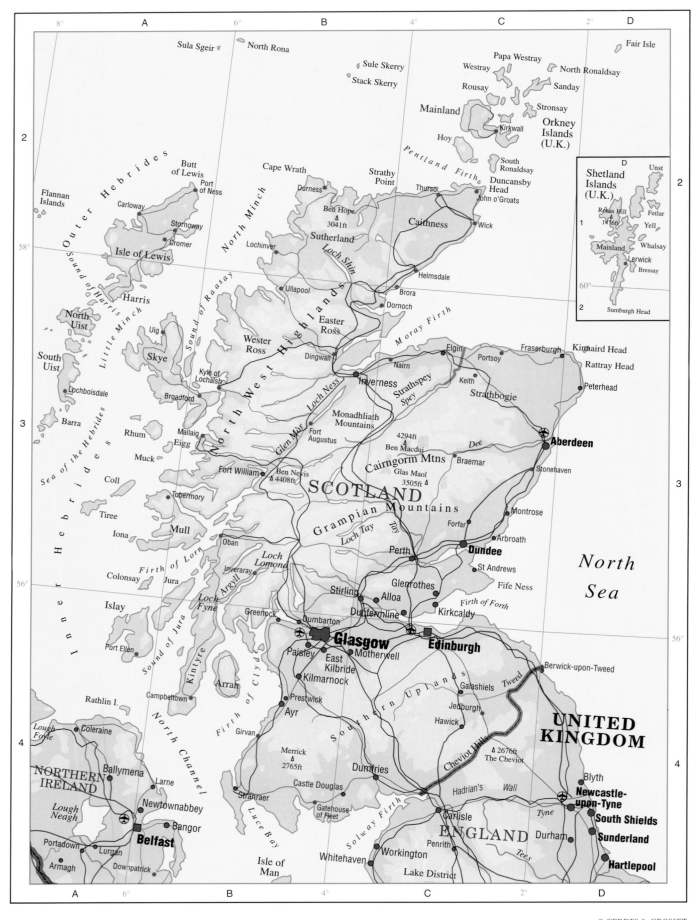

Scale 1: 2 435 000

© GEDDES & GROSSET

Scale 1: 2 605 000

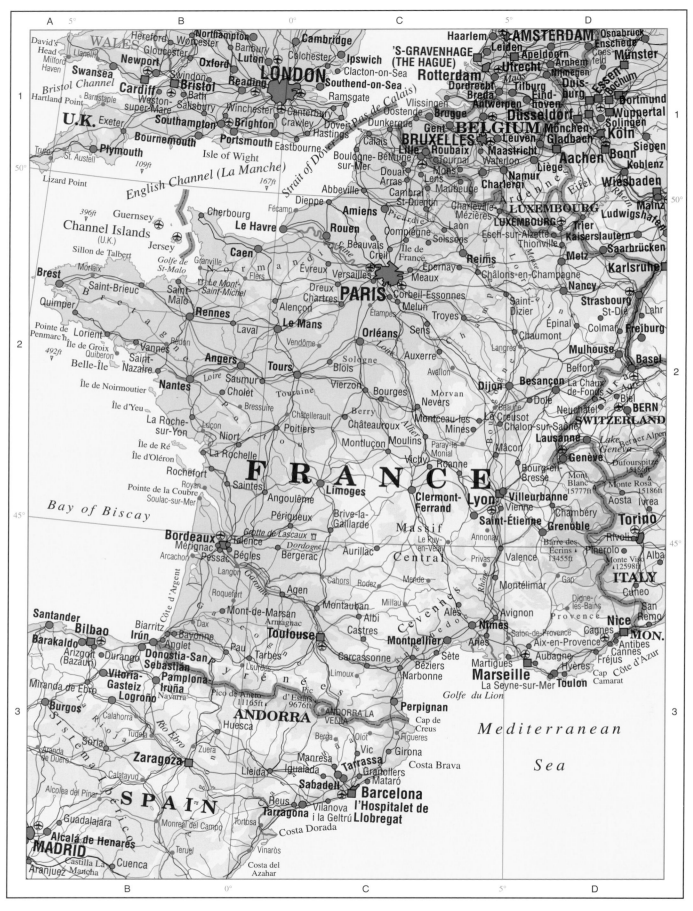

© GEDDES & GROSSET

Scale 1: 15 024 000

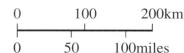

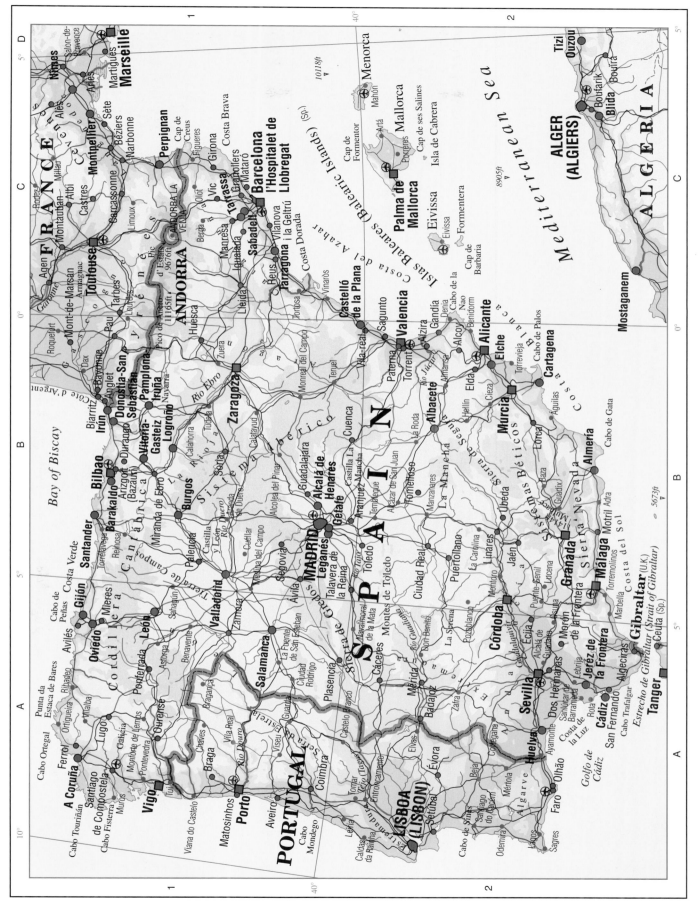

Scale 1: 5 580 000

0     100     200km

0     50     100miles

© GEDDES & GROSSET

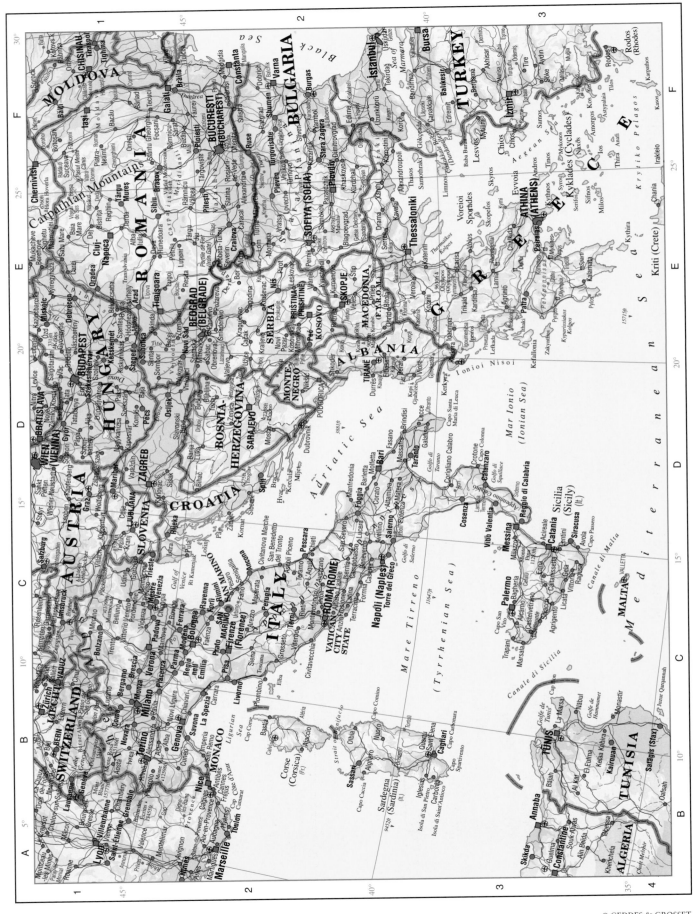

Scale 1: 8 510 000

0      200      400km

0      100      200miles

© GEDDES & GROSSET

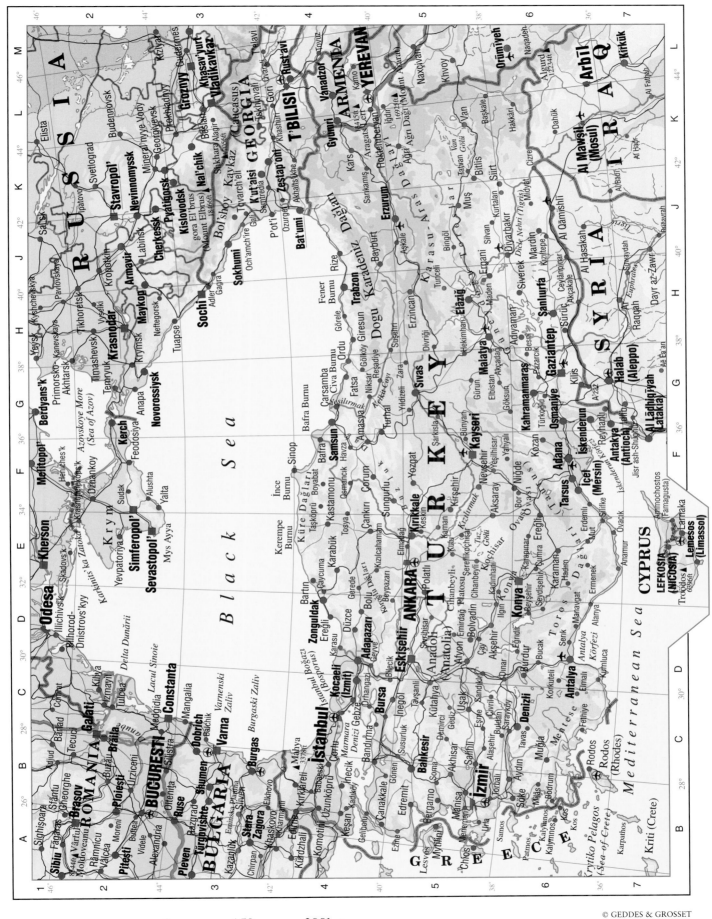

Scale 1: 7 692 000

```
0        150        300km
0      75      150miles
```

Scale 1: 6 250 000

| 0 | 150 | 300km |
| 0 | 75 | 150miles |

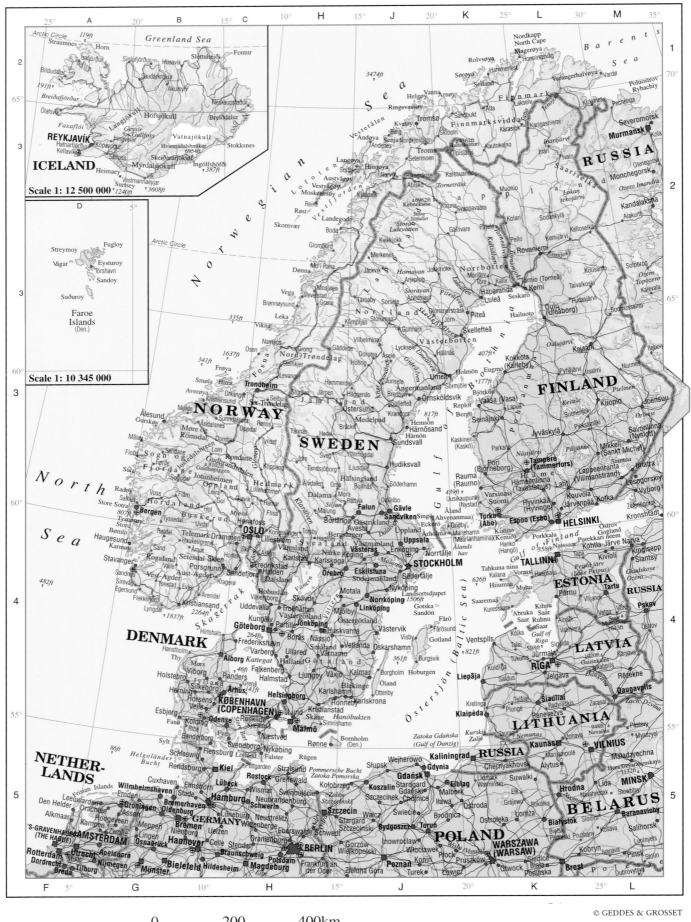

## ICELAND
Scale 1: 12 500 000

Faroe Islands (Den.)
Scale 1: 10 345 000

NORWAY

SWEDEN

FINLAND

RUSSIA

DENMARK

NETHER-LANDS

GERMANY

POLAND

ESTONIA

LATVIA

LITHUANIA

RUSSIA

BELARUS

*Norwegian Sea*

*North Sea*

*Barents Sea*

Östersjön (Baltic Sea)

© GEDDES & GROSSET

Scale 1: 9 766 000

0    200    400km

0    100    200miles

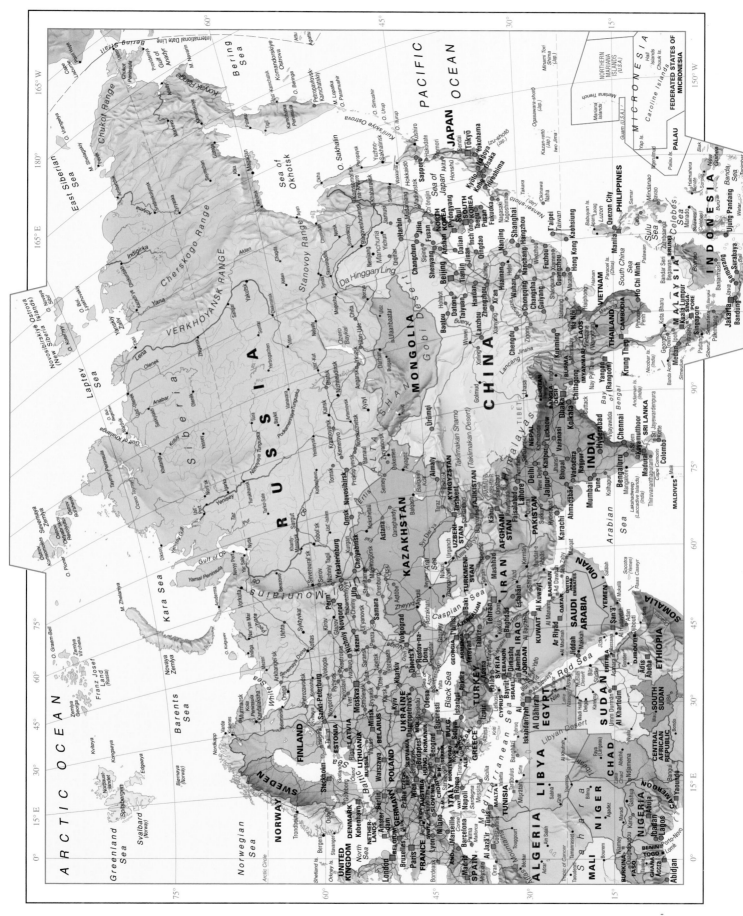

Scale 1: 14 141 000

| 0 | 250 | 500km |
|---|---|---|
| 0 | 150 | 300miles |

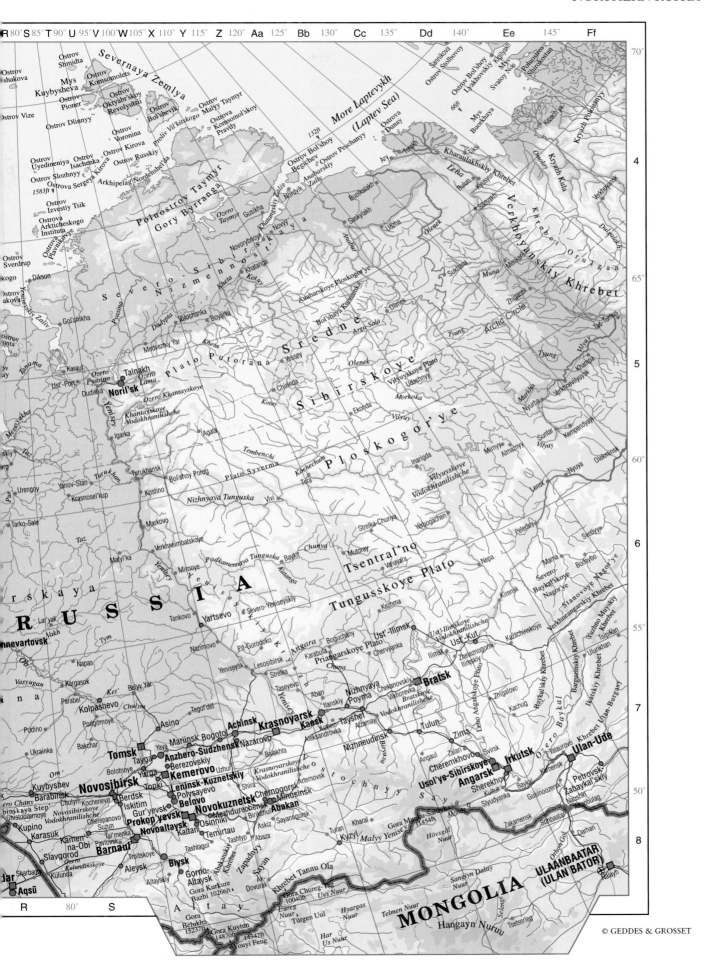

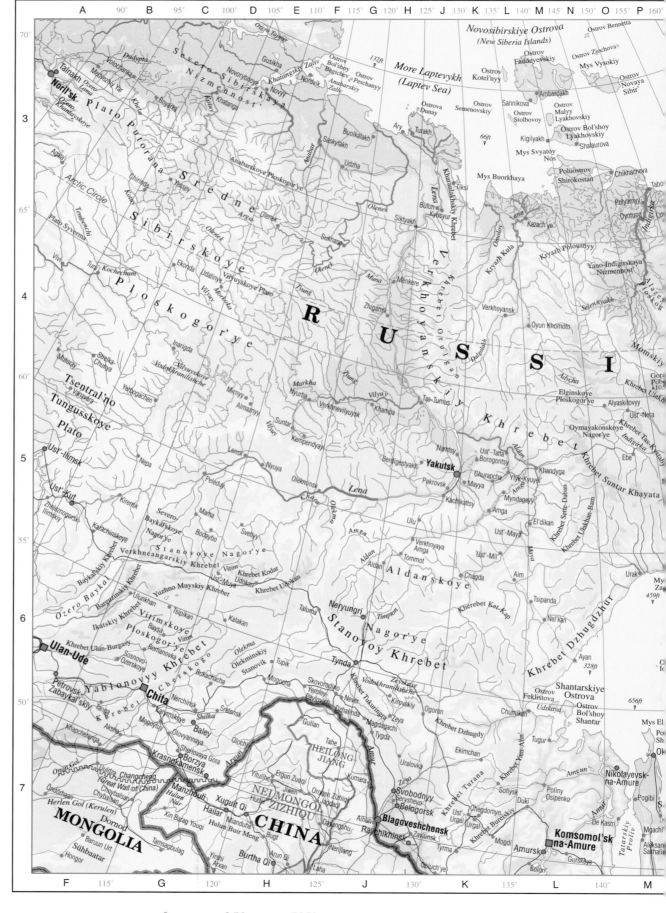

Scale 1: 13 889 000

```
0        250        500km
|----+----|----+----|
0      150        300miles
```

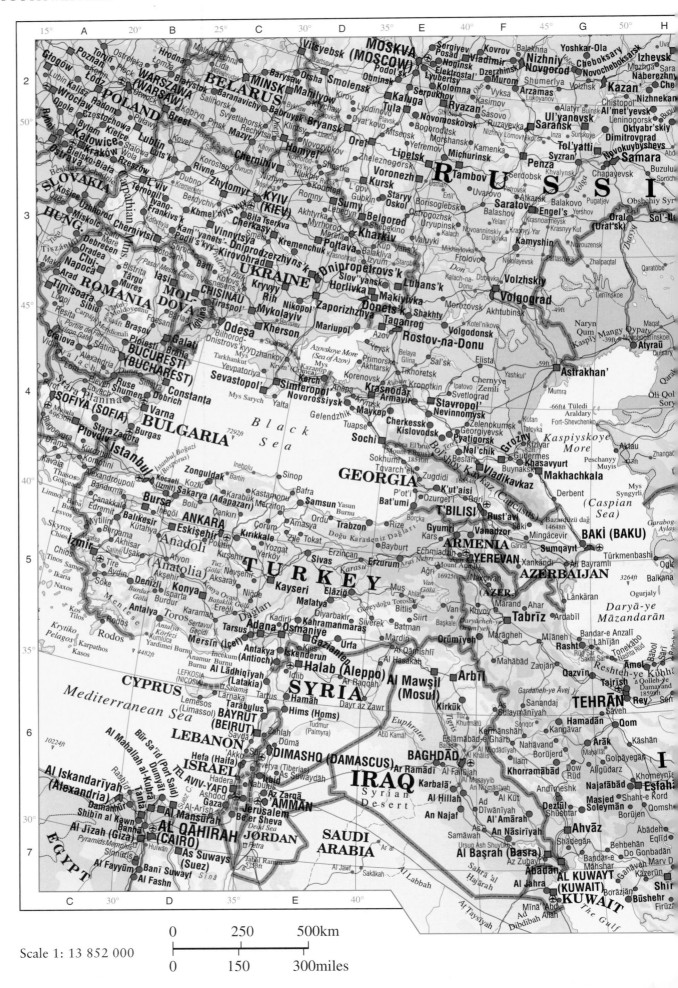

Scale 1: 13 852 000

| 0 | 250 | 500km |
|---|-----|-------|
| 0 | 150 | 300miles |

Scale 1: 27 710 000

Scale 1: 15 035 000

| 0 | 250 | 500km |
|---|-----|-------|
| 0 | 150 | 300miles |

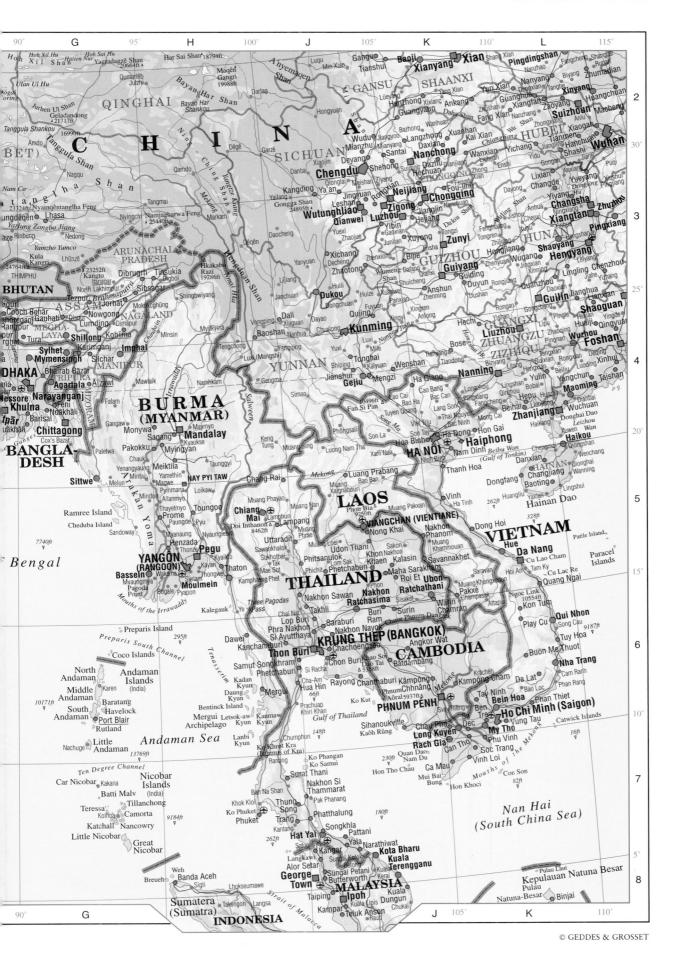

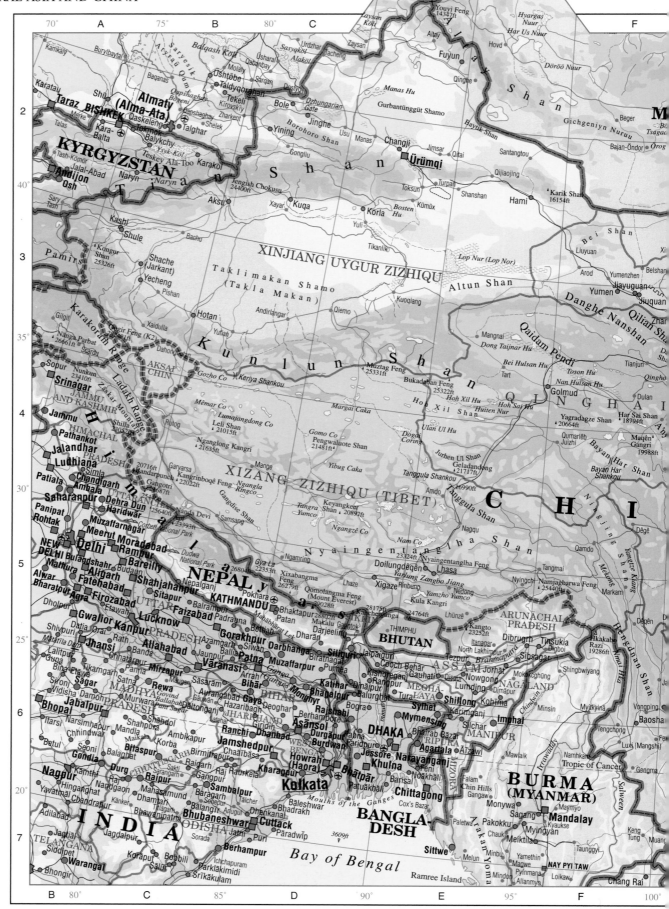

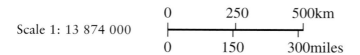

Scale 1: 13 874 000

| 0 | 250 | 500km |
|---|-----|-------|
| 0 | 150 | 300miles |

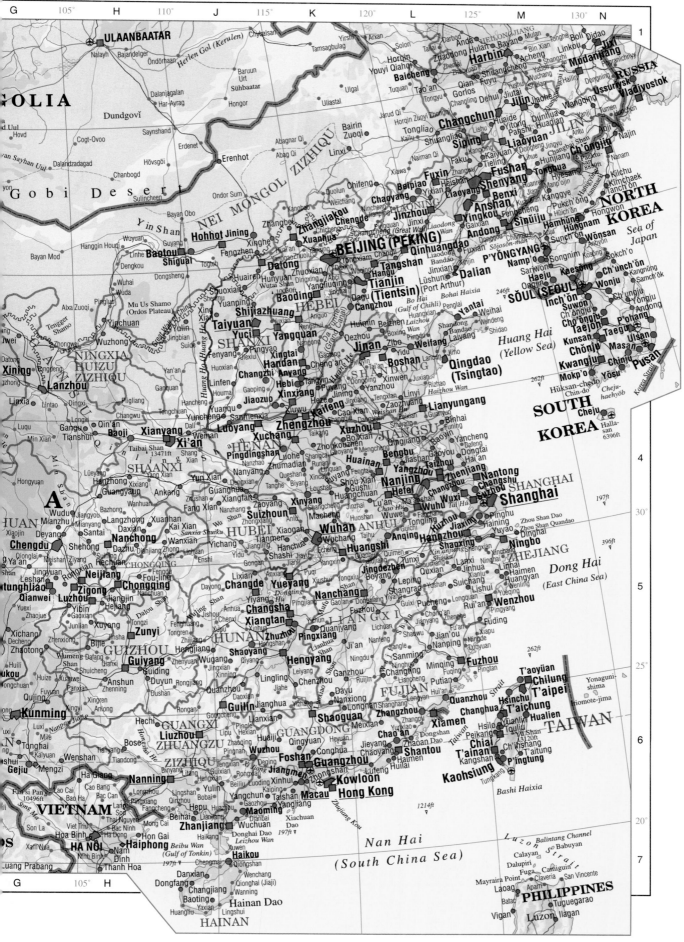

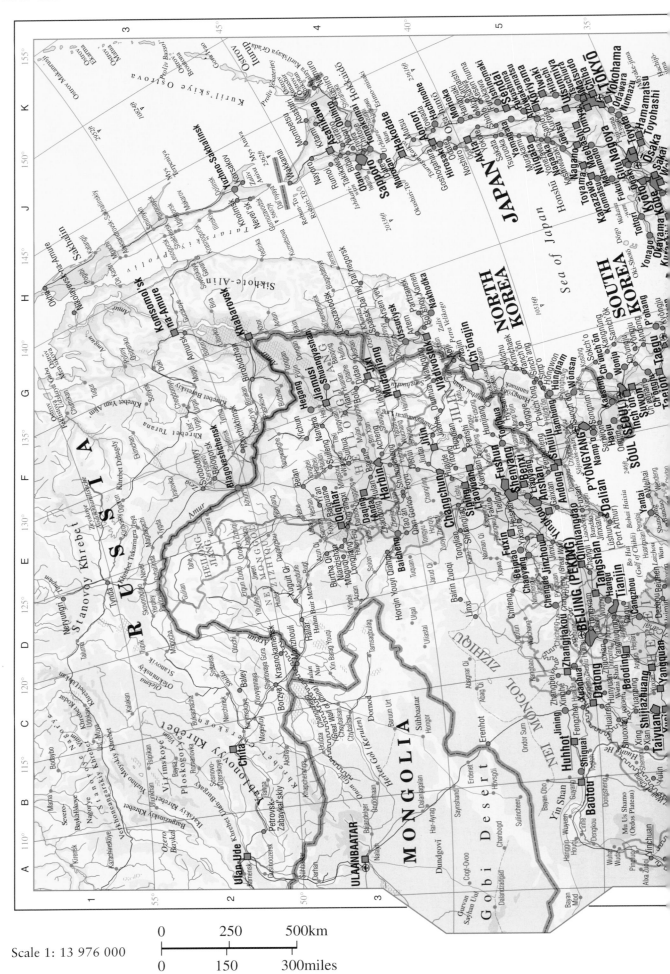

Scale 1: 13 976 000

| 0 | 250 | 500km |
| 0 | 150 | 300miles |

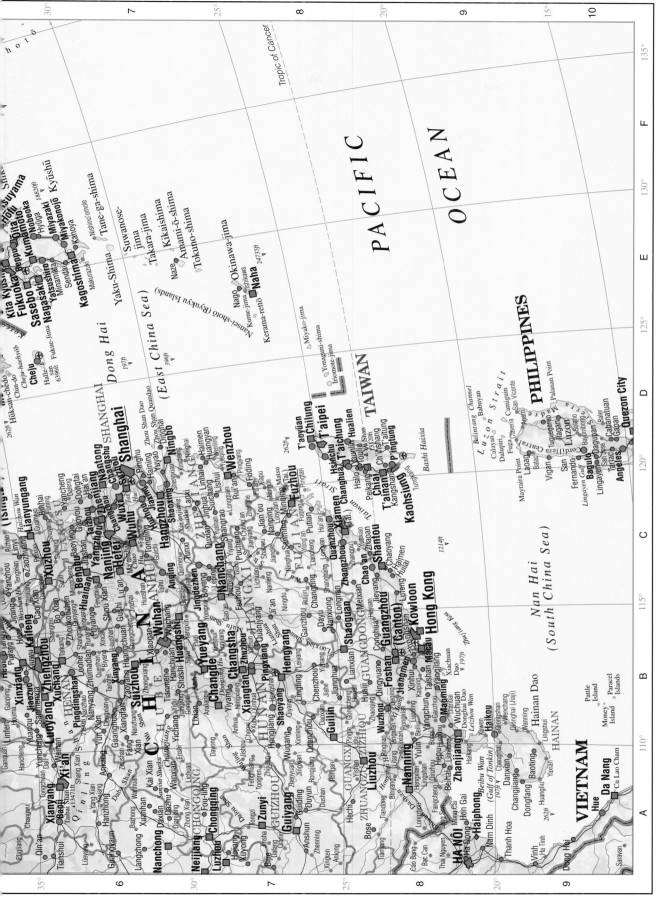

155

Scale 1: 13 889 000

| 0 | 250 | 500km |
| 0 | 150 | 300miles |

Scale 1: 9 766 000

0    200    400km

0    100    200miles

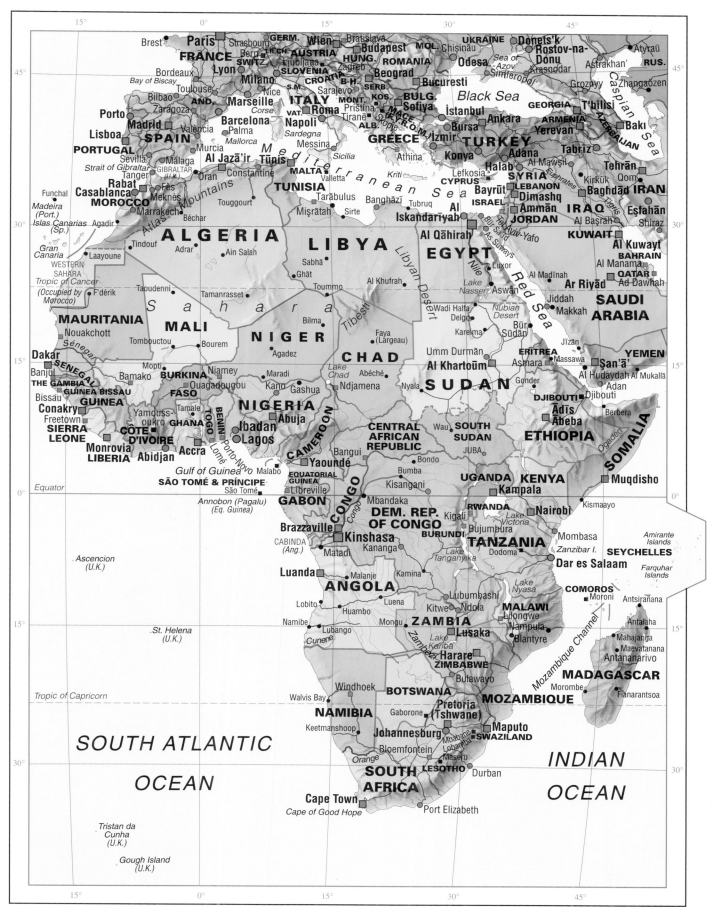

Scale 1: 21 230 000

| 0 | 500 | 1000km |
| 0 | 300 | 600miles |

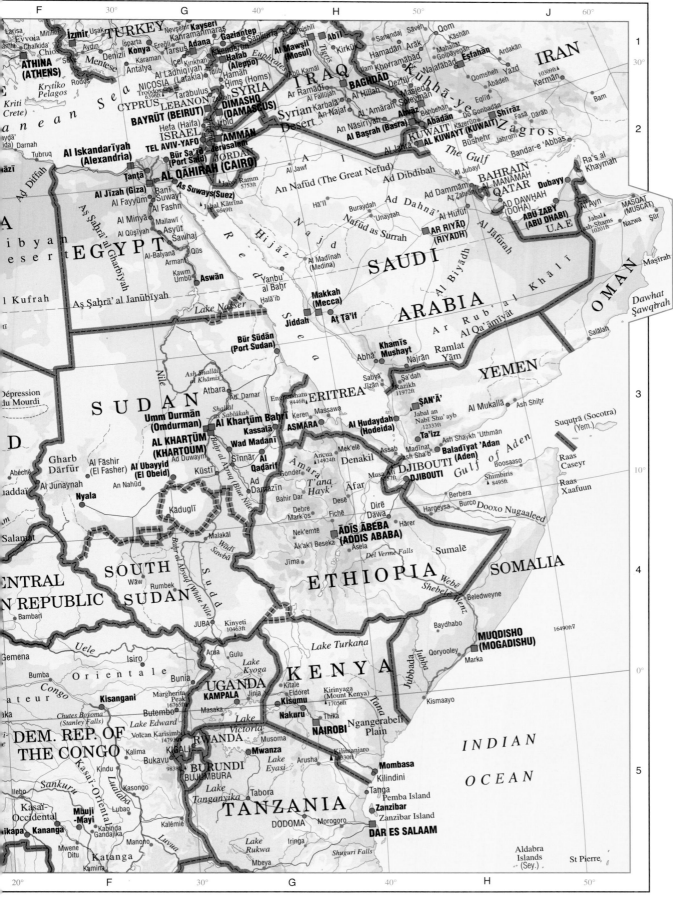

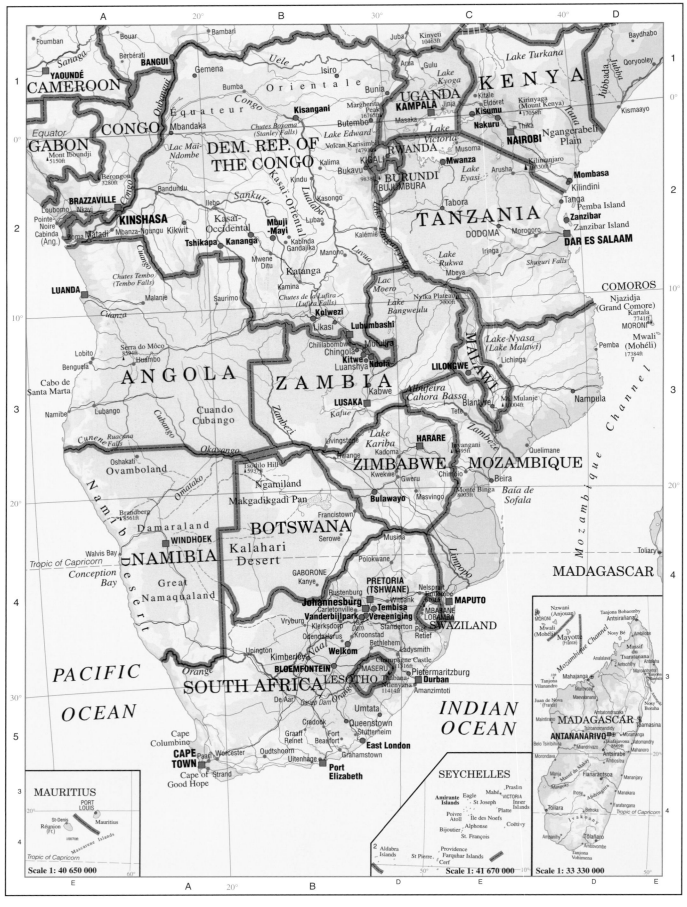

CAMEROON
YAOUNDÉ
Foumban
Bouar
Bambari
Bangui
BANGUI
Gemena
Isiro
Uele
Juba
Kinyeti
10463ft
Lake Turkana
Baydhabo

CONGO
Berbérati
Sanaga
Obangui
Bumba
Orientale
Gulu
Ania
Qoryooley

GABON
Equator
Equateur
Mbandaka
Congo
Kisangani
Chutes Boyoma
(Stanley Falls)
Butembo
Margherita
Peak
16765ft
Masaka
Volcan Karisimbi
14791ft
Lake Edward
KAMPALA
UGANDA
Jinja
Kitale
Eldoret
17065ft
Kirinyaga
(Mount Kenya)
KENYA
Kismaayo

Mont Iboundji
5150ft
Lac Maï-
Ndombe
Kalima
Kindu
Bukavu
9380ft
KIGALI
RWANDA
BURUNDI
BUJUMBURA
Musoma
NAIROBI
Nakuru
Kisumu
Lake
Victoria
Kilimanjaro
19330ft
Arusha
Ngangerabeli
Plain
Jubba

Berongou
3280ft
BRAZZAVILLE
Bandundu
Ilebo
Sankuru
Kasongo
Kalémié
Mwanza
Lake
Eyasi
Mombasa
Kilindini
Tanga
Pemba Island

Louboma
Nkayi
KINSHASA
Kikwit
Kasai-
Occidental
Lubao
Manono
Luvua
Tabora
DODOMA
TANZANIA
Morogoro
Zanzibar
Zanzibar Island
DAR ES SALAAM

Pointe-
Noire
Cabinda
(Ang.)
Boma
Matadi
Mbanza-Ngungu
Tshikapa
MBUJI-MAYI
Kananga
Kabinda
Gandajika
Mwene
Ditu
Katanga
Kamina
Iringa
Mbeya
Lake
Rukwa
Shuguri Falls
COMOROS
Njazidja
(Grand Comore)
Kartala
7741ft
MORONI

LUANDA
Cuanza
Malanje
Saurimo
Chutes Tembo
(Tembo Falls)
Chutes de la Lufira
(Lufira Falls)
Kolwezi
Likasi
LUBUMBASHI
Chililabombwe
Mufulira
Chingola
Kitwe
Ndola
Luanshya
Lake
Bangweulu
Nyika Plateau
7600ft
Lake
Moero
Lichinga
Lake Nyasa
(Lake Malawi)
Pemba
Mwali
(Mohéli)
17384ft

Lobito
Benguela
Serra do Môco
8594ft
Huambo
ANGOLA
ZAMBIA
Kabwe
LUSAKA
Kafue
Mutanda
LILONGWE
MALAWI
Blantyre
Mt Mulanje
10004ft
Nampula

Cabo de
Santa Marta
Namibe
Lubango
Cuando
Cubango
Cunene
Ruacana
Falls
Zambezi
Livingstone
Lake
Kariba
Albufeira
Cahora Bassa
Tete
Inyangani
8495ft
Quelimane

Namibe
Okavango
Hwange
Kadoma
HARARE
MOZAMBIQUE
Oshakati
Ovamboland
Omatako
Tsodilo Hill
5931ft
Ngamiland
ZIMBABWE
Kwekwe
Gweru
Chimoio
Beira
Monte Binga
8003ft
Baía de
Sofala

Brandberg
8561ft
Damaraland
Makgadikgadi Pan
Francistown
BOTSWANA
Serowe
Bulawayo
Masvingo
Musina

WINDHOEK
Walvis Bay
Tropic of Capricorn
Conception
Bay
NAMIBIA
Kalahari
Desert
Great
Namaqualand
GABORONE
Kanye
Rustenburg
Polokwane
PRETORIA
(TSHWANE)
Nelspruit
Embalenhle
Limpopo
MADAGASCAR

PACIFIC
OCEAN
Johannesburg
Carletonville
Tembisa
Vanderbijlpark
Vereeniging
Witbank
MBABANE
LOBAMBA
MAPUTO
SWAZILAND
Klerksdorp
Standerton
Piet
Retief

Vryburg
Odendaalsrus
Welkom
Kroonstad
Bethlehem
Ladysmith
Champagne Castle
11316ft
Pietermaritzburg

Upington
Kimberley
Vaal
BLOEMFONTEIN
MASERU
LESOTHO
Thabana
Ntlenyana
11414ft
Durban
Amanzimtoti

Orange
SOUTH AFRICA
De Aar
Gariep Dam
Orange
Umtata
Queenstown
Stutterheim
INDIAN
OCEAN

Cape
Columbine
Cradock
Fort
Beaufort
East London
Graaff
Reinet

CAPE
TOWN
Paarl
Worcester
Oudtshoorn
Uitenhage
Grahamstown
Port
Elizabeth

Cape of
Good Hope
Strand

MAURITIUS
PORT
LOUIS
St-Denis
Réunion
(Fr.)
10070ft
Mauritius
Mascarene Islands
Tropic of Capricorn
**Scale 1: 40 650 000**

SEYCHELLES
Amirante
Islands
Eagle
Mahé
Praslin
VICTORIA
St Joseph
Inner
Islands
Poivre
Atoll
Île des Noefs
Platte
Alphonse
Coëtivy
St François
Bijoutier
Aldabra
Islands
St Pierre
Providence
Farquhar Islands
Cerf
**Scale 1: 41 670 000**

MADAGASCAR
Nzwani
(Anjouan)
Mwali
(Mohéli)
Mayotte
(France)
Tanjona Bobaomby
Antsiranana
Nosy Bé
Ambilobe
Massif
du
Tsaratanana
Analalava
Antsohihy
Mahajanga
Maintirano
ANTANANARIVO
8669ft
Antsirabe
Fianarantsoa
Tropic of Capricorn
Toliara
**Scale 1: 33 330 000**

© GEDDES & GROSSET

0      500      1000km

**Scale 1: 21 703 000**
0      300      600miles

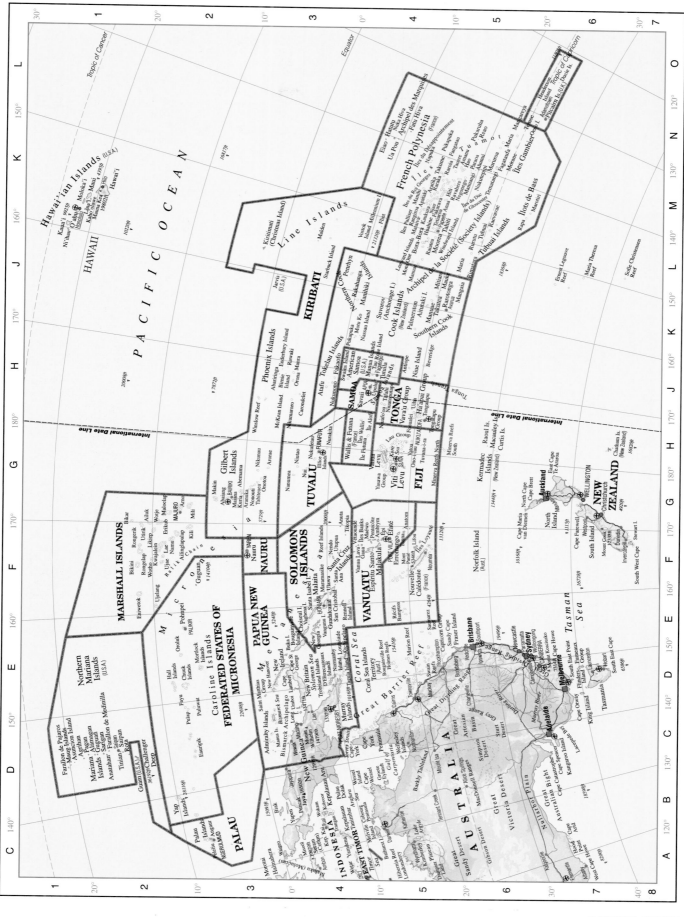

Scale 1: 50 373 000

| 0 | 1000 | 2000km |
|---|------|--------|

| 0 | 600 | 1200miles |
|---|-----|-----------|

Scale 1: 14 205 000

| 0 | 300 | 600km |
|---|-----|-------|

| 0 | 150 | 300miles |
|---|-----|----------|

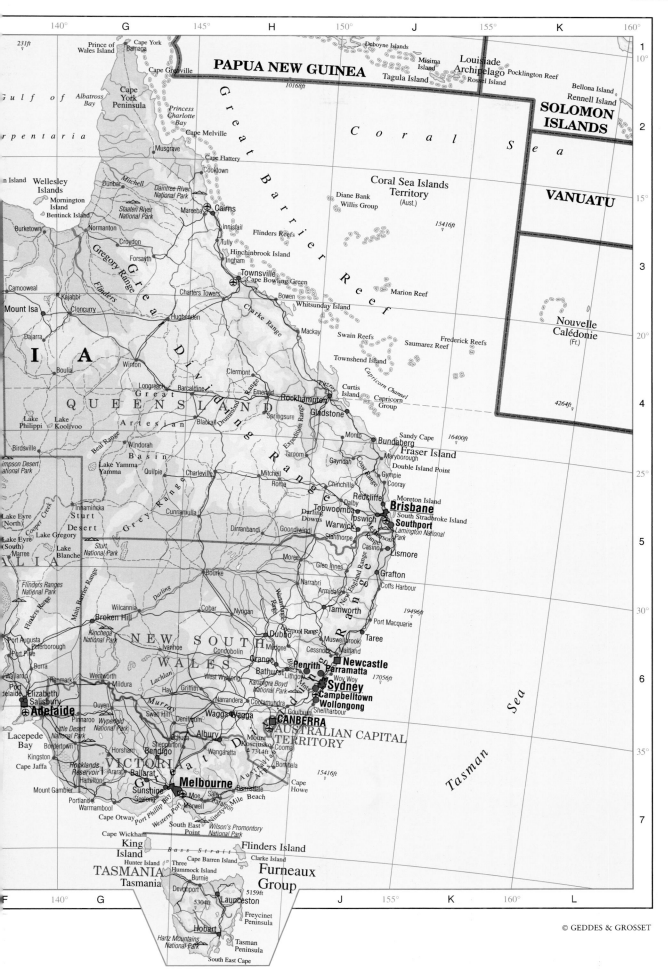

## NEW ZEALAND

Three Kings Islands
Cape Maria
van Diemen
North Cape
*Parengarenga Harbour*
Te Kao
*Rangaunu Bay*
Awanui
Kaitaia
Cape Brett
Kawakawa
Russell
Whangarei
Waiotira
Needles Point
*Hauraki*
*Gulf*
Great Barrier Island
Dargaville
Paparoa
Port Jackson
*Colville Channel*
*Kaipara Harbour*
Helensville
East Coast Bays
Mount Roskill
Takapuna
Waitemata
**Auckland**
**Manukau**
Thames
Cape
Runaway
*Bay of Plenty*
Paeroa
Tauranga
Te Araroa
**North Island**
Hamilton
Matata
Whakatane
East
Cape
Te Awamutu
Putaruru
Te Puia
Albatross Point
Tokoroa
Kawerau
Opotiki
*Waikato*
**Rotorua**
*Huiarau Range*
Awakino
*Lake Taupo*
Taupo
Gisborne
*North Taranaki Bight*
*Tongariro*
*National Park*
Wairoa
Mahia
Peninsula
New Plymouth
Waitara
Makorako
5665ft
*Hawke Bay*
Cape Egmont
Stratford
Δ Ruapehu
Napier
Mount Egmont
Eltham
9174ft
Cape Kidnappers
8259ft
Hawera
Taihape
Hastings
*South Taranaki Bight*
Hunterville
Wanganui
Marton
Dannevirke
Palmerston North
Castlepoint
Cape Farewell
Levin
Collingwood
Durville Is.
*Cook*
Masterton
*Abel Tasman National Park*
*Tasman*
Porirua
The Twins
*Bay*
Upper Hutt
5989ft Δ
Motueka
Lower Hutt
*Karamea Bight*
Red
Nelson
**WELLINGTON**
Mount Owen
Hill
Richmond
Cape Palliser
6150ft Δ
5871ft Δ
Blenheim
Westport
Seddon
Cape Campbell
*Buller*
Δ Manakau
Reefton
Ward
8561ft
*Spenser Mts*
*Wairau*
Mount
Travers 7669ft
Kaikoura
Greymouth
Waiau
**NEW ZEALAND**
**South Island**
Hokitika
Cheviot
*Tasman*
*Sea*
Harihari
Waipara
*Pegasus Bay*
Mount Arrowsmith
**Christchurch**
9168ft
Δ Mount Cook
Banks Peninsula
Haast
12333ft
Akaroa
Jackson Head
Ashburton
Mount Aspiring
*Canterbury*
9958ft Δ
Omarama
*Bight*
Milford Sound
Timaru
*Southern*
*Lake*
Waimate
*Lake Te*
*Wanaka*
*Anau*
Wanaka
Oamaru
*Doubtful Sound*
Alexandra
Hampden
*Fiordland*
Roxburgh
Palmerston
*National Park*
*Lake*
Waikouaiti
Resolution
Manapouri
*Wakatipu*
Port Chalmers
Island
Lumsden
**Dunedin**
Cape
Otautau
Providence
Winton
Gore
Balclutha
*Foveaux*
Riverton
Invercargill
Bluff
Mount Anglem Δ
3214ft
Oban
Stewart Island
*Port Pegasus*
Southwest Cape

35°
40°
45°

170°   175°

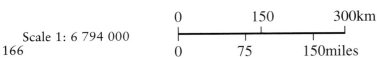

0      150      300km

Scale 1: 6 794 000

0      75      150miles

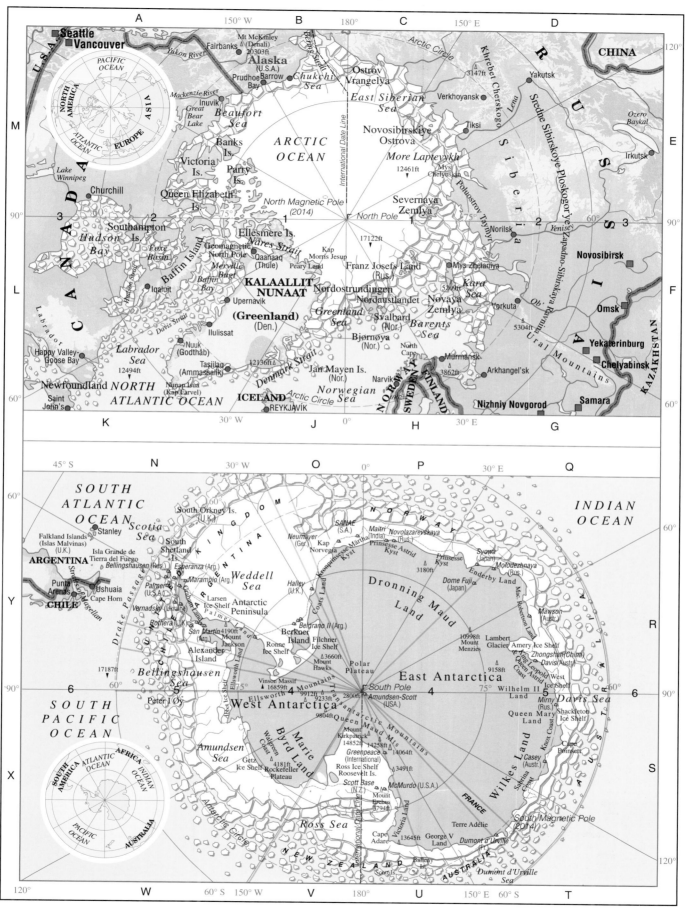

Scale 1: 42 613 000

| 0 | 1000 | 2000km |
|---|------|--------|

| 0 | 500 | 1000miles |
|---|-----|-----------|

© GEDDES & GROSSET

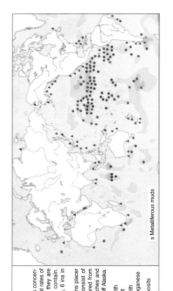

s Metalliferous muds

## Seabed treasures

In the deeper sea regions mineral exploitation has concentrated on manganese nodules. These lumps grow at rates of between 3-8 mm, .25 in each million years, and they are valuable for the copper, nickel and cobalt they contain. Granules vary in size and may be up to 150 mm, 6 ins in diameter.

On the continental shelves and near coastal regions placer deposits are often commercially viable. They consist of heavy mineral particles which have been weathered from locally occuring ore bodies and deposited on beaches and in estuaries. Gold is extracted from placer deposits off Alaska.

☐ Moderate coverage of manganese nodules
☐ Extensive coverage of manganese nodules
  Nodules with >1.8% nickel and copper
• Nodules with >1% cobalt
• Nodules with >35% manganese
• Placer deposits

## Underwater landscapes

Topography of the ocean floor can be divided into two distinct features: the continental margins and the deep sea basins.

The character of the ocean basin depends on the extent to which sediments mask the crust and also the degree of volcanic activity. The sediments may be either pelagic or terrigenous. The latter are brought down by turbidity currents which are avalanches of silt and sand from the continental shelf. These powerful currents can cut channels in the continental shelf such as the Hatteras Canyon off North America and transport material thousands of kilometres.

On the continental shelf, sediments are affected by waves, tidal currents and changes in sea level.

a. Shallow areas are most accessible, they may overlie oil and gas bearing rock.
b. The continental slope defines the edge of the continental block.
c. Deep sea floors can be very flat with gradients less than 1:1000.
d. A Guyot is a submarine volcanic mountain with a completely smooth top.
e. Volcanic islands can be higher above the seabed than Everest is above sea level.
f. Mid ocean ridges. New oceanic crust is formed along these.
g. Atolls are extinct volcanoes which have been colonized by coral.
h. Deep sea trenches. Oceanic crust is destroyed under neighbouring plates.

# FLAGS OF THE WORLD

**Afghanistan**
*Area*: 251,827 sq miles
(652,230 sq km)
*Population*: 31,108,077
*Capital*: Kabul
*Other cities*: Herat, Kandahar,
Mazar-e-Sharif
*Government*: Islamic Republic
*Main religions*: Sunni Islam,
Shia Islam
*Currency*: Afghani

**Andorra**
*Area*: 181 sq miles
(468 sq km)
*Population*: 85,293
*Capital*: Andorra la Vella
*Government*: Parliamentary
Democracy
*Main religion*: Roman Ca-
tholicism
*Currency*: Euro

**Albania**
*Area*: 11,100 sq miles
(28,748 sq km)
*Population*: 3,011,405
*Capital*: Tirana (Tiranë)
*Other cities*: Durrës, Shkodër,
Vlorë
*Government*: Republic
*Main religions*: Islam, Alba-
nian Orthodox, Roman
Catholicism
*Currency*: Lek

**Angola**
*Area*: 481,354 sq miles
(1,246,700 sq km)
*Population*: 18,565,269
*Capital*: Luanda
*Other cities*: Huambo, Lobito,
Benguela
*Government*: Republic
*Main religions*: Roman Ca-
tholicism, traditional beliefs
*Currency*: Kwanza

**African Union**
53 Members: Algeria, Angola, Benin, Bot-
swana, Burkina Faso, Burundi, Cameroon,
Cape Verde, Central African Republic,
Chad, Comoros, Democratic Republic
of the Congo, Republic of the Congo,
Côte d'Ivoire, Djibouti, Egypt, Equatorial
Guinea, Eritrea, Ethiopia, Gabon, Gambia,
Ghana, Guinea, Guinea-Bissau, Kenya,
Lesotho, Liberia, Libya, Madagascar,
Malawi, Mali, Mauritius, Mozambique,
Namibia, Niger, Nigeria, Rwanda, Western
Sahara, São Tomé and Príncipe, Senegal,
Seychelles, Sierra Leone, Somalia, South
Africa, Sudan, Swaziland, Tanzania, Togo,
Tunisia, Uganda, Zambia, Zimbabwe

**Anguilla**
*Area*: 35 sq miles (91 sq km)
*Population*: 15,754
*Capital*: The Valley
*Government*: British Overseas
Territory
*Main religion*: Christianity
*Currency*: East Caribbean
Dollar

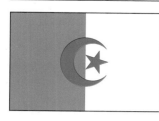

**Algeria**
*Area*: 919,595 sq miles
(2,381,741 sq km)
*Population*: 38,087,812
*Capital*: Algiers (Alger)
*Other cities*: Oran, Constan-
tine, Annaba
*Government*: Republic
*Main religion*: Sunni Islam
*Currency*: Algerian Dinar

**Antigua and Barbuda**
*Area*: 171 sq miles
(442 sq km)
*Population*: 90,156
*Capital*: St John's
*Government*: Constitutional
Monarchy
*Main religion*: Christianity
*Currency*: East Caribbean
Dollar

**American Samoa**
*Area*: 77 sq miles (199 sq km)
*Population*: 54,719
*Capital*: Pago Pago
*Government*: Unincorporated
and Unorganized Territory
of the US
*Main religion*: Christianity
*Currency*: US Dollar

**Argentina**
*Area*: 1,073,518 sq miles
(2,780,400 sq km)
*Population*: 42,610,981
*Capital*: Buenos Aires
*Other cities*: Córdoba, Rosa-
rio, Mendoza, La Plata, San
Miguel de Tucumán
*Government*: Republic
*Main religion*: Roman Ca-
tholicism
*Currency*: Peso

**Arab League**
Members: Egypt, Iraq , Jordan, Lebanon, Saudi Arabia, Syria, Yemen, Libya, Sudan, Morocco, Tunisia, Kuwait, Algeria, United Arab Emirates, Bahrain, Qatar, Oman, Mauritania, Somalia, Palestine, Djibouti, Comoros

**Azerbaijan**
*Area*: 33,436 sq miles (86,600 sq km)
*Population*: 9,590,159
*Capital*: Baku
*Other cities*: Ganja, Sumqayit
*Government*: Republic
*Main religions*: Shia Islam, Sunni Islam
*Currency*: Manat

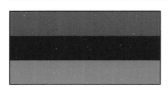

**Armenia**
*Area*: 11,484 sq miles (29,743 sq km)
*Population*: 2,974,184
*Capital*: Yerevan
*Other major city*: Gyumri
*Government*: Republic
*Main religion*: Armenian Orthodox
*Currency*: Dram

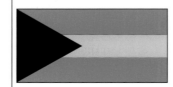

**Bahamas, The**
*Area*: 5,359 sq miles (13,8780 sq km)
*Population*: 319,031
*Capital*: Nassau
*Other major city*: Freeport
*Government*: Constitutional Monarchy
*Main religion*: Christianity
*Currency*: Bahamian Dollar

**Aruba**
*Area*: 69 sq miles (180 sq km)
*Population*: 9,153
*Capital*: Oranjestad
*Government*: Autonomous territory of the Kingdom of the Netherlands
*Main religion*: Christianity
*Currency*: Aruban Florin

**Bahrain**
*Area*: 293 sq miles (760 sq km)
*Population*: 1,281,332
*Capital*: Manama (Al Manamah)
*Government*: Constitutional Monarchy
*Main religions*: Shia Islam, Sunni Islam
*Currency*: Bahraini Dinar

**Australia**
*Area*: 2,988,902 sq miles (7,741,220 sq km)
*Population*: 22,262,501
*Capital*: Canberra
*Other cities*: Sydney, Melbourne, Brisbane, Perth, Adelaide
*Government*: Federal Parliamentary State
*Main religion*: Christianity
*Currency*: Australian Dollar

**Bangladesh**
*Area*: 55,598 sq miles (143,998 sq km)
*Population*: 163,654,860
*Capital*: Dhaka
*Other cities*: Chittagong, Khulna
*Government*: Parliamentary Democracy
*Main religions*: Sunni Islam, Hinduism
*Currency*: Taka

**Austria**
*Area*: 32,378 sq miles (83,859 sq km)
*Population*: 8,221,464
*Capital*: Vienna (Wien)
*Other cities*: Graz, Linz, Salzburg, Innsbruck
*Government*: Federal Republic
*Main religion*: Roman Catholicism
*Currency*: Euro

**Barbados**
*Area*: 166 sq miles (430 sq km)
*Population*: 288,725
*Capital*: Bridgetown
*Government*: Parliamentary Democracy
*Main religion*: Christianity
*Currency*: Barbadian Dollar

**Belarus**
*Area*: 80,155 sq miles
  (207,600 sq km)
*Population*: 9,542,883
*Capital*: Minsk
*Other cities*: Gomel, Mogilev,
  Vitebsk
*Government*: Republic
*Main religions*: Belarusian
  Orthodox
*Currency*: Belarusian Rouble

**Bhutan**
*Area*: 14,824 sq miles
  (38,394 sq km)
*Population*: 725,296
*Capital*: Thimphu
*Other city*: Phuntsholing
*Government*: Constitutional
  Monarchy
*Main religions*: Buddhism,
  Hinduism
*Currency*: Ngultrum

**Belgium**
*Area*: 11,787 sq miles
  (30,528 sq km)
*Population*: 10,444,268
*Capital*: Brussels (Bruxelles)
*Other cities*: Antwerp, Ghent,
  Charleroi, Liège, Bruges
*Government*: Constitutional
  Monarchy
*Main religion*: Roman Ca-
  tholicism
*Currency*: Euro

**Bolivia**
*Area*: 424,164 sq miles
  (1,098,581 sq km)
*Population*: 10,461,053
*Capital*: Sucre
*Other cities*: La Paz, Cocha-
  bamba, Santa Cruz, Oruro
*Government*: Republic (Social
  Unitarian State)
*Main religion*: Roman Ca-
  tholicism
*Currency*: Boliviano

**Belize**
*Area*: 8,867 sq miles
  (22,966 sq km)
*Population*: 334,297
*Capital*: Belmopan
*Other city*: Belize City
*Government*: Parliamentary
  Democracy
*Main religions*: Roman Ca-
  tholicism, Protestantism
*Currency*: Belizean Dollar

**Bosnia and Herzegovina**
*Area*: 19,767 sq miles
  (51,197 sq km)
*Population*: 3,875,723
*Capital*: Sarajevo
*Other cities*: Banja Luka,
  Mostar, Tuzla
*Government*: Federal Republic
*Main religions*: Sunni Islam,
  Eastern Orthodox, Roman
  Catholicism
*Currency*: Convertible Marka

**Benin**
*Area*: 43,484 sq miles
  (112,622 sq km)
*Population*: 9,877,292
*Capital*: Porto-Novo
*Other city*: Cotonou
*Government*: Republic
*Main religions*: Roman
  Catholicism, Sunni Islam,
  traditional beliefs (Vodun),
  Protestantism
*Currency*: CFA Franc

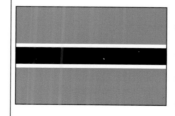

**Botswana**
*Area*: 224,607 sq miles
  (581,730 sq km)
*Population*: 2,127,825
*Capital*: Gaborone
*Other cities*: Francistown,
  Molepolole
*Government*: Parliamentary
  Republic
*Main religions*: Christianity,
  traditional beliefs
*Currency*: Pula

**Bermuda**
*Area*: 21 sq miles (54 sq km)
*Population*: 69,467
*Capital*: Hamilton
*Government*: British Overseas
  Territory
*Main religions*: Protestantism,
  Roman Catholicism
*Currency*: Bermudian Dollar

**Brazil**
*Area*: 3,287,612 sq miles
  (8,514,877 sq km)
*Population*: 201,009,622
*Capital*: Brasília
*Other cities*: Fortaleza, Recife,
  Rio de Janeiro, Salvador,
  São Paulo
*Government*: Federal Republic
*Main religion*: Roman Ca-
  tholicism
*Currency*: Real

**British Indian Ocean Territory**
The Chagos Archipelago, a group of five coral atolls in the middle of the Indian Ocean. A British colony.
*Area*: 20 sq miles/52 sq km.)

**Burundi**
*Area*: 10,745 sq miles
(27,830 sq km)
*Population*: 10,888,321
*Capital*: Bujumbura
*Government*: Republic
*Main religions*: Roman Catholicism, Protestantism, traditional beliefs
*Currency*: Burundian Franc

**Brunei**
*Area*: 2,226 sq miles
(5,765 sq km)
*Population*: 415,717
*Capital*: Bandar Seri Begawan
*Other cities*: Kuala Belait, Seria
*Government*: Monarchy (Constitutional Sultanate)
*Main religions*: Sunni Islam, Buddhism, Christianity
*Currency*: Brunei Dollar

**Cambodia**
*Area*: 69,898 sq miles
(181,035 sq km)
*Population*: 15,205,539
*Capital*: Phnom Penh
*Other city*: Battambang
*Government*: Constitutional Monarchy
*Main religion*: Buddhism
*Currency*: Riel

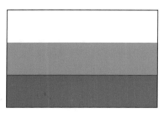

**Bulgaria**
*Area*: 42,811 sq miles
(110,879 sq km)
*Population*: 6,981,642
*Capital*: Sofia
*Other cities*: Burgas, Plovdiv, Ruse, Varna
*Government*: Parliamentary Republic
*Main religion*: Bulgarian Orthodox
*Currency*: Lev

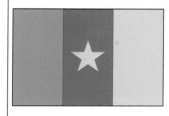

**Cameroon**
*Area*: 183,568 sq miles
(475,440 sq km)
*Population*: 20,549,221
*Capital*: Yaoundé
*Other major city*: Douala
*Government*: Republic
*Main religions*: Traditional beliefs, Christianity, Sunni Islam
*Currency*: CFA Franc

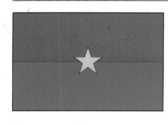

**Burkina Faso (Burkina)**
*Area*: 105,869 sq miles
(274,200 sq km)
*Population*: 17,812,961
*Capital*: Ouagadougou
*Other city*: Bobo-Dioulasso
*Government*: Republic
*Main religions*: Sunni Islam, Roman Catholicism, traditional beliefs
*Currency*: CFA Franc

**Canada**
*Area*: 3,855,103 sq miles
(9,984,670 sq km)
*Population*: 34,568,211
*Capital*: Ottawa
*Other cities*: Calgary, Toronto, Montreal, Vancouver
*Government*: Federal Parliamentary State
*Main religions*: Roman Catholicism, United Church of Canada, Anglicanism
*Currency*: Canadian Dollar

**Burma (Myanmar)**
*Area*: 261,228 sq miles
(676,578 sq km)
*Population*: 55,167,330
*Capital*: Nay Pyi Taw
*Other cities*: Yangon, Mandalay
*Government*: Constitutional Republic
*Main religion*: Buddhism
*Currency*: Kyat

**Cape Verde**
*Area*: 1,557 sq miles
(4,033 sq km)
*Population*: 531,046
*Capital*: Praia
*Government*: Republic
*Main religions*: Roman Catholicism, Traditional Beliefs, Protestantism
*Currency*: Cape Verdean Escudo

### Cayman Islands
*Area*: 102 sq miles (264 sq km)
*Population*: 53,737
*Capital*: George Town, on Grand Cayman
*Government*: British Overseas Territory
*Main religion*: Christianity
*Currency*: Cayman Islands Dollar

### China
*Area*: 3,705,407 sq miles (9,596,961 sq km)
*Population*: 1,349,585,838
*Capital*: Beijing
*Other cities*: Chengdu, Guangzhou, Shanghai
*Government*: People's Republic (Single-Party Communist State)
*Main religions*: Traditionally Taoism, Buddhism
*Currency*: Yuan

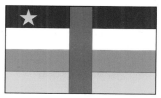

### Central African Republic
*Area*: 240,535 sq miles (622,984 sq km)
*Population*: 5,166,510
*Capital*: Bangui
*Other cities*: Bambari, Bangassou
*Government*: Republic
*Main religions*: Traditional beliefs, Christianity, Islam
*Currency*: CFA Franc

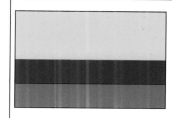

### Colombia
*Area*: 439,736 sq miles (1,138,910 sq km)
*Population*: 45,745,783
*Capital*: Bogotá
*Other cities*: Barranquilla, Cali, Cartagena, Medellín
*Government*: Republic
*Main religion*: Roman Catholicism
*Currency*: Colombian Peso

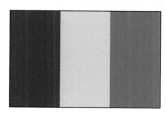

### Chad
*Area*: 495,755 sq miles (1,284,000 sq km)
*Population*: 11,193,452
*Capital*: N'Djamena
*Other cities*: Sarh, Moundou, Abéché
*Government*: Republic
*Main religions*: Sunni Islam, Christianity, traditional beliefs
*Currency*: CFA Franc

### Commonwealth of Independent States (CIS)
A confederation of 11 former Soviet Republics: Armenia, Azerbaijan, Belarus, Georgia, Kazakhstan, Kyrgyzstan, Moldova, Russia, Tajikistan, Ukraine, and Uzbekistan. Turkmenistan discontinued permanent membership as of August 2005 and is now an associate member

### Channel Islands
*Area*: 75 square miles/194 square km
*Population*: 143,000
*Main islands*: Jersey (top flag), Guernsey (bottom), also Alderney, Sark, Herm and Brechou.
*Government*: British Crown dependencies.
*Religion*: Christianity
*Currency*: Pound sterling

### Comoros
*Area*: 863 sq miles (2,235 sq km) excluding Mayotte
*Population*: 752,288
*Capital*: Moroni
*Government*: Federal Islamic Republic
*Main religion*: Sunni Islam
*Currency*: Comorian Franc

### Chile
*Area*: 291,933 sq miles (756,102 sq km)
*Population*: 17,216,945
*Capital*: Santiago
*Other cities*: Arica, Concepción, Valparaíso, Viña del Mar
*Government*: Republic
*Main religion*: Roman Catholicism
*Currency*: Chilean Peso

### Congo, Democratic Republic of the
*Area*: 905,355 sq miles (2,344,858 sq km)
*Population*: 75,507,308
*Capital*: Kinshasa
*Other cities*: Lubumbashi, Goma, Mbuji-Mayi, Kananga, Kisangani
*Government*: Republic
*Main religions*: Roman Catholicism, Protestantism, Islam, traditional beliefs
*Currency*: Congolese Franc

### Congo, Republic of the
*Area*: 132,047 sq miles
(342,000 sq km)
*Population*: 4,492,689
*Capital*: Brazzaville
*Other major city*: Pointe-Noire
*Government*: Republic
*Main religions*: Christianity,
traditional beliefs
*Currency*: CFA Franc

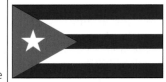

### Cuba
*Area*: 42,803 sq miles
(110,860 sq km)
*Population*: 11,061,886
*Capital*: Havana (La Habana)
*Other cities*: Santiago de
Cuba, Camagüey, Holguín,
Santa Clara
*Government*: Marxist-Leninist
Single-Party State
*Main religion*: Traditionally
Roman Catholicism
*Currency*: Cuban Peso

### Cook Islands
*Area*: 91 sq miles (236 sq km)
*Population*: 10,447
*Capital*: Avarua (on Raro-
tonga)
*Government*: Self-governing
parliamentary democracy in
free association with New
Zealand
*Main religion*: Christianity
*Currency*: Cook Islands Dollar/
New Zealand Dollar

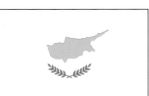

### Cyprus (Republic of)
*Area*: 3,572 sq miles
(9,251 sq km)
*Population*: 1,155,403
*Capital*: Nicosia
*Other cities*: Famagusta,
Limassol, Larnaca, Paphos
*Government*: Republic
*Main religions*: Greek Ortho-
dox, Sunni Islam
*Currency*: Euro

### Costa Rica
*Area*: 19,730 sq miles
(51,100 sq km)
*Population*: 4,695,942
*Capital*: San José
*Other cities*: Alajuela, Limón,
Puntarenas
*Government*: Republic
*Main religion*: Roman Ca-
tholicism
*Currency*: Costa Rican Colón

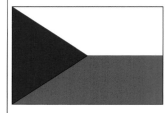

### Czech Republic
*Area*: 30,451 sq miles
(78,867 sq km)
*Population*: 10,162,921
*Capital*: Prague (Praha)
*Other cities*: Brno, Olomouc,
Ostrava
*Government*: Parliamentary
Republic
*Main religions*: Roman Ca-
tholicism, Protestantism
*Currency*: Koruna

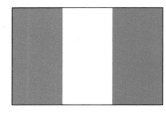

### Côte d'Ivoire (Ivory Coast)
*Area*: 124,504 sq miles
(322,463 sq km)
*Population*: 22,400,835
*Capital*: Yamoussoukro
*Other cities*: Abidjan, Bouaké,
Daloa
*Government*: Republic
*Main religions*: Sunni Islam,
Christianity, traditional
beliefs
*Currency*: CFA Franc

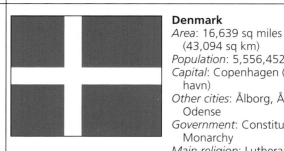

### Denmark
*Area*: 16,639 sq miles
(43,094 sq km)
*Population*: 5,556,452
*Capital*: Copenhagen (Køben-
havn)
*Other cities*: Ålborg, Århus,
Odense
*Government*: Constitutional
Monarchy
*Main religion*: Lutheranism
*Currency*: Danish Krone

### Croatia
*Area*: 21,851 sq miles
(56,594 sq km)
*Population*: 4,475,611
*Capital*: Zagreb
*Other cities*: Osijek, Rijeka,
Split
*Government*: Parliamentary
Republic
*Main religion*: Roman Ca-
tholicism
*Currency*: Kuna

### Djibouti
*Area*: 8,958 sq miles
(23,200 sq km)
*Population*: 792,198
*Capital*: Djibouti
*Government*: Republic
*Main religion*: Sunni Islam
*Currency*: Djiboutian Franc

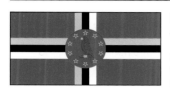

### Dominica
*Area*: 290 sq miles
(751 sq km)
*Population*: 73,286
*Capital*: Roseau
*Government*: Republic
*Main religion*: Roman Catholicism, Protestantism
*Currency*: East Caribbean Dollar

### Equatorial Guinea
*Area*: 10,831 sq miles
(28,051 sq km)
*Population*: 704,001
*Capital*: Malabo
*Other major city*: Bata
*Government*: Republic
*Main religion*: Roman Catholicism
*Currency*: CFA Franc

### Dominican Republic
*Area*: 18,792 sq miles
(48,670 sq km)
*Population*: 10,088,598
*Capital*: Santo Domingo
*Other cities*: Santiago, Puerto Plata, La Romana, Barahona
*Government*: Republic
*Main religion*: Roman Catholicism
*Currency*: Dominican Peso

### Eritrea
*Area*: 45,406 sq miles
(117,600 sq km)
*Population*: 6,233,682
*Capital*: Asmara (Asmera)
*Other cities*: Keren, Massawa, Assab
*Government*: Republic
*Main religions*: Sunni Islam, Christianity
*Currency*: Nakfa

### Ecuador
*Area*: 109,484 sq miles
(283,561 sq km)
*Population*: 15,439,429
*Capital*: Quito
*Other cities*: Guayaquil, Cuenca, Machala, Manta, Ambato
*Government*: Republic
*Main religion*: Roman Catholicism
*Currency*: US Dollar

### Estonia
*Area*: 17,463 sq miles
(45,228 sq km)
*Population*: 1,266,375
*Capital*: Tallinn
*Other cities*: Narva, Pärnu
*Government*: Parliamentary Republic
*Main religions*: Lutheranism, Eastern Orthodox
*Currency*: Euro

### Egypt
*Area*: 386,662 sq miles
(1,001,450 sq km)
*Population*: 85,294,388
*Capital*: Cairo
*Other cities*: Alexandria, Giza, Port Said, Suez
*Government*: Republic
*Main religion*: Sunni Islam
*Currency*: Egyptian Pound

### Ethiopia
*Area*: 426,373 sq miles
(1,104,300 sq km)
*Population*: 93,877,025
*Capital*: Addis Ababa (Addis Abeba)
*Other cities*: Dire Dawa, Gonder, Jima
*Government*: Federal Republic
*Main religions*: Ethiopian Orthodox, Sunni Islam, Protestantism
*Currency*: Ethiopian Birr

### El Salvador
*Area*: 8,124 sq miles
(21,041 sq km)
*Population*: 6,108,590
*Capital*: San Salvador
*Other cities*: Santa Ana, San Miguel
*Government*: Republic
*Main religion*: Roman Catholicism, Protestantism
*Currency*: US Dollar

### European Union (EU)
A union of 28 European countries. Members: Austria, Belgium, Bulgaria, Croatia, Cyprus, Czech Republic, Denmark, Estonia, Finland, France, Germany, Greece, Hungary, Ireland, Italy, Latvia, Lithuania, Luxembourg, Malta, Netherlands, Portugal, Romania, Slovakia, Slovenia, Spain, Sweden, United Kingdom

### Falkland Islands (Islas Malvinas)
*Area*: 4,700 sq miles (12,173 sq km)
*Population*: 3,140
*Capital*: Stanley
*Government*: British Overseas Territory
*Main religion*: Christianity
*Currency*: Falkland Islands Pound

### French Polynesia
*Area*: 1,609 sq miles (4,167 sq km)
*Population*: 277,293
*Capital*: Papeete
*Government*: Overseas Collectivity of France
*Main religions*: Protestantism, Roman Catholicism
*Currency*: CFP Franc

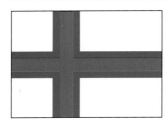

### Faroe Islands (Føroyar)
*Area*: 538 sq miles (1,393 sq km)
*Population*: 49,709
*Capital*: Tórshavn
*Government*: Self-governing Region of Denmark
*Main religion*: Lutheranism
*Currency*: Faroese Króna

### French Southern and Antarctic Territories
Territories in Antarctica and the Antarctic Ocean administered by France. They include the Crozet Islands and Kerguelen.

### Fiji
*Area*: 7,056 sq miles (18,274 sq km)
*Population*: 896,758
*Capital*: Suva
*Government*: Republic
*Main religions*: Christianity, Hinduism
*Currency*: Fijian Dollar

### Gabon
*Area*: 103,347 sq miles (267,667 sq km)
*Population*: 1,640,286
*Capital*: Libreville
*Other major city*: Port-Gentil
*Government*: Republic
*Main religions*: Christianity, traditional beliefs
*Currency*: CFA Franc

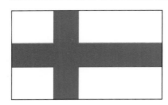

### Finland
*Area*: 130,559 sq miles (338,145 sq km)
*Population*: 5,266,114
*Capital*: Helsinki
*Other cities*: Turku, Tampere
*Government*: Republic
*Main religion*: Lutheran Church of Finland
*Currency*: Euro

### Gambia, The
*Area*: 4,361 sq miles (11,295 sq km)
*Population*: 1,883,051
*Capital*: Banjul
*Government*: Republic
*Main religion*: Sunni Islam
*Currency*: Dalasi

### France
*Area*: 212,935 sq miles (551,500 sq km)
*Population*: 65,951,611
*Capital*: Paris
*Other cities*: Bordeaux, Lyon, Marseille, Nantes, Nice, Toulouse, Strasbourg
*Government*: Republic
*Main religion*: Roman Catholicism
*Currency*: Euro

### Gaza Strip
*Area*: 139 sq miles (360 sq km)
*Population*: 1,763,387
*Government*: Under the control of Hamas
*Main religion*: Sunni Islam
*Currency*: New Israeli Shekel

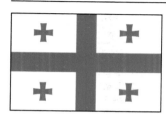

**Georgia**
*Area*: 26,911 sq miles
(69,700 sq km)
*Population*: 4,555,911
*Capital*: Tbilisi
*Other cities*: Kutaisi, Batumi,
Rustavi
*Government*: Republic
*Main religions*: Orthodox
Christianity, Sunni Islam
*Currency*: Lari

**Greenland (Kalaallit
Nunaat)**
*Area*: 840,000 sq mi
(2,175,600 sq km)
*Population*: 58,200
*Capital*: Gothåb (Nuuk)
*Government*: Self-governing
region of Denmark
*Religion*: Lutheranism
*Currency*: Danish krone

**Germany**
*Area*: 137,847 sq miles
(357,022 sq km)
*Population*: 81,147,265
*Capital*: Berlin
*Other cities*: Bonn, Cologne
(Köln), Dortmund, Düs-
seldorf, Essen, Frankfurt,
Hamburg, Leipzig, Munich
(München), Stuttgart
*Government*: Federal Republic
*Main religion*: Christianity
*Currency*: Euro

**Grenada**
*Area*: 133 sq miles
(344 sq km)
*Population*: 109,590
*Capital*: Saint George's
*Government*: Independent
State within the Common-
wealth
*Main religion*: Christianity
*Currency*: East Caribbean
Dollar

**Ghana**
*Area*: 92,098 sq miles
(238,533 sq km)
*Population*: 25,199,609
*Capital*: Accra
*Other cities*: Kumasi, Tamale,
Sekondi-Takoradi
*Government*: Republic
*Main religions*: Christianity,
Sunni Islam, traditional
beliefs
*Currency*: Ghana Cedi

**Guadeloupe**
*Area*: 658 sq mi (1,705 sq km)
*Population*: 431,000
*Capital*: Basse Terre
*Other main town*: Pointe-à-
Pitre
*Government*: French overseas-
department
*Religion*: Roman Catholicism
*Currency*: Euro
NB.The pictured flag is local
but unofficial. The French flag
is official.

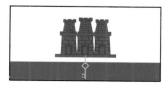

**Gibraltar**
*Area*: 2.5 sq miles (6.5 sq km)
*Population*: 29,111
*Capital*: Gibraltar
*Government*: Self-governing
British Overseas Territory
*Main religion*: Roman Ca-
tholicism
*Currency*: Gibraltar Pound

**Guam**
*Area*: 210 sq miles
(544 sq km)
*Population*: 160,378
*Capital*: Hagåtña
*Government*: Organized
Unincorporated Territory of
the US
*Main religion*: Roman Ca-
tholicism
*Currency*: US Dollar

**Greece**
*Area*: 50,949 sq miles
(131,957 sq km)
*Population*: 10,772,967
*Capital*: Athens (Athína)
*Other cities*: Thessalonki,
Heraklion, Larissa
*Government*: Parliamentary
Republic
*Main religion*: Greek Ortho-
dox
*Currency*: Euro

**Guatemala**
*Area*: 42,042 sq miles
(108,889 sq km)
*Population*: 14,373,472
*Capital*: Guatemala City
*Other city*: Quetzaltenango
*Government*: Republic
*Main religions*: Christianity,
traditional beliefs
*Currency*: Quetzal

**Guiana (French) or Guyane**
*Area*: 34,749 sq mi (90,000 sq km)
*Population*: 153,000
*Capital*: Cayenne
*Government*: French Overseas Department
*Religion*: Roman Catholicism
*Currency*: Euro

**Honduras**
*Area*: 43,278 sq miles (112,090 sq km)
*Population*: 8,448,465
*Capital*: Tegucigalpa
*Other cities*: San Pedro Sula, La Ceiba
*Government*: Republic
*Main religion*: Roman Catholicism
*Currency*: Lempira

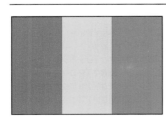

**Guinea**
*Area*: 94,926 sq miles (245,857 sq km)
*Population*: 11,176,026
*Capital*: Conakry
*Other cities*: Kankan, Kindia, Labé
*Government*: Republic
*Main religion*: Sunni Islam
*Currency*: Guinean Franc

**Hong Kong**
*Area*: 426 sq miles (1,104 sq km)
*Population*: 7,182,724
*Government*: Special Administrative Region of China
*Main religions*: Mix of local religions, Christianity
*Currency*: Hong Kong Dollar

**Guinea-Bissau**
*Area*: 13,948 sq miles (36,125 sq km)
*Population*: 1,660,870
*Capital*: Bissau
*Government*: Republic
*Main religions*: Sunni Islam, traditional beliefs
*Currency*: CFA Franc

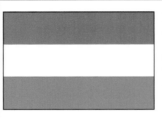

**Hungary**
*Area*: 35,918 sq miles (93,028 sq km)
*Population*: 9,939,470
*Capital*: Budapest
*Other cities*: Debrecen, Miskolc, Pécs, Szeged
*Government*: Parliamentary Democracy
*Main religion*: Christianity
*Currency*: Forint

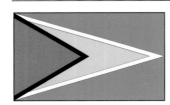

**Guyana**
*Area*: 83,000 sq miles (214,969 sq km)
*Population*: 741,908
*Capital*: Georgetown
*Other cities*: Linden, New Amsterdam
*Government*: Cooperative Republic
*Main religions*: Christianity, Hinduism
*Currency*: Guyanese Dollar

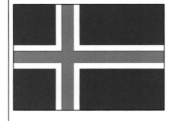

**Iceland**
*Area*: 39,769 sq miles (103,000 sq km)
*Population*: 315,281
*Capital*: Reykjavík
*Other towns*: Akureyri, Kópavogur
*Government*: Republic
*Main religion*: Lutheran Church of Iceland
*Currency*: Icelandic Króna

**Haiti**
*Area*: 10,714 sq miles (27,750 sq km)
*Population*: 9,893,934
*Capital*: Port-au-Prince
*Other towns*: Cap-Haïtien, Les Cayes, Gonaïves
*Government*: Republic
*Main religions*: Christianity, Voodooism
*Currency*: Gourde

**India**
*Area*: 1,269,219 sq miles (3,287,263 sq km)
*Population*: 1,220,800,359
*Capital*: New Delhi
*Other cities*: Mumbai (Bombay), Delhi, Bangalore, Hyderabad, Amdavad (Ahmadabad), Chennai (Madras), Kolkata (Calcutta)
*Government*: Federal Republic
*Main religions*: Hinduism, Islam
*Currency*: Indian Rupee

**Indonesia**
*Area*: 735,358 sq miles
  (1,904,569 sq km)
*Population*: 251,160,124
*Capital*: Jakarta
*Other cities*: Bandung, Med-
an, Palembang, Semarang,
Surabaya
*Government*: Republic
*Main religion*: Sunni Islam
*Currency*: Indonesian Rupiah

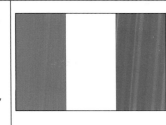

**Italy**
*Area*: 116,348 sq miles
  (301,340 sq km)
*Population*: 61,482,297
*Capital*: Rome (Roma)
*Other cities*: Milan (Milano),
Naples (Napoli), Turin (To-
rino), Genoa (Genova),
Palermo, Florence (Firenze)
*Government*: Republic
*Main religion*: Roman Ca-
tholicism
*Currency*: Euro

**Iran**
*Area*: 636,372 sq miles
  (1,648,195 sq km)
*Population*: 79,853,900
*Capital*: Tehran
*Other cities*: Esfahan, Mash-
had, Tabríz
*Government*: Islamic Republic
*Main religion*: Shia Islam
*Currency*: Iranian Rial

**Jamaica**
*Area*: 4,244 sq miles
  (10,991 sq km)
*Population*: 2,909,714
*Capital*: Kingston
*Other city:* Montego Bay
*Government*: Parliamentary
Democracy
*Main religion*: Protestantism
*Currency*: Jamaican Dollar

**Iraq**
*Area*: 169,235 sq miles
  (438,317 sq km)
*Population*: 31,858,481
*Capital*: Baghdad
*Other cities*: Al Basrah, Al
Mawsil
*Government*: Parlimentary
Republic
*Main religions*: Shia Islam,
Sunni Islam
*Currency*: Iraqi Dinar

**Japan**
*Area*: 145,914 sq miles
  (377,915 sq km)
*Population*: 127,253,075
*Capital*: Tokyo
*Other cities*: Osaka, Nagoya,
Sapporo, Kobe, Kyoto,
Yokohama
*Government*: Constitutional
Monarchy
*Main religions*: Shintoism,
Buddhism
*Currency*: Yen

**Ireland, Republic of**
*Area*: 27,133 sq miles
  (70,273 sq km)
*Population*: 4,775,982
*Capital*: Dublin (Baile Átha
Cliath)
*Other cities*: Cork, Galway,
Limerick, Waterford
*Government*: Republic
*Main religion*: Roman Ca-
tholicism
*Currency*: Euro

**Jordan**
*Area*: 34,495 sq miles
  (89,342 sq km)
*Population*: 6,482,081
*Capital*: Amman
*Other cities*: Aqaba, Irbid,
Zarqa
*Government*: Constitutional
Monarchy
*Main religion*: Sunni Islam
*Currency*: Jordanian Dinar

**Israel**
*Area*: 8,019 sq miles
  (20,770 sq km)
*Population*: 7,707,042
*Capital*: Jerusalem (UN-recog-
nized capital Tel Aviv)
*Other cities*: Haifa, Ashdod,
Netanya
*Government*: Parliamentary
Democracy
*Main religions*: Judaism, Sunni
Islam
*Currency*: New Israeli Shekel

**Kazakhstan**
*Area*: 1,052,090 sq miles
  (2,724,900 sq km)
*Population*: 17,736,896
*Capital*: Astana
*Other cities*: Almaty, Shym-
kent (Chimkent), Kara-
ganda
*Government*: Republic
*Main religions*: Sunni Islam,
Russian Orthodox
*Currency*: Tenge

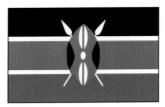

### Kenya
*Area*: 224,081 sq miles
  (580,367 sq km)
*Population*: 44,037,656
*Capital*: Nairobi
*Other cities*: Mombasa,
  Eldoret, Kisumu
*Government*: Republic
*Main religions*: Christianity,
  Islam, traditional beliefs
*Currency*: Kenyan Shilling

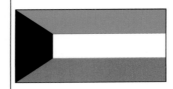

### Kuwait
*Area*: 6,880 sq miles
  (17,818 sq km)
*Population*: 2,695,316
*Capital*: Kuwait City (Al
  Kuwayt)
*Government*: Constitutional
  Hereditary Emirate
*Main religions*: Sunni Islam,
  Shia Islam
*Currency*: Kuwaiti Dinar

### Kiribati
*Area*: 313 sq miles
  (811 sq km)
*Population*: 103,248
*Capital*: Tarawa
*Government*: Republic
*Main religion*: Christianity
*Currency*: Australian Dollar

### Kyrgyzstan
*Area*: 77,202 sq miles
  (199,951 sq km)
*Population*: 5,548,042
*Capital*: Bishkek
*Other cities*: Osh, Namangan
*Government*: Republic
*Main religions*: Sunni Islam,
  Russian Orthodox
*Currency*: Som

### Korea, North (Democratic People's Republic of)
*Area*: 46,540 sq miles
  (120,538 sq km)
*Population*: 24,589,122
*Capital*: Pyongyang
*Other cities*: Chongjin, Wonsan
*Government*: Officially Socialist
  Republic (One-man Dictator-
  ship)
*Main religion*: Traditionally
  Buddhist, Confucionist
*Currency*: North Korean Won

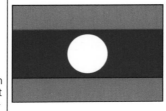

### Laos
*Area*: 91,429 sq miles
  (236,800 sq km)
*Population*: 6,695,166
*Capital*: Vientiane
*Other cities*: Luang Prabang,
  Savannakhét, Paksé
*Government*: People's Demo-
  cratic Republic (Communist
  State)
*Main religions*: Buddhism,
  traditional beliefs
*Currency*: New Kip

### Korea, South (Republic of)
*Area*: 38,502 sq miles
  (99,720 sq km)
*Population*: 48,955,203
*Capital*: Seoul (Soul)
*Other cities*: Pusan, Taegu
*Government*: Republic
*Main religions*: Christianity,
  Buddhism
*Currency*: South Korean Won

### Latvia
*Area*: 24,938 sq miles
  (64,589 sq km)
*Population*: 2,178,443
*Capital*: Riga
*Other cities*: Liepaja, Dau-
  gavpils
*Government*: Parliamentary
  Republic
*Main religion*: Christianity
*Currency*: Latvian Lat

### Kosovo
*Area*: 4,203 sq miles
  (10,887 sq km)
*Population*: 1,847,708
*Capital*: Pristina
*Other cities*: Kosovska-Mitro-
  vica, Pec, Uroševac
*Government*: Republic
*Main religions*: Islam, Serbian
  Orthodox, Roman Catholic
*Currency*: Euro

### Lebanon
*Area*: 4,015 sq miles
  (10,400 sq km)
*Population*: 4,140,289
*Capital*: Beirut (Beyrouth)
*Other cities*: Tripoli (Tarabu-
  lus), Sidon (Saïda)
*Government*: Republic
*Main religions*: Islam, Chris-
  tianity
*Currency*: Lebanese Pound

**Lesotho**
*Area*: 11,720 sq miles
(30,355 sq km)
*Population*: 1,936,181
*Capital*: Maseru
*Government*: Parliamentary
Constitutional Monarchy
*Main religions*: Christianity,
traditional beliefs
*Currency*: Loti/South African
Rand

**Luxembourg**
*Area*: 998 sq miles
(2,586 sq km)
*Population*: 514,862
*Capital*: Luxembourg
*Government*: Constitutional
Monarchy
*Main religion*: Roman Ca-
tholicism
*Currency*: Euro

**Liberia**
*Area*: 43,000 sq miles
(111,369 sq km)
*Population*: 3,887,886
*Capital*: Monrovia
*Other major city*: Buchanan
*Government*: Republic
*Main religions*: Christianity,
Sunni Islam
*Currency*: Liberian Dollar

**Macao (Macau)**
*Area*: 10.9 sq miles (28.2
sq km)
*Population*: 583,003
*Government*: Special Admin-
istrative Region of China
*Main religions*: Buddhism,
Roman Catholicism
*Currency*: Pataca

**Libya**
*Area*: 679,362 sq miles
(1,759,540 sq km)
*Population*: 6,002,347
*Capital*: Tripoli (Tarabulus)
*Other cities*: Benghazi (Bang-
hazi), Misrata (Misrātah)
*Government*: (In transition)
*Main religion*: Sunni Islam
*Currency*: Libyan Dinar

**Macedonia, the former
Republic of (FYROM)**
*Area*: 9,928 sq miles
(25,713 sq km)
*Population*: 2,087,171
*Capital*: Skopje
*Other cities*: Kumanovo,
Ohrid
*Government*: Parliamentary
Democracy
*Main religions*: Macedonian
Orthodox, Islam
*Currency*: Macedonian Dinar

**Liechtenstein**
*Area*: 62 sq miles (160 sq km)
*Population*: 37,009
*Capital*: Vaduz
*Government*: Constitutional
Monarchy
*Main religion*: Roman Ca-
tholicism
*Currency*: Swiss Franc

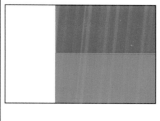

**Madagascar**
*Area*: 226,658 sq miles
(587,041 sq km)
*Population*: 22,599,098
*Capital*: Antananarivo
*Other cities*: Fianarantsoa,
Manakara
*Government*: Republic
*Main religions*: Traditional
beliefs, Christianity
*Currency*: Madagascar Ariary

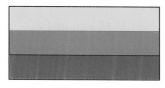

**Lithuania**
*Area*: 25,212 sq miles
(65,300 sq km)
*Population*: 3,515,858
*Capital*: Vilnius
*Other cities*: Kaunas, Šiauliai
*Government*: Parliamentary
Democracy
*Main religion*: Roman Ca-
tholicism
*Currency*: Litas

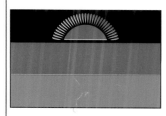

**Malawi**
*Area*: 45,747 sq miles
(118,484 sq km)
*Population*: 16,323,044
*Capital*: Lilongwe
*Other cities*: Blantyre, Zomba
*Government*: Republic
*Main religions*: Christianity,
Islam
*Currency*: Malawian Kwacha

**Malaysia**
*Area*: 127,320 sq miles
　(329,847 sq km)
*Population*: 29,628,392
*Capital*: Kuala Lumpur
*Other cities*: Ipoh, George
　Town, Johor Baharu
*Government*: Federal Consti-
　tutional Monarchy
*Main religions*: Islam, Bud-
　dhism
*Currency*: Ringgit (Malaysian
　Dollar)

**Martinique**
*Area*: 425 sq mi
　(1,102 sq km)
*Population*: 384,000
*Capital*: Fort-de-France
*Government*:Overseas
Department of France
*Religion*: Roman Catholicism
*Currency*: Euro

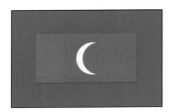

**Maldives, Republic of**
*Area*: 115 sq miles
　(298 sq km)
*Population*: 393,988
*Capital*: Malé
*Government*: Republic
*Main religion*: Sunni Islam
*Currency*: Rufiyaa

**Mauritania**
*Area*: 397,955 sq miles
　(1,030,700 sq km)
*Population*: 3,437,610
*Capital*: Nouakchott
*Other cities*: Kaédi, Tidjikdja
*Government*: Islamic Republic
*Main religion*: Sunni Islam
*Currency*: Ouguiya

**Mali**
*Area*: 478,841 sq miles
　(1,240,192 sq km)
*Population*: 15,968,882
*Capital*: Bamako
*Other towns*: Gao, Kayes,
　Ségou, Mopti
*Government*: Republic
*Main religion*: Sunni Islam
*Currency*: CFA Franc

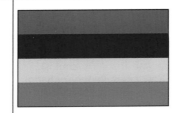

**Mauritius**
*Area*: 788 sq miles
　(2,040 sq km)
*Population*: 1,322,328
*Capital*: Port Louis
*Government*: Parliamentary
　Republic
*Main religions*: Hinduism,
　Roman Catholicism, Sunni
　Islam
*Currency*: Mauritian Rupee

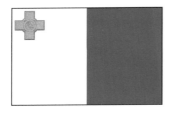

**Malta**
*Area*: 122 sq miles
　(316 sq km)
*Population*: 411,277
*Capital*: Valletta
*Government*: Republic
*Main religion*: Roman Ca-
　tholicism
*Currency*: Euro

**Mexico**
*Area*: 758,449 sq miles
　(1,964,375 sq km)
*Population*: 116,220,947
*Capital*: México City
*Other cities*: Guadalajara,
　Monterrey, León, Puebla,
　Tijuana
*Government*: Federal Republic
*Main religion*: Roman Ca-
　tholicism
*Currency*: Mexican Peso

**Marshall Islands**
*Area*: 70 sq miles (181 sq km)
*Population*: 68,480
*Capital*: Majuro
*Government*: Constitutional
　Government in Free As-
　sociation with the US
*Main religion*: Christianity
*Currency*: US Dollar

**Micronesia, Federated
　States of**
*Area*: 271 sq miles
　(702 sq km)
*Population*: 106,104
*Capital*: Palikir
*Government*: Constitutional
　Government in Free As-
　sociation with the US
*Main religion*: Christianity
*Currency*: US Dollar

**Moldova**
*Area*: 13,012 sq miles
 (33,851 sq km)
*Population*: 3,619,925
*Capital*: Chisinau
*Other cities*: Bel'tsy, Tiraspol,
 Tighina
*Government*: Republic
*Main religion*: Eastern
 Orthodox
*Currency*: Moldovan Leu

**Morocco**
*Area*: 172,414 sq miles
 (446,550 sq km)
*Population*: 32,649,130
*Capital*: Rabat
*Other cities*: Dar el Beida,
 Casablanca (Dar el Beida),
 Marrakech, Agadir
*Government*: Constitutional
 Monarchy
*Main religion*: Sunni Islam
*Currency*: Moroccan Dirham

**Monaco**
*Area*: 0.77 sq mile (2 sq km)
*Population*: 30,500
*Capital*: Monaco
*Government*: Constitutional
 Monarchy
*Main religion*: Roman Ca-
 tholicism
*Currency*: Euro

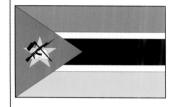

**Mozambique**
*Area*: 308,642 sq miles
 (799,380 sq km)
*Population*: 24,096,669
*Capital*: Maputo
*Other towns*: Beira, Nampula
*Government*: Republic
*Main religions*: Christianity,
 Sunni Islam
*Currency*: Metical

**Mongolia**
*Area*: 603,909 sq miles
 (1,564,116 sq km)
*Population*: 3,226,516
*Capital*: Ulan Bator (Ulaan-
 baatar)
*Other cities*: Altay, Saynshand,
 Hovd, Choybalsan, Tsetserleg
*Government*: Parliamentary
 Republic
*Main religion*: Lamaist Bud-
 dhism
*Currency*: Togrok/Tugrik

**Namibia**
*Area*: 318,261 sq miles
 (824,292 sq km)
*Population*: 2,182,852
*Capital*: Windhoek
*Other cities*: Gobabis, Swa-
 kopmund, Keetmanshoop
*Government*: Republic
*Main religions*: Christianity,
 traditional beliefs
*Currency*: Namibian Dollar

**Montenegro**
*Area*: 5,333 sq miles
 (13,812 sq km)
*Population*: 653,474
*Capital*: Podgorica
*Other cities*: Nikši, Pljevljia
*Government*: Republic
*Main religions*: Eastern
 Orthodox, Islam
*Currency*: Euro

**Nauru**
*Area*: 8 sq miles (21 sq km)
*Population*: 9,434
*Administrative Centre*: Yaren
*Government*: Republic
*Main religion*: Christianity
*Currency*: Australian Dollar

**Montserrat**
*Area*: 91 sq km
*Population*: 8,400
*Capital*: Plymouth (aban-
 doned; destroyed by
 volcanic eruption
*Government*: British overseas
 territory
*Religions*: Christian denomi-
 nations
*Currency*: East Carribean
 Dollar

**Nepal, Republic of**
*Area*: 56,827 sq miles
 (147,181 sq km)
*Population*: 30,430,267
*Capital*: Kathmandu
*Other cities*: Biratnagar,
 Lalitpur
*Government*: Federal Demo-
 cratic Republic
*Main religions*: Hinduism,
 Buddhism
*Currency*: Nepalese Rupee

**Netherlands**
*Area*: 16,040 sq miles
(41,543 sq km)
*Population*: 16,805,037
*Capital*: Amsterdam
*Seat of government*: The
Hague (s'Gravenhage)
*Other cities*: Rotterdam,
Eindhoven
*Government*: Constitutional
Monarchy
*Main religion*: Christianity
*Currency*: Euro

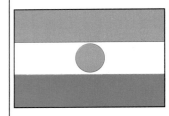

**Niger**
*Area*: 489,191 sq miles
(1,267,000 sq km)
*Population*: 16,899,327
*Capital*: Niamey
*Other cities*: Agadez, Maradi,
Tahoua, Zinder
*Government*: Republic
*Main religions*: Sunni Islam,
Christianity, traditional
beliefs
*Currency*: CFA Franc

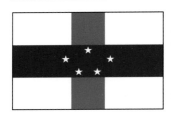

**Netherlands Antilles**
*Area*: 309 sq mi (800 sq km)
*Population*: 207,300
*Capital*: Willemstad
*Government*: Self-governing
Dutch Territory
*Religion*: Roman Catholicism
*Currency*: Netherlands
Antilles guilder

**Nigeria**
*Area*: 356,669 sq miles
(923,768 sq km)
*Population*: 174,507,539
*Capital*: Abuja
*Other cities*: Lagos, Onitsha,
Enugu, Kano, Ogbomosho
*Government*: Federal Republic
*Main religions*: Sunni Islam,
Christianity, traditional
beliefs
*Currency*: Naira

**New Caledonia**
*Area*: 7,172 sq miles (18,575
sq km)
*Population*: 264,022
*Capital*: Nouméa
*Government*: Self-governing
Territorial Collectivity of
France
*Main religion*: Christianity
*Currency*: CFP Franc

**Niue**
*Area*: 260 km
*Population*: 2,145
*Capital*: Alofi
*Government*: Self-governing
in free association with
New Zealand
*Religions*: Ekalesia Niue,
Latter- Day Saints, Ro-
man Catholic, Jehovah's
Witnesses, Seventh-Day
Adventist
*Currency*: New Zealand Dollar

**New Zealand**
*Area*: 104,454 sq miles
(267,710 sq km)
*Population*: 4,365,113
*Capital*: Wellington
*Other cities*: Auckland,
Christchurch
*Government*: Parliamentary
Democracy
*Main religion*: Christianity
*Currency*: New Zealand Dollar

**Norfolk Island**
*Area*: 34.6 sq km
*Population*: 1853
*Capital*: Kingston
*Government*: Constitutional
monarchy. Non-selfgoverning
territory of Australia. (Some
claim it was actually
granted independence by
Queen Victoria.)
*Religion*: Christianity
*Currency*: Australian dollar

**Nicaragua**
*Area*: 50,336 sq miles
(130,370 sq km)
*Population*: 5,788,531
*Capital*: Managua
*Other cities*: Léon, Masaya
*Government*: Republic
*Main religion*: Christianity
*Currency*: Gold Cordoba

**Northern Mariana Islands**
*Area*: 179 sq miles (464 sq
km)
*Population*: 51,170
*Capital*: Saipan
*Government*: Common-
wealth in Political Union
with the US
*Main religions*: Roman Ca-
tholicism, traditional beliefs
*Currency*: US Dollar

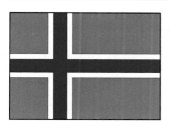

## Norway
*Area*: 125,021 sq miles
(323,802 sq km)
*Population*: 4,722,701
*Capital*: Oslo
*Other cities*: Bergen,
Trondheim, Frederikstad,
Kristiansand, Tromsö
*Government*: Constitutional
Monarchy
*Main religion*: Church of
Norway
*Currency*: Norwegian Krone

## Panama
*Area*: 29,120 sq miles
(75,420 sq km)
*Population*: 3,59,408
*Capital*: Panama City
*Other cities*: Colón, Puerto
Armuelles, David
*Government*: Constitutional
Democracy
*Main religion*: Roman Ca-
tholicism
*Currency*: Balboa

## Oman
*Area*: 119,499 sq miles
(309,500 sq km)
*Population*: 3,154,134
*Capital*: Muscat (Musqat)
*Other city:* Salalah
*Government*: Monarchy
*Main religion*: Ibadhi Islam
*Currency*: Omani Rial

## Papua New Guinea
*Area*: 178,704 sq miles
(462,840 sq km)
*Population*: 6,431,902
*Capital*: Port Moresby
*Government*: Constitutional
Parliamentary Democracy
*Main religions*: Protestantism,
Roman Catholicism
*Currency*: Kina

## Organization of Islamic Conference (OIC)
57 members, including: Afghanistan,
Algeria, Chad, Egypt,Guinea, Indone-
sia, Iran, Jordan,Kuwait, Lebanon,
Libya, Malaysia, Mali, Morocco, Ni-
ger, Pakistan, Palestine, Yemen, Saudi
Arabia, Senegal, Sudan, Somalia,
Tunisia,Turkey, Bahrain, Oman,Qatar,
Syria, UAE, Sierra Leone, Bangladesh,
Gambia, Uganda, Cameroon, Iraq,
Maldives, Benin, Brunei, Nigeria,
Azerbaijan, Albania, Kyrgyzstan, Ta-
jikistan, Turkmenistan, Mozambique,
Kazakhstan, Uzbekistan, Suriname,
Guyana, Côte d'Ivoire.

## Paraguay
*Area*: 157,048 sq miles
(406,752 sq km)
*Population*: 6,623,252
*Capital*: Asunción
*Other cities*: Concepción,
Encarnación
*Government*: Constitutional
Republic
*Main religion*: Roman Ca-
tholicism
*Currency*: Guarani

## Pakistan
*Area*: 307,374 sq miles
(796,095 sq km)
*Population*: 193,238,868
*Capital*: Islamabad
*Other cities*: Lahore, Faisal-
abad, Hyderabad, Karachi,
Rawalpindi
*Government*: Federal Islamic
Republic
*Main religions*: Sunni Islam,
Shia Islam
*Currency*: Pakistan Rupee

## Peru
*Area*: 496,225 sq miles
(1,285,216 sq km)
*Population*: 29,849,303
*Capital*: Lima
*Other cities*: Arequipa,
Trujillo, Callao, Chiclayo,
Iquitos, Cuzco
*Government*: Constitutional
Republic
*Main religion*: Roman Ca-
tholicism
*Currency*: Nuevo Sol

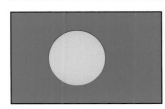

## Palau
*Area*: 177 sq miles
(459 sq km)
*Population*: 21,108
*Capital*: Melekeok
*Government*: Constitutional
Government in Free As-
sociation with the US
*Main religion*: Christianity,
Modekngei
*Currency*: US Dollar

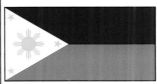

## Philippines
*Area*: 115,831 sq miles
(300,000 sq km)
*Population*: 105,720,644
*Capital*: Manila
*Other cities*: Cebu, Davao,
Quezon City, Zamboanga,
Butuan
*Government*: Republic
*Main religion*: Roman Ca-
tholicism
*Currency*: Philippine Peso

**Pitcairn Islands**
*Area*: 18 sq miles (47 sq km)
*Population*: 48
*Capital*: Adamstown
*Government*: British Overseas
　Territory
*Main religion*: Seventh-Day
　Adventism
*Currency*: New Zealand Dollar

**Romania**
*Area*: 92,043 sq miles
　(238,391 sq km)
*Population*: 21,790,479
*Capital*: Bucharest (Bucuresti)
*Other cities*: Cluj-Napoca,
　Timisoara, Constanta, Iasi
*Government*: Republic
*Main religion*: Eastern
　Orthodox
*Currency*: New Leu

**Poland**
*Area*: 120,728 sq miles
　(312,685 sq km)
*Population*: 38,383,809
*Capital*: Warsaw (Warszawa)
*Other cities*: Gdansk, Kraków,
　Lódz, Poznan, Wroclaw
*Government*: Republic
*Main religion*: Roman Ca-
　tholicism
*Currency*: Polish Zloty

**Russia (Russian Federation)**
*Area*: 6,601,668 sq miles
　(17,098,242 sq km)
*Population*: 142,500,482
*Capital*: Moscow (Moskva)
*Other cities*: St Petersburg,
　Novosibirsk, Nizhniy
　Novgorod, Yekaterinburg
*Government*: Federation
*Main religions*: Russian
　Orthodox, Islam
*Currency*: Russian Rouble

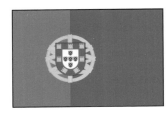

**Portugal**
*Area*: 35,556 sq miles
　(92,090 sq km)
*Population*: 10,799,270
*Capital*: Lisbon (Lisboa)
*Other cities*: Porto, Braga,
　Faro
*Government*: Republican
　Parliamentary Democracy
*Main religion*: Roman Ca-
　tholicism
*Currency*: Euro

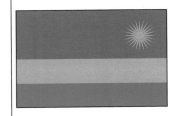

**Rwanda**
*Area*: 10,169 sq miles
　(26,338 sq km)
*Population*: 12,012,589
*Capital*: Kigali
*Other city*: Butare
*Government*: Republic
*Main religion*: Christianity
*Currency*: Rwandan Franc

**Qatar**
*Area*: 4,473 sq miles
　(11,586 sq km)
*Population*: 2,042,444
*Capital*: Doha (Ad Dawhah)
*Government*: Emirate
*Main religion*: Sunni Islam
*Currency*: Qatari Riyal

**St Helena, Ascension and
Tristan Da Cunha**
*Area*: 119 sq miles (308 sq
　km)
*Population*: 7,754
*Capital*: Jamestown
*Government*: British Overseas
　Territory
*Main religion*: Christianity
*Currency*: St Helenian Pound

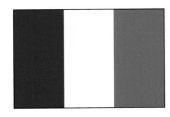

**Réunion**
*Area*: 969 sq mi (2,510 sq
　km)
*Population*: 664,000
*Capital*: St Denis
*Government*: French overseas
　department
*Religion*: Roman Catholicism
*Currency*: Euro

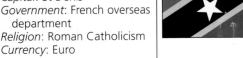

**St Kitts and Nevis**
*Area*: 101 sq miles
　(261 sq km)
*Population*: 51,134
*Capital*: Basseterre
*Other major city*: Charles-
　town
*Government*: Parliamentary
　Democracy
*Main religion*: Christianity
*Currency*: East Caribbean
　Dollar

**St Lucia**
*Area*: 238 sq miles
(616 sq km)
*Population*: 162,178
*Capital*: Castries
*Government*: Parliamentary
Democracy
*Main religion*: Christianity
*Currency*: East Caribbean
Dollar

**Samoa**
*Area*: 1,093 sq miles
(2,831 sq km)
*Population*: 179,186
*Capital*: Apia
*Government*: Unitary Parlia-
mentary Republic
*Main religion*: Christianity
*Currency*: Tala

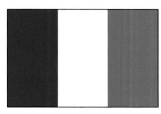

**St Martin**
*Area*: 21 sq miles (54.4 sq
km)
*Population*: 31,264
*Capital*: Marigot
*Government*: French Self-gov-
erning Territorial Overseas
Collectivity
*Main religions*: Christianity,
Hinduism
*Currency*: Euro

**San Marino**
*Area*: 24 sq miles (61 sq km)
*Population*: 32,448
*Capital*: San Marino
*Other cities*: Borgo Maggiore,
Serravalle
*Government*: Republic
*Main religion*: Roman Ca-
tholicism
*Currency*: Euro

**St Martin (Sint Maarten)**
*Area*: 13 sq miles (34 sq km)
*Population*: 39,689
*Capital*: Philipsburg
*Government*: Estates of Sint
Maarten (Island Council)
*Main religion*: Christianity
*Currency*: Netherlands Antil-
lean Guilders

**São Tomé and Príncipe**
*Area*: 372 sq miles
(964 sq km)
*Population*: 186,817
*Capital*: São Tomé
*Government*: Republic
*Main religion*: Roman Ca-
tholicism
*Currency*: Dobra

**St Pierre and Miquelon**
*Area*: 93 sq mi (240 sq km)
*Population*: 6,300
*Capital*: Saint Pierre
*Government*: French overseas
territory
*Religion*: Roman Catholicism
*Currency*: Euro

**Saudi Arabia**
*Area*: 830,000 sq miles
(2,149,690 sq km)
*Population*: 26,939,583
*Capital*: Riyadh (Ar Riyād)
*Other cities*: Ad Dammam,
Mecca (Makkah), Jed-
dah (Jiddah), Medina (Al
Madimah)
*Government*: Monarchy
*Main religions*: Wahhabi Islam,
Sunni Islam, Shia Islam
*Currency*: Saudi Riyal

**St Vincent and the
Grenadines**
*Area*: 150 sq miles
(389 sq km)
*Population*: 103,220
*Capital*: Kingstown
*Government*: Parliamentary
Democracy
*Main religion*: Christianity
*Currency*: East Caribbean
Dollar

**Senegal**
*Area*: 75,955 sq miles
(196,722 sq km)
*Population*: 13,300,410
*Capital*: Dakar
*Other cities*: Kaolack, Thiès,
St Louis
*Government*: Republic
*Main religion*: Sunni Islam
*Currency*: CFA Franc

**Serbia**
*Area*: 29,913 sq miles
   (77,474 sq km)
*Population*: 7,243,007
*Capital*: Belgrade (Beograd)
*Other cities*: Novi Sad, Nis
*Government*: Republic
*Main religion*: Serbian
   Orthodox
*Currency*: Serbian Dinar

**Slovenia**
*Area*: 7,827 sq miles
   (20,273 sq km)
*Population*: 1,992,690
*Capital*: Ljubljana
*Other cities*: Maribor, Kranj
*Government*: Parliamentary
   Republic
*Main religion*: Roman Ca-
   tholicism
*Currency*: Euro

**Seychelles**
*Area*: 176 sq miles
   (455 sq km)
*Population*: 90,846
*Capital*: Victoria
*Government*: Republic
*Main religion*: Roman Ca-
   tholicism
*Currency*: Seychelles Rupee

**Solomon Islands**
*Area*: 11,157 sq miles
   (28,896 sq km)
*Population*: 597,248
*Capital*: Honiara
*Government*: Parliamentary
   Democracy
*Main religion*: Christianity
*Currency*: Solomon Islands
   Dollar

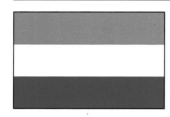

**Sierra Leone**
*Area*: 27,699 sq miles
   (71,740 sq km)
*Population*: 5,612,685
*Capital*: Freetown
*Other cities*: Bo, Kenema
*Government*: Constitutional
   Democracy
*Main religions*: Sunni Islam,
   traditional beliefs, Chris-
   tianity
*Currency*: Leone

**Somalia**
*Area*: 246,201 sq miles
   (637,657 sq km)
*Population*: 10,251,568
*Capital*: Mogadishu
   (Muqdisho)
*Other cities*: Hargeysa, Burco
*Government*: Transitional
   Parliamentary Federal (no
   permanent central govern-
   ment)
*Main religion*: Sunni Islam
*Currency*: Somali Shilling

**Singapore**
*Area*: 269 sq miles
   (697 sq km)
*Population*: 5,460,302
*Capital*: Singapore
*Government*: Parliamentary
   Republic
*Main religions*: Buddhism,
   Sunni Islam, Christianity
*Currency*: Singapore Dollar

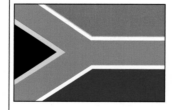

**South Africa**
*Area*: 470,693 sq miles
   (1,219,090 sq km)
*Population*: 48,601,098
*Capital*: Pretoria (Tshwane)
*Other cities*: Johannesburg,
   Soweto, Cape Town, Dur-
   ban, Port Elizabeth
*Government*: Republic
*Main religion*: Christianity
*Currency*: Rand

**Slovakia**
*Area*: 18,933 sq miles
   (49,035 sq km)
*Population*: 5,488,339
*Capital*: Bratislava
*Other cities*: Kosice, Zilina,
   Nitra
*Government*: Parliamentary
   Democracy
*Main religion*: Roman Ca-
   tholicism
*Currency*: Euro

**South Sudan**
*Area*: 248,777 sq miles
   (644,329 sq km)
*Population*: 11,090,104
*Capital*: Juba
*Other cities*: Malakal, Wau
*Government*: Republic
*Main religions*: Traditional
   beliefs, Christianity
*Currency*: South Sudanese
   Pound

### Spain
*Area*: 195,124 sq miles
(505,370 sq km)
*Population*: 47,370,542
*Capital*: Madrid
*Other cities*: Barcelona, Valencia, Seville, Bilbao, Malaga
*Government*: Constitutional Monarchy
*Main religion*: Roman Catholicism
*Currency*: Euro

### Sweden
*Area*: 173,860 sq miles
(450,295 sq km)
*Population*: 9,119,423
*Capital*: Stockholm
*Other cities*: Göteborg (Gothenburg), Malmö, Uppsala
*Government*: Constitutional Monarchy
*Main religion*: Lutheranism
*Currency*: Swedish Krona

### Sri Lanka
*Area*: 25,332 sq miles
(65,610 sq km)
*Population*: 21,675,648
*Capital*: Colombo
*Other cities*: Trincomalee, Jaffna, Kandy
*Government*: Democratic Socialist Republic
*Main religion*: Buddhism
*Currency*: Sri Lankan Rupee

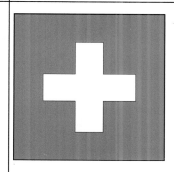

### Switzerland
*Area*: 15,937 sq miles
(41,277 sq km)
*Population*: 7,996,026
*Capital*: Bern
*Other cities*: Zürich, Basle (Basel), Geneva (Genève)
*Government*: Federal Parliamentary Republic
*Main religion*: Christianity
*Currency*: Swiss Franc

### Sudan
*Area*: 718,723 sq miles
(1,861,484 sq km)
*Population*: 34,847,910
*Capital*: Khartoum (El Khartum)
*Other cities*: Omdurman, Khartoum North, Nyala, Port Sudan
*Government*: Republic
*Main religion*: Sunni Islam
*Currency*: Sudanese Pound

### Syria
*Area*: 71,498 sq miles
(185,180 sq km)
*Population*: 22,457,336
*Capital*: Damascus (Dimashq)
*Other cities*: Aleppo, Homs (Hims), Lataka (Al Ladhiqiyah), Hama
*Government*: Republic
*Main religion*: Sunni Islam
*Currency*: Syrian Pound

### Suriname
*Area*: 63,251 sq miles
(163,820 sq km)
*Population*: 566,846
*Capital*: Paramaribo
*Government*: Constitutional Democracy
*Main religions*: Christianity, Hinduism, Sunni Islam
*Currency*: Surinamese Dollar

### Taiwan
*Area*: 13,892 sq miles
(35,980 sq km)
*Population*: 23,299,716
*Capital*: Taipei (T'ai-pei)
*Other cities*: New Taipei, Kaohsiung, Taichung
*Government*: Multiparty Democracy
*Main religions*: Taoism, Buddhism
*Currency*: New Taiwan Dollar

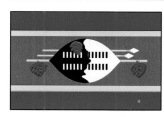

### Swaziland
*Area*: 6,704 sq miles
(17,364 sq km)
*Population*: 1,403,362
*Capital*: Mbabane
*Other towns*: Big Bend, Manzini, Mankayane, Lobamba
*Government*: Monarchy
*Main religions*: Zionist Church, Roman Catholicism, Islam
*Currency*: Lilangeni

### Tajikistan
*Area*: 55,251 sq miles
(143,100 sq km)
*Population*: 7,910,041
*Capital*: Dushanbe
*Other cities*: Khujand (Khudzhand), Kulob
*Government*: Republic
*Main religion*: Sunni Islam
*Currency*: Tajikistani Somoni

**Tanzania**
*Area*: 365,755 sq miles
(947,300 sq km)
*Population*: 48,261,942
*Capital*: Dodoma
*Other cities*: Dar es Salaam,
Mwanza, Arusha, Dodoma
*Government*: Republic
*Main religions*: Sunni Islam,
Christianity, traditional
beliefs
*Currency*: Tanzanian Shilling

**Trinidad and Tobago**
*Area*: 1,980 sq miles
(5,128 sq km)
*Population*: 1,226,383
*Capital*: Port of Spain
*Other cities*: Chaguanas, San
Fernando, Arima
*Government*: Parliamentary
Democracy
*Main religions*: Christianity,
Hinduism, Sunni Islam
*Currency*: Trinidad and
Tobago Dollar

**Thailand**
*Area*: 198,117 sq miles
(513,126 sq km)
*Population*: 67,448,120
*Capital*: Bangkok
*Other cities*: Chiang Mai,
Nakhon, Ratchasima
*Government*: Constitutional
Monarchy
*Main religion*: Buddhism
*Currency*: Baht

**Tunisia**
*Area*: 63,170 sq miles
(163,610 sq km)
*Population*: 10,835,873
*Capital*: Tunis
*Other cities*: Sfax, Kairouan,
Sousse
*Government*: Republic
*Main religion*: Sunni Islam
*Currency*: Tunisian Dinar

**Timor-Leste (East Timor)**
*Area*: 5,743 sq miles
(14,874 sq km)
*Population*: 1,172,390
*Capital*: Dili
*Government*: Democratic
Republic
*Main religion*: Roman Ca-
tholicism
*Currency*: US Dollar

**Turkey**
*Area*: 302,535 sq miles
(783,562 sq km)
*Population*: 80,694,485
*Capital*: Ankara
*Other cities*: Istanbul, Izmir,
Adana
*Government*: Republican
Parliamentary Democracy
*Main religion*: Sunni Islam
*Currency*: Turkish Lira

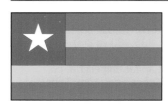

**Togo**
*Area*: 21,925 sq miles
(56,785 sq km)
*Population*: 7,154,237
*Capital*: Lomé
*Other major city*: Sokodé
*Government*: Republic under
transition to Multiparty
Democracy
*Main religions*: Traditional
beliefs, Christianity, Sunni
Islam
*Currency*: CFA Franc

**Turkmenistan**
*Area*: 188,456 sq miles
(488,100 sq km)
*Population*: 5,113,040
*Capital*: Ashkhabad (Asgabat)
*Other cities*: Chardzhou,
Türkmenabat, Mary, Turk-
menbashi (Türkmenbasy)
*Government*: Presidential
Republic Single-party State
*Main religion*: Sunni Islam
*Currency*: Turkmen Manat

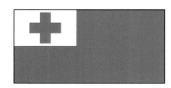

**Tonga**
*Area*: 288 sq miles
(747 sq km)
*Population*: 106,322
*Capital*: Nuku'alofa
*Government*: Constitutional
Monarchy
*Main religion*: Christianity
*Currency*: Pa'anga

**Turks and Caicos Islands**
*Area*: 166 sq miles
(430 sq km)
*Population*: 46,335
*Capital*: Cockburn Town on
Grand Turk
*Government*: British Overseas
Territory
*Main religion*: Christianity
*Currency*: US Dollar

**Tuvalu**
*Area*: 10 sq miles (26 sq km)
*Population*: 10,698
*Capital*: Funafuti
*Government*: Parliamentary
Democracy
*Main religion*: Christianity
*Currency*: Tuvaluan Dollar/
Australian Dollar

**United States of America
(USA)**
*Area*: 3,794,100 sq miles
(9,826,675 sq km)
*Population*: 316,668,567
*Capital*: Washington, DC
*Other cities*: New York, Chi-
cago, Detroit, Los Angeles,
Philadelphia, San Diego
*Government*: Constitution-
based Federal Republic
*Main religion*: Christianity
*Currency*: US Dollar

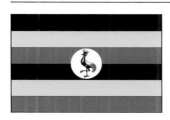

**Uganda**
*Area*: 93,065 sq miles
(241,038 sq km)
*Population*: 34,758,809
*Capital*: Kampala
*Other cities*: Entebbe, Jinja,
Soroti
*Government*: Republic
*Main religions*: Christianity,
Sunni Islam
*Currency*: Ugandan Shilling

**Uruguay**
*Area*: 68,500 sq miles
(176,215 sq km)
*Population*: 3,324,460
*Capital*: Montevideo
*Other cities*: Salto, Melo
*Government*: Constitutional
Republic
*Main religion*: Christianity
*Currency*: Uruguayan Peso

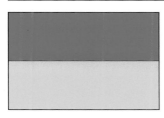

**Ukraine**
*Area*: 233,032 sq miles
(603,550 sq km)
*Population*: 44,573,205
*Capital*: Kiev (Kyiv)
*Other cities*: Dnepropetrovsk,
Donetsk, Khar'kov, Odessa
*Government*: Republic
*Main religion*: Ukranian
Orthodox
*Currency*: Grivna (Hryvnia)

**Uzbekistan**
*Area*: 172,742 sq miles
(447,400 sq km)
*Population*: 28,661,637
*Capital*: Tashkent
*Other cities*: Namangan,
Samarkand, Andizhan,
Nukus, Bukhara
*Government*: Republic
*Main religion*: Sunni Islam
*Currency*: Uzbekistani Soum

**United Arab Emirates
(UAE)**
*Area*: 32,278 sq miles
(83,600 sq km)
*Population*: 5,473,972
*Capital*: Abu Zabi (Abu Dhabi)
*Government*: Federation
*Main religions*: Sunni Islam,
Shia Islam
*Currency*: Emirati Dirham

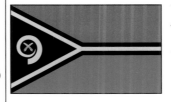

**Vanuatu**
*Area*: 4,706 sq miles
(12,189 sq km)
*Population*: 261,565
*Capital*: Port Vila
*Government*: Parliamentary
Republic
*Main religion*: Christianity,
traditional beliefs
*Currency*: Vatu

**United Kingdom of Great
Britain and Northern
Ireland (UK)**
*Area*: 94,058 sq miles
(243,610 sq km)
*Population*: 63,395,574
*Capital*: London
*Other cities*: Birmingham, Man-
chester, Liverpool, Glasgow,
Edinburgh, Cardiff, Belfast
*Government*: Constitutional
Monarchy
*Main religion*: Christianity
*Currency*: Pound Sterling

**Vatican City (Holy See)**
*Area*: 0.17 sq miles
(0.44 sq km)
*Population*: 839
*Capital*: Vatican City
*Government*: Ecclesiastical
*Religion*: Roman Catholicism
*Currency*: Euro

**Venezuela**
*Area*: 352,144 sq miles
  (912,050 sq km)
*Population*: 28,459,085
*Capital*: Caracas
*Other cities*: Maracaibo,
  Valencia, Barquisimeto
*Government*: Federal Republic
*Main religion*: Roman Ca-
  tholicism
*Currency*: Bolivar

**West Bank**
*Area*: 2,263 sq miles (5,860
  sq km)
*Population*: 2,676,740
*Government*: (Under the con-
  trol of President Abbas and
  the Palestinian Authority)
*Main religion*: Sunni Islam,
  Judaism
*Currency*: New Israeli Shekel

**Vietnam**
*Area*: 128,066 sq miles
  (331,210 sq km)
*Population*: 92,477,857
*Capital*: Hanoi
*Other cities*: Ho Chi Minh
  City (Saigon), Haiphong,
  Hué, Dà Nang
*Government*: Socialist Repub-
  lic (communist state)
*Main religions*: Buddhism,
  Roman Catholicism
*Currency*: Dong

**Western Sahara**
*Area*: 102,703 sq miles
  (266,000 sq km)
*Population*: 522,928
*Capital*: Laâyoune (El Aaiún)
*Government*: Legal status of
  territory and issue of sover-
  eignty unresolved between
  Morocco and the Polisario
  Front [2012]
*Religion*: Sunni Islam
*Currency*: Moroccan Dirham

**Virgin Islands, British**
*Area*: 58 sq miles (151 sq km)
*Population*: 31,912
*Capital*: Road Town
*Government*: Self-governing
  British Overseas Territory
*Main religion*: Protestantism
*Currency*: US Dollar

**Yemen**
*Area*: 203,850 sq miles
  (527,968 sq km)
*Population*: 25,408,288
*Capital*: Sana'a
*Other cities*: Ta'izz, Aden
  (Adan), Al Hudaydah
*Government*: Republic
*Main religions*: Sunni Islam,
  Shia Islam
*Currency*: Yemeni Riyal

**Virgin Islands, US**
*Area*: 737 sq miles (1,910
  sq km)
*Population*: 104,737
*Capital*: Charlotte Amalie
*Government*: Organized,
  Unincorporated Territory of
  the US
*Main religion*: Christianity
*Currency*: US Dollar

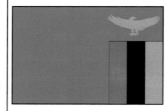

**Zambia**
*Area*: 290,587 sq miles
  (752,618 sq km)
*Population*: 14,3222,233
*Capital*: Lusaka
*Other cities*: Ndola, Kitwe,
  Chingola
*Government*: Republic
*Main religions*: Christianity,
  Islam, Hinduism
*Currency*: Zambian Kwacha

**Wallis and Futuna Islands**
*Area*: 55 sq miles (142 sq km)
*Population*: 15,507
*Capital*: Mata-Utu
*Government*: French Overseas
  Territory
*Main religion*: Roman Ca-
  tholicism
*Currency*: CFP Franc

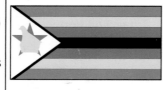

**Zimbabwe**
*Area*: 150,872 sq miles
  (390,757 sq km)
*Population*: 13,182,908
*Capital*: Harare
*Other cities*: Bulawayo, Mutare
*Government*: Parliamentary
  Democracy
*Main religions*: Traditional beliefs,
  Christianity
*Currency*: South African Rand,
  Botswana Pula, Pound Sterling,
  Euro, and the United States Dol-
  lar (use of Zimbabwean Dollar
  abandoned 2009)